THREE
HISTORICAL PHILOSOPHIES
OF
EDUCATION

ARISTOTLE, KANT, DEWEY

WILLIAM K. FRANKENA
University of Michigan

KEYSTONES OF EDUCATION SERIES

ACADEMIC EDITORS

MERLE L. BORROWMAN, *University of Wisconsin*
ISRAEL SCHEFFLER, *Harvard University*
EDWARD JOSEPH SHOBEN, JR., *University of Cincinnati*

144456

SCOTT, FORESMAN AND COMPANY

To My Teachers

The author gratefully acknowledges the cooperation of the following publishers for permission to reprint material in this book:

Bureau of Publications, Teachers College, Columbia University: for excerpts from John Dewey, *Dewey on Education*, Martin S. Dworkin, editor. New York: Bureau of Publications, Teachers College, Columbia University, 1959.

Harper & Row, Publishers, Incorporated: for excerpts from *The Doctrine of Virtue* by Immanuel Kant copyright © by Mary J. Gregor. Reprinted by permission of Harper & Row, Publishers, Incorporated.

Holt, Rinehart and Winston, Inc.: for excerpts from *Ethics*, Revised, by John Dewey and J. H. Tufts (Part Two, *Theory of the Moral Life*, by John Dewey, published separately), copyright © 1936, by John Dewey and James H. Tufts. Reprinted by permission of Holt, Rinehart and Winston, Inc.

The Macmillan Company: for excerpts from *Democracy and Education* by John Dewey copyright © 1961.

Putnam's & Coward-McCann: for excerpts from *The Quest for Certainty* by John Dewey, © 1929, Minton, Balch & Company.

The University of Michigan Press: for excerpts from *Education* by Immanuel Kant, translated by Annette Churton copyright © 1961.

The study of education is today in a state of ferment. With the expansion of educational horizons in American society, specialists of various sorts—historians, philosophers, psychologists, sociologists, political scientists—are to an ever greater extent joining with professional educators in inquiries into the nature of our educational ideas and institutions. Together, these scholars are enhancing the vitality, authority, and inspiration required of educational concepts in a revolutionary era of social change and scientific discovery.

In some small measure, the Keystones of Education Series is intended to reflect and, hopefully, to advance this educational development. It brings to instructors and students, indeed to all those concerned with education, a unique group of relatively brief but authoritative books, selective in content so as to develop in considerable depth key areas of knowledge. Each book is an original treatment of its special topic. The series may be profitably used in both introductory and advanced courses, for the instructor is free to construct a course with the content, emphasis, and sequence he desires, by selecting a combination of books to serve as text material. Because of the distinguished academic consultants and authorship, instructors can confidently take full advantage of the flexibility of the series without fear of uneven quality, superficiality, or duplication.

The Keystones of Education Series will for the first time make available a variety of superior materials, in convenient and inexpensive format, for the entire pre-service education program at colleges and universities.

The Publishers

TABLE OF CONTENTS

PREFACE vi

INTRODUCTION vii

CHAPTER ONE 1
THE PHILOSOPHY OF EDUCATION AND ITS PROBLEMS
The Human Problem
The Role of Education
The Nature and Aim of Education
Philosophy of Education
The Plan of This Book

CHAPTER TWO 15
ARISTOTLE'S PHILOSOPHY OF EDUCATION
Preliminaries
Views on the Philosophy of Education
The Ultimate Aim of Education
The Dispositions to Be Cultivated
Methods and Curriculum

CHAPTER THREE 79
KANT'S PHILOSOPHY OF EDUCATION
Approach to Kant's Thought
Views on Philosophy of Education
Dispositions to Be Fostered
The Aims of Education
The Methods and Practices of Education

CHAPTER FOUR 135
DEWEY'S PHILOSOPHY OF EDUCATION
    Preliminaries
    The Nature of Philosophy of Education
    The Dispositions to be Formed
    Reasons for Forming These Dispositions
    The Methods and Practices of Education

CHAPTER FIVE 192
COMPARISON OF THE PHILOSOPHIES
    Comparisons on Three Basic Questions
    Some General Comparisons
    Concluding Unphilosophical Postscript

FOOTNOTES 201

BIBLIOGRAPHICAL ESSAY 208

INDEX 211

PREFACE

Philosophy, unlike the sciences, never fully outgrows its history. The arguments and conceptions of past thinkers retain a fundamental relevance for contemporary philosophy even as it struggles to find new ways for itself. Unlike the student of science, therefore, the student of philosophy cannot be trained wholly out of current textbooks and journals, nor rely wholly upon the current consensus they reflect. Indeed, he cannot properly learn to philosophize at all unless he comes to appreciate the force of those overpowering constructions represented by the great philosophies of the past, and to develop, at the same time, a rational attitude toward their basic conceptions and claims to truth.

The philosophy of education has for a long time urgently needed studies of the history of the subject which not only meet the highest standards of serious scholarship but which are also analytic and critical in approach, encouraging the student to philosophize for himself as he develops a richer sense of his intellectual heritage. Professor Frankena's book is just such a study. Not only does it provide an original, intensive scholarly introduction to three outstanding systems of educational philosophy; it also trains the student to attend critically to their basic ideas, crucial assumptions and fundamental questions, to the logic by which these systems are built and through which their claims to truth are articulated. In writing with sympathy and lucidity about complex matters of deep human concern, as well as in providing an analytical account of three important historical expressions of this concern, Professor Frankena has produced a masterly introduction to a great subject.

Israel Scheffler

This book is an introduction to three important philosophies of education: those of Aristotle, Kant, and Dewey. Its main purpose, however, is to help teach the student how to do philosophy of education, though it will also teach him something—I hope a good deal—about its history. One way to prepare a student to do philosophy of education is to teach him philosophy in general and then set him to thinking about education. This is presumably what happened in the lives of our three authors themselves, except that Aristotle may actually have heard Plato doing philosophy of education. Another way is to work out a philosophy of education oneself and present it to the student in a book or lectures for him to master and think about. This is what Aristotle, Kant, and Dewey did. A third way is to review for and with him the whole history of man's philosophizing about education.

In this book a fourth way is taken—that of giving an account of the questions and logic of a philosophy of education and a full statement of three historical ones. This way has some of the virtues of the others: it teaches some philosophy for use in thinking about education, it presents an actual philosophy of education (three of them), and it covers some of the history of the philosophy of education. It also has some advantages over the others: as against the first, it actually deals with education; as against the second, it presents alternative philosophies of education, not only the one espoused by the teacher or author; and, as against the third, while it covers less, it goes more deeply.

However, this book represents not so much a rival of or substitute for approaches of the other three kinds as a supplement to them. It can be used independently, but it can also be used in conjunction with books in which the first or second approach is taken or, along with other works, as part of a course in the history of its subject. Used independently of other philosophical texts, it may, of course, serve as the philosophy part of a course in the foundations of education. One other way of using it may be worth mentioning—that it be studied in conjunction with readings in the ethical and educational writings of each of the three philosophers with whom it deals. Those are, after all, the writings on which it is based.

William K. Frankena

•

CHAPTER ONE

The Philosophy of Education

and

Its Problems

•

THE HUMAN PROBLEM

A crucial part of the human problem, for both individuals and societies, is the acquisition and transmission of excellences of body, mind, and character. This is a problem for human beings because such excellences are neither innate nor automatically acquired in the course of their natural experiences. Knowledge of one's language is almost automatically acquired in the course of social experience, and so are moral habits in a tradition-bound society, but only because social life has an educational aspect built into it. The cultivation of excellences is only part of the human problem because more is needed for the life and well-being of an individual or society than the mere possession of certain abilities and traits. Needed also, as Aristotle pointed out, are adequate native endowment, favorable physical conditions, and a not too brief span of life.

In saying this, I am assuming, of course, that the goal or task of human beings is not simply to acquire a certain group of excellences, moral or otherwise—as Kant and others sometimes seem to imply. It seems to me Aristotle is right when he says that our goal or task cannot be merely to *have* excellences or to *be* excellent, since a man may be excellent or have all the excellences and yet be asleep or unconscious. In short, I believe that the point of having an excellence is that it is necessary for engaging in worthwhile activities of a waking and conscious sort, just as the point of being able to play chess is to play it on occasion. Excellences, like the Sabbath, are made for man, not vice versa. Even if I am wrong about this, however, the formation of the required excellences remains a problem for human beings.

It may be asked at this point: Why should we worry at all about the acquisition or transmission of such things as abilities and traits? Why are any such things necessary or desirable? Why should we not simply go ahead and engage in the worthwhile activities that constitute the good or happy life? One might reply shortly by remarking that this would be like playing chess without learning how. This answer is, in fact, correct, but it needs to be spelled out. We must try to see what kind of a thing an excellence is and why it is necessary and desirable for us to acquire such things, since we are not born with them.

(1) When a man is said to know geometry or to be just, he is being said to have an excellence (if we assume that knowing geometry and being just are in fact desirable). But it is not being said that he is engaged in doing geometry or in doing just actions; it is not being said that he is engaged in any activities or having any experiences or feelings at all. He may, as Aristotle remarked, be asleep or unconscious and yet be correctly said to know geometry or to be just. What is being said, rather, is that *if* he is awake, *then* he *can* do things like proving the Pythagorean theorem if he is asked or decides to, or that, *when* he is awake, he *tends* to act justly in situations where this is called for. That is, an excellence is not an activity, action, experience, or feeling; it is what Aristotle calls a *hexis* and Dewey a "habit." A *hexis* is a disposition or dispositional property of a mind or person, something that need not be activated at a given time and yet may correctly be said to be present. One may know how to play chess when one is not playing it or even thinking about it. All such things as abilities, habits, skills, and traits of character or personality are dispositions in this wide sense. All excellences, then, are dispositions of this sort, though, of course, not all such dispositions are excellences, since some of them are bad or undesirable—like being unjust or ignorant, or indifferent—like the habit of tying the left shoestring first.

A word about my terminology is needed here. It is convenient in thinking about education to have one word for all of the desirable abilities, skills, states, traits, etc., to be produced or fostered, and words like "character" and "virtue" are too purely moral in connotation to include such things as an ability to speak French or a knowledge of geography. Some writers use the term "values" to refer to such desirable abilities, etc.—for example, in discussing "moral and spiritual values" in education. But the term "values" is much too vague and much too broad. For one thing, it covers not only desirable abilities, traits, etc., but also what I have called worthwhile *activities* (i.e., not only what Aristotle called *hexis* but what he called *energeiai*). I have therefore decided to use the term "excellences" as I have. It has the incidental advantage of fitting in with the concern about excellence in education today.

It is also convenient to have a word to cover both desirable and undesirable abilities, traits, etc., of all kinds, and I have elected to use the term "dispositions" for this purpose. Ordinarily we use "disposition" in a narrower sense, as in saying that Jones has a sunny disposition and Smith a disposition to be bashful or to waste time. We should not ordinarily say that being able to skate and having a knowledge of mathematics were dispositions. But philosophers do sometimes use terms like "disposition" and "dispositional property" in a wider sense, and since we need a term to use in this wide way and have no ordinary one to do the job, I shall do likewise. That "dispositions" is being used in this way must, however, be constantly remembered in what follows.

What I am calling dispositions and excellences may be of various sorts. Sunniness and bashfulness are dispositions, and the former is also an excellence. Qualities of personality like charm, traits of character like benevolence, skills like knowing how to dance, and states like having a knowledge of the kings of Britain—different as these are, they are all dispositions in my sense and presumably excellences as well. Their opposites, of course, are also dispositions but presumably not excellences.

(2) Now, why is it desirable or necessary that we have any dispositions at all other than those we may be born with? In a way, this is an academic question, because, as many writers have pointed out, including those we shall be studying, the formation of habits and other kinds of dispositions is inevitable in the course of our lives. As William James puts it:

> Could the young but realize how soon they will become mere walking bundles of habits, they would give more heed to their conduct while in the plastic state. . . . Every smallest stroke of virtue or of vice leaves its never so little scar. . . . Nothing we ever do is, in strict scientific literalness, wiped out.[1]

Such is our nature (or, according to James, our nervous system) that we form dispositions of one sort or another willy-nilly; the question really is not whether we shall have dispositions but which ones we shall have.

There is, however, something more to be said than merely that, since we must have dispositions, we might as well cultivate desirable ones. This is that we cannot, in any case, simply go ahead and enjoy or engage in the worthwhile activities and experiences that make up the good or happy life. Except possibly for purely passive perceptions and pleasures, if these exist, we cannot enjoy or engage in these valuable activities and experiences unless we first develop certain abilities, habits, or traits rather than others. To play chess or prove the Pythagorean theorem, I must first develop a number of abilities. I must also learn self-control so as not to be diverted by other attractions. Moreover, being finite and unable to do everything I wish to do or ought to do at the same time, I must have the capacity, as it were, to store one thing away while I do something else, and to control its return when I want it again. God, at least in one view, is pure act and is infinite; He can have no dispositions and has no need of them. He engages eternally in all worthwhile activities all at once, and has no problem of learning or control or storing away. We human beings, however, are not so blessed, and hence must regard certain dispositions as not only necessary but desirable because they are the condition and underpinning of the good life. We must acquire them in order to put ourselves in the position of engaging in worthwhile activities if and when we choose to.

The matter also has a social side. If any given individual is to be able to enjoy and engage in desirable experiences and activities, then not only must he have certain dispositions, but so must others. They must be disposed to treat him in certain ways, for example, with some tolerance, and they must have abilities and habits which maintain and provide the best possible environment for him to live in. He himself, on his part, must acquire corresponding dispositions that bear on the goodness of their lives. Hence, as Dewey says, society must be concerned to transmit

> habits of doing, thinking, and feeling from the older to the younger. Without this communication of ideals, hopes, expectations, standards, opinions, from those members of society who are passing out of the group life to those who are coming into it, social life could not survive.[2]

Society could not even maintain life, let alone promote worthwhile activities and experiences for its members.

THE ROLE OF EDUCATION

If both individuals and societies must be thus concerned about the acquisition and transmission of certain dispositions rather than others, or of what we have termed excellences, then the next question is: How are excellences acquired? Can they be transmitted from the older to the younger at all, and, if so, how? This question was nicely posed by the Greeks, who were the first to really see how crucial it is. Plato's *Meno* begins with Meno asking Socrates,

> Can you tell me whether [excellence] can be taught or is acquired by practice, not teaching; or, if neither by practice nor by learning, whether it comes to men by nature or in some other way [such as luck or divine gift]?[3]

Here four possibilities are recognized: (a) excellences are transmitted by being taught and acquired by being learned, (b) they are transmitted and acquired by practice, (c) they are natural or innate, (d) they are gifts of fortune or of the gods (or God). Socrates, who holds that excellence is knowledge, would like to say (a), but in the *Meno* at any rate he settles for (d). He neglects (b), which is taken seriously by Aristotle. Christianity holds to (d) for all or at least some of the excellences. Kant's position is rather difficult to make out, as we shall see, but his mentor, Rousseau, roughly speaking, was betting on (c). Dewey, like Plato (in the *Republic*) and Aristotle, is betting on a combination of (a) and (b).

To me, as to Socrates, Plato, and Aristotle, it seems clear that such excellences as we need are not innate, except in potentiality, or even automatically acquired. To say, however, that these excellences depend entirely on fortune and luck is to say that the solution of the human problem is entirely beyond the scope of our endeavor—and this simply is not true, though it is true that its solution is not wholly in our hands. We must allow that the achievement of the good life, whether on earth or in heaven, does depend, in part at least, on fortune or on something besides ourselves, and perhaps even that the acquisition and possession of at least some excellences, possibly of all of them, depends in some degree on something not ourselves that makes for excellence. But our hope may and must still lie, in large part, in (a) and (b)—that is, in education. Even if one believes, as Christians do, that something in the way of a divine gift or regeneration is required for certain excellences like faith and perhaps also for the perfecting of any excellence, it does not follow that the human effort of education is unnecessary as a condition of other excellences or of the divine gift itself. Certainly Christianity has in general not drawn this conclusion about education, though Christians have often held rather strict views of the kinds of excellence that are necessary or desirable. In fact, Christianity has usually regarded "the propagation of the gospel in foreign parts" and Christian education at home as duties and even as normal preconditions of the action of divine grace. For civilized man, at any rate, Christian or not, the question is not whether education is necessary and effective in the acquisition of excellences, but which excellences are to be cultivated or prepared for by education (teaching or practice), and how, when, and why.

THE NATURE AND AIM OF EDUCATION

We come, thus, to the subject of education. What is it? Actually the term "education" is ambiguous and may mean any one of four things:

(1) the *activity of educating* carried on by teachers, schools, and parents (or by oneself),

(2) the *process of being educated* (or learning) which goes on in the pupil or child,

(3) the *result*, actual or intended, of (1) and (2),

(4) the *discipline* or field of enquiry that studies or reflects on (1), (2), and (3) and is taught in schools of education.

We may begin to define education in sense (1) by saying that it is the activity of fostering or transmitting excellences. It is true that we sometimes use "education" in a wider sense to mean any shaping of a mind or character; in this sense Rousseau said that education comes to us from nature, from men, and from things. But in this wider sense, we are being educated no matter what dispositions are being fostered in us. In a narrower and more usual sense, however, we decline to call anything education unless it fosters or is intended to foster desirable dispositions and not undesirable ones, and this is the usage which is important for the philosophy of education and which we must try to define. One addition must be made to this definition. If the desired excellences could be produced by giving drugs, we probably would not call this way of producing them education (though we might then resort to the drugstore instead of the schoolhouse). To complete our definition we must say that education in sense (1) is the use of certain kinds of methods to foster excellences or desirable dispositions—namely, those belonging to the family which includes teaching, instruction, training, learning, practice, and the like. For a really careful definition all of these methods would, of course, have to be defined further, but this statement will suffice for present purposes.

Bertrand Russell once wrote,

> Education, in the sense in which I mean it, may be defined as the *formation, by means of instruction, of certain mental habits and a certain outlook on life and the world*.[4]

If we take "instruction" to cover the whole family of methods mentioned before and read "desirable" for "certain," this will serve very well as a definition of education in sense (1). Then education in sense (2) is the *acquisition by learning* of desirable dispositions or excellences, and education in sense (3) is the *possession* of excellent dispositions. Education in sense (4) is different; it is not an activity of teaching or a process of learning, it is a *field of study* like history or physics—namely, the field of study and thought *about* education in the other three senses. Many other definitions of education have, of course, been given, but I think it can be shown that they are either inadequate, unclear, mistaken, or compatible with those just stated. Ours certainly fit the views of Aristotle, Kant, and Dewey, as we shall see.

If all this is so, then whatever we may think about the *ultimate* aim or aims of education, we must take as its *proximate* aim the formation or fostering of excellent dispositions. As Aristotle put the matter, though the *end* of political science (which for him includes the art or science of education) is the highest good,

> the principal care of this science is to produce a certain [disposition] in the citizens, namely, to make them [excellent] and capable of performing noble actions.[5]

Or, if we say that the *immediate* aim of education is to do the things that will form or foster excellences of disposition, as Dewey's follower W. H. Kilpatrick does, then we may prefer his way of stating it:

> The *remoter* and inclusive guiding aim of education is to rear the young *to live the full good life*, both individual and social. The *intermediate* aim is to build such character in the young as will guarantee, so far as this is possible, that they *can* and *will* live the desirable good life.[6]

My only objection to this statement is that it uses the term "character" for the intermediate aim of education—just as Kant, Ruskin, Mill, and many others, including Dewey sometimes, do. This suggests that the *moral* excellences constitute the whole intermediate aim of education, unless it is carefully explained that "character" is being used to cover all of what I am calling excellences, which is not usually done by those who use it in talking about education. Now, it may be true that education should concern itself only to promote the moral virtues. But this must be shown and cannot be taken for granted at this point in the discussion. I think, in fact, that it is false, but here, at any rate, we must leave open the question which dispositions are to be cultivated. I should, therefore, amend Kilpatrick's statement by substituting "dispositions" for "character," thus allowing for the cultivation of a knowledge of physics or an ability to paint or do geometry, as well as of courage, integrity, and the like.

PHILOSOPHY OF EDUCATION

The philosophy of education is part of the discipline of education as defined earlier. It may be either *analytical* or *normative*. It is normative insofar as it is concerned to propose ends or values for education to promote, principles for it to follow, excellences for it to foster, or methods, contents, programs, etc., for it to adopt or employ, in general or in specific situations. It is analytical insofar as it is concerned merely to analyze, clarify, or elucidate, or to criticize and evaluate, our thinking about education—the concepts or terms we employ, the arguments we use, the assumptions we make, the slogans we proclaim, the theories we formulate. In this introduction I am doing mainly analytical philosophy of education. Aristotle, Kant and Dewey, however, did normative philosophy of education primarily, though in the course of doing so they included a good deal of analytical discussion. Some recent philosophers— for example, C. D. Hardie and D. J. O'Connor—believe that philosophy should be confined to logical analysis and so have been advocating a purely analytical approach to the philosophy of education. Since we mean to study the educational philosophies of Aristotle, Kant, and Dewey, however, we must take seriously the notion of a normative philosophy of education.

From what was said in the previous section it follows that there are three questions for any normative philosophy of education:

(1) *What* dispositions are to be cultivated? *Which* dispositions are excellences?

(2) *Why* are these dispositions to be regarded as excellences and cultivated? What are the aims or principles of education that require their cultivation?

(3) *How* or by what methods or processes are they to be cultivated?

The first two questions clearly go together. For to tell which dispositions are to be fostered, we need a criterion or rationale, and in order to have such a criterion or rationale, we must have an answer to the second question. I should like now to exhibit the general logic of such a rationale—one by which an answer to the first question is justified via an answer to the second. First, however, we must observe that some theories of education seem to rest simply on the premise that an educational system should promote the dispositions regarded as excellent by its supporting society—by Catholics if it is a Catholic system, by Americans if it is a public system in the United States. But if this answer to our question is to have the status of a *philosophy* of education, its proponent must explain why we should promote whatever dispositions are considered excellent in our society, and then his rationale will have much the same logic that I shall describe. In general, if one's culture has passed the stage of being purely tradition-bound and directed, as ours has, one cannot escape doing at least a minimum of philosophy. At any rate, even if an actual system of education must in a sense take as its business the implementation and transmission of the ideals of its supporting church, state, or class, the task of a normative philosopher of education is still to say what ought to be done and why, even if in doing so he only expresses the ethos of his group.

For the logic involved in a normative theory of education I shall adapt what John Stuart Mill says in his *System of Logic* (1843), Book VI, Chapters V and XII. According to this conception, one must begin one's educational thinking with one or more premises stating what the basic ends or principles of human action are. For Mill the basic principle is that of utility: do what will promote the greatest balance of pleasure over pain in the universe as a whole. For Kant (in one formulation) it is to do what you can will to be done by all rational beings in the kind of situation you are in. Whatever one's basic premises, it follows that certain dispositions are to be cultivated. First, we must cultivate the dispositions to act for the ends or on the principles affirmed; for instance, in Mill's view, we must promote the disposition to act for the greatest general happiness. Second, we must cultivate whatever dispositions are required for promoting the end or carrying out the principles in question. Both Mill and Kant think, for example, that it follows from their premises, different as they are, that we should develop our intellectual abilities and a will to be honest.

In general, one's thinking here will take the form of a kind of "practical syllogism," as Aristotle called it. (a) The major premise will consist of a normative statement of basic ends or principles. (b) The minor premise will consist of factual beliefs about life, human beings, and the world, taken from psychology, sociology, history, or from metaphysics, epistemology, or theology. (c) The conclusion will be a normative judgment about the dispositions to be fostered by education. In the case of Mill, for example, the reasoning will be as follows:

(a) We ought to do what is conducive to the greatest general happiness.
(b) The development of our intellects, honesty, etc., are conducive to the greatest general happiness.
(c) Therefore we should develop our intellects, be honest, etc.

The other question for a normative philosophy of education is *how* to foster the dispositions or excellences thus decided on—what practically is to be done or not done, when, in what way, with what means, in what order, by whom, and so on. Here enter all of the rules of teaching, learning, educational policy, curriculum, and school administration, from fairly general ones like Aristotle's "Use practice to realize the moral excellences" or Dewey's "Always relate what is done to the interests of the child" to rather specific ones like Kant's "If a child tells a lie, a look of contempt is punishment enough," but not including completely particular instructions like "Do . . . now." Such particular conclusions about what to do are, of course, the final outcome and application of the whole process of educational reasoning, but they are not part of the philosophy involved. Philosophy, as I once overheard a student remark, is always "in general."

For thinking about this second, practical question the logic is again that of a kind of practical syllogism. This time the major premise is usually a normative statement about an excellence or set of excellences to be fostered. The major premise will, in fact, normally be a conclusion (c) from a piece of reasoning of the sort just described. The minor premise (d) consists again of one or more factual propositions taken from psychology, history, or some natural or social science (including educational science and experimentation), or perhaps from metaphysics, epistemology, or theology. And (e) the conclusion is what Mill calls a "practical precept" for the guidance of the teacher, parent, child, or administrator. Thus Kant's reasoning in connection with the precept just quoted might be:

(c) We ought to cultivate a disposition of honesty.
(d) Looks of contempt help to cultivate such dispositions.
(e) Therefore, if a child tells a lie, we should give him a look of contempt.

The two stages of reasoning we have been analyzing may, of course, be combined as follows:

(a) We ought to promote the greatest general happiness.
(b) Dispositions of honesty, etc., promote the greatest general happiness.
(c) Therefore we ought to cultivate honesty, etc.
(d) Looks of contempt help to cultivate honesty.
(e) Therefore, if a child lies, we should give him a look of contempt.

Kant would not accept the opening utilitarian line of argument here given for (c), as we shall see, but Mill, if he is willing to agree to (d), could accept this entire chain of thought from first principle to practical precept.

In practice, educational thinking cannot be quite so simple and straightforward as this. Whether we should actually give a lying child a look of contempt does not depend merely on (a), (b), (c), and (d); it depends also on further considerations. It may be, for instance, that giving looks of contempt is ruled out by some basic ethical principle other than (a); or it may be that it would have such undesirable concomitant effects that it should be avoided even on utilitarian grounds. That is, its total effect on the child's dispositions may be so undesirable that it is better to use some other way of fostering honesty. Such possible complications must always be kept in mind, but the model of reasoning presented remains instructive nevertheless.

The model at least makes it clear that a normative philosophy of education, if it is completely worked out, must include:

1. A list of dispositions or excellences to be cultivated, with definitions,
2. A statement of the basic ends or principles taken as normative *premises*,
   a. for showing why these dispositions should be cultivated (or that they are excellences),
   b. for showing what is to be done or not done in cultivating them,
3. Factual *premises*, empirical, philosophical, or theological,
   a. for showing what dispositions are excellent and to be cultivated,
   b. for showing what is to be done, and how, in order to cultivate these excellences,
4. Normative *conclusions* about what to do, and how and when, in cultivating them.

Thus the schema we borrowed from Mill can be used in the analysis of any given normative philosophy of education, as well as in the development and exposition of one's own. It is also useful in comparing philosophies of education, in seeing the issues between them and in judging the merits of one as against another; for it exhibits the points at which different normative philosophies of education may disagree. (1) They may differ in the lists of dispositions they regard as desirable—i.e. in their lists of excellences. Or even if they agree in their verbal lists, they may still define their terms differently; they may both hold integrity to be an excellence but mean different things by "integrity." (2) They may differ in the

ends or principles they take to be basic in moral, social, and educational thinking, as Mill and Kant do. If so, they will give different
rationales for their lists of excellences to be cultivated, even if their
lists are the same. (3) They may differ in their factual premises—
that is, their authors may have different views as to the relevant
facts about the universe, human nature, child psychology, learning,
motivation, the effects of corporal punishment, etc. Then, even if
their basic ends or principles are the same, they will advocate different lists of excellences and/or different concrete precepts about how
to foster them. Here we must notice that different philosophers have
different views about the *kinds* of factual premises that may be used.
Confident metaphysicians and speculative philosophers like Aristotle
will regard metaphysical premises as admissible, but positivists and
agnostics will not. Kant holds metaphysics to be impossible, and
Dewey rules out all metaphysical premises that cannot be interpreted pragmatically. Mill admits only empirically verifiable premises.
A religious thinker may be willing to use premises based on authority,
revelation, or faith—as Christian philosophers of education do—but
Aristotle and Dewey are against doing so, though Kant, in a sense,
is not.

(4) And, of course, philosophers of education may differ in their
practical conclusions about teaching methods, curriculum, school
administration, and so on. However, unless they are simply illogical,
they should not differ in their conclusions about such matters unless
they also differ somewhere in their normative or factual premises
(they might differ in their definitions of terms, but if they differ
only in this way they are disagreeing only verbally, not in substance).
On the other hand, they may agree completely or at least to a very
considerable extent in their working conclusions, even though they
differ fundamentally in their normative and/or factual premises;
then they will agree in practice but differ in their rationales. In
short, different normative philosophies of education must disagree in
at least one of the categories, (1) to (4), and may disagree in more
than one; if they disagree in (4), they must disagree in one of the
others, but they may agree in any one of them and yet disagree
in all the others.

THE PLAN OF THIS BOOK

As was indicated earlier, this book will be a study, largely ex-
pository and interpretative, of three historical normative philosophies
of education—namely, those of Aristotle, Immanuel Kant, and John
Dewey. The first represents the culture and thought of Greece in
ancient times, the second that of northern Europe in the Enlightenment, and the third that of America in the twentieth century. Three

authors have been chosen in order to get some breadth of representation in time and point of view and some basis for interesting comparisons and debate; only three have been chosen in order that the treatments might be as full as possible and yet provide some variety. The result, of course, is not a full review of the history of educational ideas and philosophies, but it will furnish at least a partial introduction to their history, since it presents three of the historically important types of educational philosophy and gives some account of their origins and influences. The main point of this study, however, is not a historical but a philosophical one. It is to provide the student or reader, in a fair degree of depth, with some of the background knowledge of different positions, and some of the experience in thinking about them, that will help him to work out a normative philosophy of education of his own. It will probably turn out that he will learn something for his own thinking from each of our three authors, but the purpose is not to make him an eclectic. It is rather to show him what some great uneclectic philosophies are like, with the admonition, "Go thou, and do likewise!" He may borrow from the writers he studies here, but hopefully in the same spirit in which they themselves borrowed from Plato, Rousseau, or James. He may also not come out with as original a position as they do; what matters is not so much that he achieve novelty and originality as that he achieve a position of his own and that it be thought out with all the care, clarity, and insight he can muster. As Socrates put it, what matters is the examined life. Today as never before we are being asked to examine our educational life and, since this is a democracy, to make decisions about it; and while we are all bound to have some views about and some effect on what is done, it surely behooves us to see that these are as intelligent as possible.

Our choice of philosophers needs some explanation. Dewey is almost a must, given the contemporary situation in American education. But why not Plato, Rousseau, and Dewey? Plato and Rousseau have been more important in the history of educational philosophy than Aristotle and Kant, and they are perhaps more original. Aristotle has been chosen here in preference to Plato, partly because he is less often studied in courses on education, partly because Plato is being discussed to a considerable extent in R. S. Peters' volume in this series, and partly because so much of the opposition to Dewey today is more or less inspired by Aristotle—for example, the thought of M. J. Adler, R. M. Hutchins, H. S. Broudy, J. D. Wild, and that of Jacques Maritain and Catholic Neo-Thomists in general. As for Kant, he has been preferred here over Rousseau partly because he represents a somewhat similar point of view, partly because his position is nevertheless more different from those of Aristotle and

Dewey than Rousseau's, and partly because it is harder for non-philosophers to read and interpret and hence is less familiar in educational circles. We must remember, too, that Aristotle represents the culmination of Greek thought and the doorway to that of the later Middle Ages, and that Kant similarly represents the outcome of seventeenth- and eighteenth-century thought and the entrance to that of the nineteenth and twentieth centuries.

The rest of the book will consist, then, of chapters on each of these three philosophies of education, plus a final chapter. In the chapters on the three philosophies I shall not, in expounding them, follow the model presented above in any mechanical way. To some extent I shall let my exposition and discussion be dictated by my materials. I shall, however, make my account such that it will be relatively easy for the reader to interpret it in accordance with the model. I shall also in each of these chapters include some observations by way of comparing the position expounded with the others, and a brief indication of its historical influence.

I do not propose in these chapters to give systematic expositions of the entire philosophies of the authors dealt with, as some books in the philosophy of education do. This is not a book on the philosophies of Aristotle, Kant, and Dewey in general. It is a book on their philosophies *of education*, and I shall limit myself rather strictly to what the reader must know to understand and think about this part of their philosophies. It is, of course, desirable that educators know more about the views of our three authors, but I shall not try to provide this additional information here. I am concerned that we should do our thinking about education well, or—as Aristotle would say—excellently, and it seems to me confusing to present material that is not strictly relevant to education as if it were relevant. Much is relevant, but not everything (except as a possible content of the curriculum); at least it must be shown to be relevant and how, if it is introduced into the discussion at all. Philosophers of education should certainly know their philosophy in general, and perhaps teachers and administrators should also, but it should not be presented to them as philosophy of education.

In the final chapter I shall do something more by way of comparing our three philosophies of education than can be done in the chapters that deal with them individually. I shall also try to show briefly the direction in which I for one am disposed to go when I read Aristotle, Kant, and Dewey and when I obey the admonition to do likewise.

•

CHAPTER TWO

Aristotle's Philosophy

of

Education

•

The Greeks were the first to think philosophically about education; indeed, one of the central concerns of Athenian philosophy in its great age was with education. The problem of education, as the Greeks saw it, was that of the transmission and acquisition of something for which they used the word *arete*, which has usually been translated by "virtue" but is better translated by "excellence." The Greeks originally meant by it the manly excellences of the athlete and warrior and later came to mean by it all the dispositions which, as their culture deepened and widened, they came to regard as desirable—intellectual and moral, as well as physical and warlike ones— not only strength and courage, but temperance, justice, and wisdom as well. Rarely, if ever, did they mean by *arete* only the moral dispositions that we associate with the word "virtue." In other words, they thought of the problem of education, or *paideia*, as they called it, as that of the acquisition or transmission of excellences. Their society was no longer tradition-directed as it had once been, and their culture was in crisis (as ours is often said to be), and so they were troubled about the question of acquiring and passing on the excellence they put such store in. They wondered how they could secure its acquisition by a process they could control. Indeed, they even raised the more drastic questions: What is it? and Can its acquisition be controlled by any process of education?

All of this is nicely illustrated in such Platonic dialogues as the *Laches*, *Protagoras*, and *Meno*. In the *Laches*, for instance, the company has just been watching a man fighting in armor, and two of them explain why they have brought the others there. "We have two sons," they say,

> and we have resolved to give them our most constant care and not let them run loose as their fancy leads them. We thought that you above all men must have concerned your-selves with the question of the kind of upbringing that would make the best of them . . . we are considering what lessons or pursuits will lead them to the highest attainable excellence. . . . That is the question which we wanted to discuss with you. And we look to you now to give us your advice, first as to whether you think this accomplishment [fighting in armor] should be learned or not, and then as to any other such art or pursuit that you can recommend for a young man. . . .[1]

Socrates then takes the lead in a somewhat inconclusive discussion of the nature of courage, moral as well as physical. In the *Protagoras* and *Meno* he raises the broader question of the nature of excellence in general and whether it is teachable, coming reluctantly to the conclusion noted in Chapter I. Meanwhile the poet Pindar, speaking for more traditional aristocrats, was arguing in his *Odes* that certain men have excellence virtually by nature, while the rest are by nature incapable of it. In this view the education for excellence that both contemporary democrats and Socrates were searching for would be either unnecessary or impossible. The philosophers, however, though not believing in democracy, put their faith more and more in educa-tion and became increasingly confident that they understood the nature of excellence and could see, at least in principle, how it might and should be taught. Their opponents, the sophists and rhetoricians, though they proposed different programs, were even more confident. While the Greek city-states were going down to military and political defeat, they were producing the greatest suc-cession of educational philosophers in history.

This is the setting for the educational thought of Aristotle. His concern is with *arete*, and, though less radical, he is even surer than Plato that he can define the various excellences and outline a feasible program for producing them, for, while he has the question of the *Meno* constantly in mind, he does not really doubt that excellence is transmitted and acquired by a kind of education. He is also concerned to work out a rationale for the whole enterprise—what excellences are to be produced and why and how—which is what makes him a philosopher of education. He has not the local Athenian patriotism or reforming zeal of Socrates and Plato and is rather more of a spectator of the Greek condition than they were—more the scientist and philosopher than the evangelist or reconstructionist—but, perhaps for this very reason, he was able to present a more systematically formulated and reasoned philosophy than they did. His philosophy borrows a great deal from them, but it is nevertheless different in important ways, both in method and in conclusion and not merely in motivation or tone—different enough to make it a significant historical philosophy of education.

VIEWS ON THE PHILOSOPHY OF EDUCATION

POLITIKE

Although our primary interest is in Aristotle's normative philosophy of education, we must glance at his views about the nature and function of a philosophy of education. One might call this his metaphilosophy of education. Except for an occasional passage elsewhere, Aristotle presents his thinking about education as a part of what he calls politics (*politike*). In fact, his specific discussion of education, itself incomplete, forms the last part of the incomplete work called *Politics*. Whether it was intended to be the concluding or climactic part of that work we do not know; it may well have been, for Aristotle says over and over that the main business of a statesman is to make the citizens good—that is, to give them *arete*—in other words, to educate them. In any case, the *Politics* is for him only the second part of his whole enquiry into politics; the first part consists of what he calls ethics and also has something to say about education. Of this the *Nicomachean Ethics* is the last and best version, but there are one or two others. The *Ethics* and the *Politics* together make up *politike* proper and present virtually the whole line of thought about education that we are to review.

For Aristotle this *politike* is the supreme practical science, or normative discipline. He distinguishes three kinds of disciplines. (1) A *theoretical* science employs the scientific or theoretical part of our rational faculty and has as its end simply to know the truth about the world for its own sake. The theoretical sciences are mathematics, physics (which includes biology and psychology for Aristotle), and "theology" or metaphysics. (2) A *productive* science or art employs the "deliberative" part of our rational faculty and also involves a kind of knowledge, but its purpose is the making of something useful or beautiful—for example, the arts of shipbuilding, medicine, or writing tragedy. (3) *Practical* science also employs the "deliberative" part of our reason and seeks a kind of knowledge, but its end is action or "doing" (not "making") and so it seeks knowledge in relation to desire or as a guide to conduct.

> . . . in the practical sciences the end is not to attain a theoretical knowledge of any subject, but rather to act in a certain way. . . . to know what excellence is, is not enough; we must endeavor to acquire it and to act accordingly. . . .[2]

Politike is a practical science in this sense, not a productive or a theoretical one; its end is not knowledge for its own sake but action, and its end is not the making of something besides action, like a house or a statue, but "doing" itself, action for its own sake.

Every productive art and practical science aims at some good, such as health in the case of medicine, and the end of politics is the highest or supreme good for man. Politics includes all other practical sciences like ethics and economics as parts of itself; it uses the productive arts as instruments; it even has a kind of hegemony over the theoretical sciences, for, while it cannot determine their premises or conclusions, it does or should determine whether they are to be studied or not, by whom, and to what extent. Its end is to realize the good, but its central concern in doing this is to make men virtuous.

> . . . the supreme good [is] the end of political science, but the principal care of this science is to produce a certain disposition in the citizens, namely to make them good and disposed to do what is noble.[3]

Why politics must be so concerned to make men virtuous if its end is the good, we shall see shortly. The point now is that it must make education its principal care and must, therefore, include the philosophy of education as its central part.

By implication Aristotle asserts that a complete philosophy of education must answer four questions:[4]

(a) What kind of education is the best—i.e. appropriate to an individual or a people with the best natural endowment (intelligence and spirit) living in the most favorable circumstances?

(b) What kind of education is best for a given individual or people—i.e. best relatively to them?

(c) What kind of education is best for the majority of peoples?

(d) What kind of education will produce the dispositions desired by a given individual or people?

Actually Aristotle presents his theory of education in the *Politics* as an answer to the first question—that is, as an account of the best education for a people with sufficient intelligence and spirit living in fortunate circumstances (in short, for Greeks)—and it is simply an application of what he says in the *Ethics*. Presumably he would say, however, that if one has an answer to question (a), then one will have a pattern in the light of which to answer questions (b) and (c). He does not deal with question (d) at all, though it is the one that many people would regard as primary. Probably this is because he holds that what matters is what is best for us, which is what we really desire, not what we think we desire.

It is worth noticing, as a part of Aristotle's philosophy of education, that he believes young men (and all women!) to be unfit for the study of *politike*.

> . . . the man who has been educated in a subject is a good judge of that subject, and the man who has received an all-around education is a good judge in general. Hence a young man is not a proper hearer of lectures on *politike* [including ethics], for he is inexperienced . . . and tends to follow his passions. . . .[5]

Perhaps Aristotle was remembering his experiences with Alexander when he wrote this. At any rate, he thinks that the study of ethics and politics should not come until relatively late, when one has acquired a considerable experience of life and has learned, by a program of habituation, to control one's passions. Fortunately, he adds that this is not so much a question of time as of character, and so perhaps we may assume that today's college student has reached this stage. At any rate, I shall let the reader judge whether he is prepared for the study we are engaged in, which is something Aristotle probably would not have done. As Barker says, "Plato and Aristotle perhaps treated their contemporaries too much as if they were 'always children.' "[6]

ITS CERTAINTY

Aristotle also says that in *politike*—and hence in ethics and in the philosophy of education—we cannot have and must not expect the same accuracy and certainty that can be had in mathematics or the other theoretical sciences. Partly this is because *politike* raises questions about excellence, justice, and the good which involve "much difference of opinion and uncertainty"; and partly it is because *politike* is concerned with human action and with things that can be affected or effected by human action, matters into which an element of unpredictability may enter, so that "our subjects and our premises are merely generalities." It is not clear that Aristotle means that even his basic views about the end or about happiness are not completely accurate or certain, but at any rate we must remember this statement as we go along. Indeed, Aristotle remarks that

> . . . it is the mark of an educated mind to expect that amount of exactness in each kind which the nature of the particular subject admits. It is equally unreasonable to accept merely probable conclusions from a mathematician and to demand strict demonstration from an orator.[7]

We may note, however, that this remark is two-edged, and that, if we must not expect mathematical accuracy and certainty in social and educational philosophy, we must still demand of them all the exactness and demonstration of which they do admit. This demand, too, is the mark of an educated mind, though it is not always met in writings on education.

THE ULTIMATE AIM OF EDUCATION

THE GOOD

We saw in Chapter I that a normative philosophy of education must answer three questions: (1) What dispositions are to be fostered by education? (2) Why? (3) How? Now, it happens that Aristotle in effect answers the second question first. While he is in a sense primarily concerned with excellences and their ·acquisition or transmission, he does not begin his discussion in either the *Ethics* or the *Politics* with excellence. The end of politics (and ultimately of education) is the good and the good is not *arete*, since *arete* in all its forms is something (a disposition) that one can have when one is asleep, and the good life is not. The good, according to Aristotle, is happiness or "living well" (*eudaimonia*). *Politike*, therefore, including ethics and the theory of education, is first of all the science of happiness; the excellences come in and are to be cultivated only if and because they are prerequisites of the good or happy life. Hence Aristotle begins the *Ethics* with a discussion of the good, goes on to a description of the excellences to be cultivated, and ends the *Politics* with a treatment of education. Since his approach is so nicely systematic, our account of his philosophy of education will best take the questions in the order in which he deals with them.

A thing is good, Aristotle maintains, if it is desired or aimed at, and he means that it is good if and because it is desired or aimed at, not, as Plato does, that it is desired or aimed at if and because it is good. The highest or supreme good, then, if there is such a thing, must be something which is (a) such that it is sought for its own sake while other things are sought for the sake of it, and (b) such that, if it were attained, nothing more would be sought after. Is there such a good? Aristotle thinks there is and that it is happiness. Happiness is the ultimate goal of all human striving; it fulfills both of the conditions stated, and therefore it is the highest good.

Here a note on Aristotle's use of terms is necessary to prevent misunderstanding. He does not mean by happiness or "living well" what is sometimes meant by it. His *eudaimonia* is not pleasure, enjoyment, or contentment, and it certainly is not "living it up." Aristotle does think that *eudaimonia* is a life we will find pleasant and be contented with if we achieve it, but he means by *eudaimonia*, not the pleasure or contentment involved, but the kind of life or activity that yields this pleasure or contentment. Our word "happiness" is therefore not a wholly satisfactory translation for his word *eudaimonia*, since we are apt to take it to mean a certain state of feeling. However, when we ask what happiness is, we ourselves often answer, not by saying it is pleasure, but by describing the kind of life or activity we think to be desirable. Aristotle, so to speak, takes this sort of answer quite literally, and identifies happiness with the kind of life or activity that is desirable, not with the enjoyment that may accompany it. With this understanding we may continue to use "happiness" as our term for what he is talking about.

HAPPINESS

That happiness in this sense is our ultimate goal Aristotle thinks no one will question. But, still, What is happiness? Some say it is pleasure, some honor, some *arete*, some money making, and some contemplation. But, excepting possibly contemplation, to which we shall recur, none of these fulfills the above conditions for being the supreme good. Besides, happiness is an activity (*energeia*), not a capacity (*dynamis*) or a disposition (*hexis*), and therefore cannot be identified with *arete*, the possession of which is compatible with being asleep, inactive, or miserable. Well, pleasure is an activity of sorts. Why cannot it be identified with happiness? In reply Aristotle argues, among other things, that pleasures may be bad—for example, those that accompany bad activities. His main point, however, is that pleasure simply is not strictly speaking what we are aiming at in life; what we aim at is activity of certain kinds, and pleasure is really only an accompaniment, an added bloom which is not what we are after but accrues to and completes the sought-after activities we engage in. Happiness is only a certain kind of activity, namely, activity that is sought for its own sake alone and can never be bad, namely, excellent activity. That is the supreme human goal and therefore the supreme human good.

Aristotle supports this conclusion by contending (1) that man has a function *qua* man, (2) that his function is to exercise the distinctive or highest capacities of his soul, that is, his intellect or reason, (3) that, therefore, the function of the good man is to exercise these capacities well or excellently, and finally, as a consequence, (4) that happiness or the human good

> . . . is an activity of the soul in accordance with excellence, or if there be several excellences, in accordance with the best and most perfect among them. . . . this activity must last a complete life-time.[8]

However, since the notion that a man has a function *qua* man, and not just *qua* carpenter or husband, is a rather implausible one, it may help to have a fuller statement of what Aristotle seems to have in mind.

According to Aristotle, a man is a living organism, a body with a soul. This does not mean that man is a conjunction of two substances, one material and one spiritual, as Plato and so many later thinkers thought. A man is a single substance, and, like all such substances, consists of matter plus a form. A book is a bit of matter with a characteristic form, and so is a man. A thing's matter represents its stuff, its potentialities; its form represents its completed nature, its actualization. In man, the body is the matter and the soul is the form or actualization of the body. The soul is the actualization of the potentialities of the body. As such it contains a number of capacities or faculties which need to be actualized in their turn:

nutrition, reproduction, sense, locomotion, imagination, desire, emotion, reason. The first two Aristotle assigns to the nutritive part of the soul, the next five to the sensitive or appetitive part, and the last to the rational part, which is the part that is really distinctive of man. All of them, of course, are capacities that may be present without being active or exercised, but they may and normally do become activated in some way or other—for example, in feelings and thoughts. Aristotle maintains, however, that this is not enough, that they must be exercised in accordance with excellence. What is wanted —quite literally—is excellent activity of one's capacities, especially of those distinctive of man. Everything has as its function, aim, or end the achievement not only of its complete form but also and especially of the excellent activities that are made possible by achieving this form. Its final actualization, toward which all of its aspiration—conscious or unconscious—tends, is simply this excellent activity of its specific faculties. The acorn and the young oak tree desire and strive for the form and activity of the full-grown oak tree, and just so does the undeveloped man aim at a life of the excellent exercise of his powers, especially of his intellect. The harp player not only wants to play the harp, he wants to play it well; the human organism not only wants to play the man, it wants to play the man well. The soul with its powers is the organism's first form or actualization, and is present already at birth, but its final form or actualization comes only when it has acquired the further excellent dispositions needed and actually exercises its powers well. In the case of the oak tree and other sub-human organisms all of this achievement transpires by nature and is virtually automatic in the absence of obstacles. But in the case of man much of it depends on his own effort in cooperation with others. He must, largely through conscious care and study, which may fail and go awry, develop his capacities and control his passions so as to ensure their excellent exercise. This means that he must develop and form the right kinds of dispositions, that is, he must be educated.

In short, man's actualization or self-realization, which is what he is aiming at in life, involves a series of stages:

(1) the body, provided at birth and requiring only growth,
(2) its first form or actualization, the soul with its powers, also provided at birth,
(3) certain dispositions or excellences of the soul, to be acquired by education,
(4) its final form or actualization = activity of excellent kinds.

The end or the good or happiness, then, is the goal of the whole process—namely, excellent activity of the soul.

Behind this striving for actualization in man and all the other substances in the world, according to Aristotle, is God, the unmoved mover in it all. God, he claims, is pure form, that is, He is completely actualized, He has no potentialities, no dispositions, no *arete*, and needs none. For He is eternally engaged in the excellent activity that everything else is striving to achieve and enjoy (which Aristotle takes to be contemplation). God does nothing about the world except to arouse in it the desire to be like Him; He is like a beautiful woman who inspires great deeds in a lover of whom she is not even aware. This is the love that "makes the world go 'round." Everything wants to live at "the top of its form," as God does.

This, as I see it, is what Aristotle has in mind when he gives us his argument about man's function. The core of it all, however, is simply the claim that what human beings aim at in life is the exercise of their powers in excellent activities, and much, if not all, of the metaphysics that Aristotle associates with it is unnecessary. The substance of his argument is this:

(a) what we aim at ultimately is excellent activity of the soul, not pleasure, virtue, honor, etc.; therefore,

(b) excellent activity of the soul is the supreme good, and

(c) happiness is excellent activity of the soul.

It may be summarized in a series of equations: the supreme good = that which is aimed at as the final end = happiness = excellent activity of the soul.

Two clauses in Aristotle's definition of happiness as an activity of the soul in accordance with excellence must be noted before we go on. In one he adds that

. . . this activity must occupy a complete lifetime; for one swallow does not make spring, nor does one fine day. . . .[9]

If a person's life lasts only a short time, according to Aristotle, we cannot correctly say, when it is over, that he was happy. (This is one of the reasons that Aristotle says children cannot be happy; the other is that they are not yet capable of excellent activity.) It follows that happiness depends, not only on a man's cultivation of the necessary excellences, but on what the Greeks called "fortune," for fortune largely controls the span of our lives. In fact, there are other things that Aristotle regards as necessary for happiness: food, health, friends, property, and especially an adequate inheritance of native capacities. To some extent one can do something about some of these requirements, and one's *polis* or state can do a good deal more (though Aristotle never envisages a welfare state except in his own terms, namely, as one that is mainly concerned to make the lives of its citizens good by making them good, that is, by educating them in the needed excellences), but mainly they are in the hands of fortune. Even whether one's state is a good one or not depends largely on fortune. The main point for our purposes is that not all of what needs to be done, as Aristotle sees it, can be done by education— not even all that the individual or the state can and must do can be done by education—even if the main part of it can be. A "little bit o' luck" is needed also.

In the other clause, having said that happiness is an activity of the soul in accordance with excellence, Aristotle adds "or, if there are several excellences, in accordance with the best and most perfect of them."[10] This clause implies that not all excellent activity of the soul is a part of happiness, but only that (those) which is (are) most excellent, whatever this (these) may turn out to be. As a result of this clause, we are faced at this point by several questions. What activities of the soul does Aristotle regard as excellent? Which of these is (are) the most excellent? And which of them are *parts* of happiness and not mere *means* to it? Only if we know Aristotle's replies to these questions can we understand his views about what excellences of disposition the statesman (and educator) is to try to foster, why he is to foster them, and in what order of priority.

> . . . inasmuch as happiness is a certain activity of soul in conformity with perfect excellence, it is necessary to investigate excellence. . . . the true statesman [or educator] would appear to be one who has made a special study of excellence, since his aim is to make the citizens good and law-abiding. . . .[11]

And it will not do to answer these questions by saying that those activities are excellent or belong to happiness which carry out our function *qua* man, realize our potentialities, or actualize our form or nature as human beings—though Aristotelians, including Aristotle himself, often do answer thus. These answers are true, in Aristotle's view, but they do not tell us what we want to know. For Aristotle, we can find out how to realize ourselves only by finding out what activities are excellent or most excellent—not the other way around.

KINDS OF ACTIVITIES

What kinds of activities are there, according to Aristotle? One is tempted to list bodily activities first, but, on his view, there are no peculiarly bodily activities; all of our "bodily" activities are activities of one or more of the parts of our souls, for example, digestion is an activity of the nutritive part, locomotion and movement of the appetitive or sensitive part. Thus we have:

(1) activities of the nutritive part: digestion, growth, reproduction, etc.;

(2) activities of the sensitive or appetitive part: sensing, imagining, remembering, desiring, locomotion, feeling various kinds of emotions;

(3) activities of the intelligent or rational part:

   (a) those of "scientific" or "theoretical" reason: theoretical thinking, reasoning, and knowing (knowing *that* something is or is not the case);

   (b) those of "deliberative" or "practical" reason: practical thinking, deliberating, reasoning, and knowing (knowing *what* to do or *how* to do it).

There are also (4) activities in which the appetitive soul and the practical reason both participate, that is, activities in which the appetitive soul is guided by the practical reason—for example, when one feels angry justifiably. For Aristotle, the activities of the appetitive soul ought all to come under this heading, that is, they ought all to be guided by or at least in conformity with practical reason. Conversely, the function of practical reason is to guide or regulate the life of the appetitive part of the soul—its desire, emotion, and action. Theoretical reason does not take part in this, or, if it does, only indirectly and by way of practical reason. For example, if I tell myself that it is no use being angry at the apple for falling, because it was only acting in accordance with the law of gravitation (adding, perhaps, that Newton would not even have discovered this law if he had not watched another apple fall), then my practical reason is using a truth borrowed from my theoretical reason in order to control my emotions. It is not clear, however, that Aristotle himself thinks that theoretical reason ever helps guide our feelings and actions even in this indirect way, for he usually confines theoretical reason to the region of the necessary and unchanging which we can only contemplate and know but cannot do anything about or make any practical use of. This is, in fact, one of the points at which Dewey attacks Aristotle's distinction between two realms of being and two kinds of thinking and knowing.

There are two kinds of activities in which the deliberative and appetitive parts of the soul may cooperate. One Aristotle calls *praxis*, practical action, or "doing," and the other *poiesis*, productive action, or "making." The latter includes the activities involved in the arts and crafts, and even medicine—all action that is aimed at making something beautiful or useful other than itself, for example, a poem, a flute, or a house, something that will continue in existence when the action is over. The former kind of activity is different, Aristotle insists. We may see how, if we compare making a flute with playing one. Making a flute is not its own end, its end is the existence of a flute; but playing a flute is or at least may be its own end, being engaged in simply for its own sake. So, says Aristotle, the end of making is to bring something into being, the end of doing is the doing itself or rather doing something well or excellently (*eupraxis*), not the production of any artifact. Doing has its value or excellence in itself, just as the theoretical activities of the scientific faculty have, while making finds its worth entirely in that of its product. Both may be excellent, but the excellence of making is borrowed while that of doing is its own. Under doing in this sense Aristotle includes especially moral, military, and political action: war, legislation, acts of liberality and justice (and possibly teaching, but not practicing medicine). Such actions have results, of course, but Aristotle seems to regard them as being noble (*kalos*) just because they are the actions they are, provided only that they are done because they are noble.

WHICH ACTIVITIES ARE EXCELLENT?

Now, all of these different kinds of activity—digesting, feeling angry, deliberating, thinking about mathematics, etc.—may be excellently or well done, but they may also be poorly done. Even activities in which the appetitive soul conforms to practical reason may be badly done, since practical reason may be mistaken in its instructions. We must, then, have some criteria for determining, in connection with each kind of activity, when it is excellent and when it is not. What, according to Aristotle, are these criteria of excellence?

In the case of the nutritive part of the soul his reply is easy. Its activities, being largely automatic and unconscious, are not good in themselves, but only as means to the life of the other parts of the soul. Hence they are excellent or well done if and only if they are conducive to the better life—in other words, excellent activity—of the other parts of the soul. This does not mean, insofar as they are susceptible of conscious care or control, that they may be in any way neglected, for they remain indispensable both to life and to the good life, but it does mean that they are not to be made objects of concern for their own sakes.

The activities of the appetitive part of the soul are excellent, according to Aristotle, if and only if they conform to practical reason when it is itself functioning excellently. These activities include making and doing. But making, as we saw, is good only as a means, and so it is excellent if and only if (a) it effectively brings about its end, the existence of that which is being made, whether it be a work of art, a bed, a pie, or a person's health, and (b) this object is itself good as a means to activities which are good in themselves or excellent in their own right. Vocational activity or "work," whether it can be called making or not—for example, farming or housekeeping —is also good only as a means, and hence is well done if and only if it is conducive to other activities that are excellent in themselves. This view about making and work is another point on which Dewey attacks Aristotle. But, again, we must notice that these activities remain important in Aristotle's view of them, even if they are "put in their place."

This leaves two kinds of activities: all sorts of action proper, or "doing," and all sorts of intellectual activity. Of these the former, if excellent at all, are excellent in themselves, though, of course, they may also be good or bad as means or because of their results. The same is true of the operations of practical reason; if well done, they are excellent in themselves, but they may be good as means to moral virtue and even as conditions of the excellent operation of theoretical reason. The operations of theoretical reason, however, if well done, are excellent, for Aristotle, wholly in themselves; they have no effects or uses and are simply their own excuse for being.

Thus, according to Aristotle, though activities of all sorts may be excellent or well done, only those of two kinds may be intrinsically excellent—namely, moral and political action and the operations of the intellect. Other excellent activities must be provided for in one's social and educational theory, but only because they are necessary or useful as means to or conditions of excellent activities of these two kinds. It follows, we must now note, that activities of other kinds—"bodily" or nutritive activities, making, work, etc.— cannot belong to happiness in the sense of being parts of it. Since they have no intrinsic value, they remain mere means to happiness, however indispensable they may be. For happiness, it will be remembered, must be something desirable entirely for its own sake, and hence must consist wholly of activities that are excellent in themselves.

We now have three more specific questions than we had before: (1) Which is the more excellent, morally excellent activity or excellent activity of the intellect? (2) Do they *both* belong to happiness in the sense of being *parts* of it? (3) What is the criterion of excellence in each case? Aristotle deals with (1) and (2) in Book X of the *Ethics*, and Book VII of the *Politics*, and with (3) throughout Books II and VII of the *Ethics*.

MORAL VS. INTELLECTUAL ACTIVITY

(1) Aristotle's answer to this question is clear: purely intellectual activity is more excellent than moral, political, or military activity.

His main arguments are as follows: that, although morally excellent action is desirable or excellent in itself, it is also desirable as a means or because of its results; that intellectually excellent activity is the only kind of activity we can ascribe to God, Who is both perfectly happy and the end of all our aspiration; that the life of contemplation is or may be self-sufficient, while that of action cannot be; and that the life of contemplation is not only more self-sufficient but also more continuous, more leisurely, and more pleasant. It should be added that Aristotle also seems to hold, on much the same grounds, that the activity of the theoretical part of the intellect is superior to that of the practical or deliberative part.

HAPPINESS AGAIN

(2) On the other hand, it seems to me that Aristotle's answer to the second question remains in the end unclear. He makes three statements bearing on it in Book X of the *Ethics* and then leaves the matter there: (a) that happiness is contemplation (activity of the theoretical intellect) or some form of contemplation, (b) that contemplation is the *highest* happiness, since it is the highest kind of excellent activity, and (c) that "doing" or excellent activity of a moral, political, or military kind constitutes a "second" sort of happiness, one which is characteristically human as compared with that of the intellect, which is "separate" or divine. Since (c) is compatible with (b) but not with (a), it follows that Aristotle may be holding either of two positions. The first is that there is only one kind of happiness and it is identical with contemplation, and that morally excellent activity is not a part of happiness at all but only a means to or a condition of it. The second is that there are two kinds or parts of happiness, namely, excellent activity of the intellect and morally excellent action or "doing," and that the first is better or higher than the second. W. D. Ross takes Aristotle to hold the first view, H. H. Joachim takes him to hold the second; I see no decisive way of deciding between them. However, the first view fits in better with the final clause in Aristotle's original definition of happiness as quoted earlier, and it seems to be the view adopted in the *Politics*, and so I shall on the whole assume that it is Aristotle's position.

(3) Aristotle does not offer us a general criterion that will cover both intellectual and moral excellence, except to say that the excellent is the praiseworthy, which gets us nowhere. We must, then, look for two criteria: one for determining which actions, or "doings," are morally excellent or right, and one for determining which acts of the intellect are excellent.

Aristotle discusses the question of the criterion of moral excellence or rightness at various places in the *Ethics*, but again, I do not find that he gives a clear and definite answer. There have been two main types of reply to this question in the history of ethics: that of the teleologist and that of the deontologist or formalist.[12] A teleologist holds that the rightness of an action depends on the amount of good produced by it or by the rule it falls under; an action is right, he maintains, if and only if it or the rule under which it falls produces at least as great a balance of good over evil as any available alternative, and wrong if and only if this is not the case. If he thinks that only the good and evil for the agent involved needs to be considered, he is an ethical egoist. If he thinks that the criterion is the greatest balance of good or evil for one's nation, he is an ethical nationalist. Finally, if he holds, as J. S. Mill does, that the criterion is the greatest balance of good over evil in the world as a whole, he is an ethical universalist or utilitarian. A deontologist, on the other hand, denies that the rightness or wrongness of an action is determined, directly or indirectly, wholly by the relative amount of good produced, whether for oneself, one's country, or the world. According to him some actions are made right or wrong by their own intrinsic properties, not just by the goodness or badness of their consequences. Some actions or rules are right, for example, because they are just. Another action perhaps is right because it keeps a promise, the rule of keeping promises being right in itself apart from its consequences.

We shall see later that Kant is a deontologist in ethics and Dewey a teleologist of a universalistic sort. What about Aristotle? Most interpreters take him to be a teleologist (either egoistic or nationalistic) almost without discussion, as both Joachim and Ross do. I am inclined to agree with them on the whole, but I think there are considerations that point to a deontological interpretation of Aristotle and that there is no decisive way of determining just what his position is.

He begins by explaining that a moral excellence or virtue like temperance is a disposition (*hexis*), not an action or activity, not an emotion like anger, not a capacity or faculty like imagination or reason. It is a disposition to act, choose, or feel in a certain way in certain kinds of situations; one may have this disposition even when one is not acting, choosing, or feeling in that way, provided that one *would* do so *if* one were in situations of the kinds in question. Moral goodness or virtue is the possession of such dispositions to act, choose, and feel in morally excellent ways. But what ways of acting are morally excellent?

... we must carry our enquiry into the realm of conduct, and ask how we are to act, for our actions determine the quality of our dispositions. . . .[13]

Aristotle answers that we may assume that morally excellent choice and action is that which is in conformity with "right principle," and he indicates that this will be further elucidated in the discussion of practical wisdom in Book VI. Meanwhile he thinks he can make some progress. He argues that moral virtue is

... a settled disposition to choose the relative mean in action and emotion, this being determined in accordance with right principle, or as the man of practical wisdom would determine it.[14]

Aristotle's notion is that in all such matters as feeling angry, dispensing money, or eating food one may err in two ways, on the side of excess or on the side of defect, and that the right course lies, therefore, in moderation or in the mean. He seeks to show then that each of the moral virtues can be exhibited as a disposition to choose the mean between excess and defect in a certain area of action or emotion. Thus, in matters of anger, the virtue of good temper is a mean between irascibility and apathy; in the giving of money, the virtue of liberality is a mean between lavishness and meanness; in the facing of danger, the virtue of courage is a mean between rashness and cowardice; and in relation to pleasure and pain, the virtue of temperance is a mean between intemperance and insensibility. For each virtue there are two vices. But the mean is not the same for everyone; it has a certain relativity, for a hot-tempered man must lean closer to the extreme of apathy than a phlegmatic man, and a man of one constitution may habitually eat more than a man of another constitution.

This is the famous doctrine of the golden mean. But does it really give us a criterion of morally excellent action? It tells us in any situation to choose the mean and act in it, and it seems to say that the mean is to be found by some kind of arithmetical formula that will find the mid-point between two extremes, for example, that one should feel medium angry (for him) all the time, or that one should feel angry every other chance one gets. But Aristotle disowns all such arithmetical formulae, as indeed he should. However, he must still give us a criterion for determining the mean. As he says in one place,

... it is hard to find the [mean] in anything . . . anybody can become angry . . . but to be angry with . . . the right person, to the right amount, at the right time . . . and in

> the right way—this . . . is not easy. . . . it is not easy to
> define in what manner and with what people and on what
> grounds and how long one ought to be angry. . . .[15]

In other words, we cannot find out what is right by looking to see
what the mean is; we must find out what the mean is by looking
to see what is right.

Of course Aristotle sees this; in his very definition of moral virtue
he tells us that the mean must be determined by "right principle"
or "as the practically wise man would determine it." What does
this mean? H. H. Joachim, who contends that Aristotle does really
give us a fixed rule for determining the relative mean, suggests an
interesting answer.[16] Using Aristotle's example of the trainer, he formulates a rule of diet for anyone to use:

> As your digestive powers are to those of the normal (ideally
> healthy) man, so is x—the amount of food which you ought
> to take—to the amount required by the normal or standard
> man.

Similarly, he holds, Aristotle's reply to the question of how to determine the right amount of emotion to feel on any occasion is this:

> As the nature and the circumstances of the given agent A. B.
> are to the nature of the . . . man of practical wisdom under
> such and such determinate circumstances, so must x (the
> amount of emotion which A. B. ought to embody in this act)
> be to the amount of emotion embodied by the man of practical
> wisdom acting under those determinate circumstances.

Here the right act is a mean determined, not by an arithmetical
formula, but by a geometrical proportion. Assuming that one can
apply this formula in practice, it does give a rule to go by. But it
assumes that one knows what the nature and circumstances of the
man of practical wisdom are, and how much emotion he will embody
in action in those circumstances. Perhaps one can learn all this from
the man of practical wisdom himself by asking him, or perhaps one
has already been taught it all by him. There still, however, remains
the question how *he* tells what amount of emotion to feel in such
circumstances. He may be my measure of morally excellent action,
but what is his criterion? The child may go to his teacher for the
answer, but how does his teacher know? What *is* the criterion of
morally excellent action?

Now and then Aristotle seems to reply by saying that the good
man is the measure of what is right, that is, that what the good man

thinks to be right is right. Perhaps it is, but then we must first have a criterion for determining who is a good man, and this is precisely our problem.

In another passage, just after the one last quoted, Aristotle talks as if the question what degree of anger to feel in a certain situation is a matter of "perception": ". . . such questions of degree depend on particular circumstances, and the decision lies with perception."[17] This suggests that there is no criterion or rule for determining the mean or right thing to do—that one can only tell this in each particular case by some kind of intuition, moral sense, or taste for excellence, which is either innate or acquired by experience and education. If this is Aristotle's final answer to our question, as it appears to be in the context, then he is not a teleologist but a deontologist of a particularistic or perceptualistic kind—that is, one who does not believe in rules. For then he does not believe that we must determine the consequences of our actions in terms of good and evil in order to determine whether they are right or wrong.

In yet other passages, however, Aristotle speaks as if we may always tell what to do in a particular case by applying a rule via a "practical syllogism." He gives as an example:[18]

> Sweet things ought to be tasted.
> This food is sweet.
> Therefore it ought to be tasted.

In this passage he seems to be thinking that there is some set of rules we are to take as our criterion. Then whether he is a deontologist or a teleologist depends on the manner in which he thinks the rules are to be determined. If he thinks that we (or men of practical wisdom) are to find out what rules to follow by looking to see which ones have the best consequences for self or society, then he is a teleologist; if not, he is a deontologist of a somewhat different kind, viz. a rule-deontologist.

Aware that he has not yet clearly answered our question, Aristotle opens Book VI of the *Ethics* as follows:

> We have said that it is right to choose the mean . . . and that the mean is determined by right principle. Now we may examine the nature of right principle. In the case of each of the dispositions discussed, there is a mark to aim at. . . a standard determining what is in the mean between excess and defect, being in accordance with right principle. But saying this, although correct, is not very helpful. . . . we must also determine what the right rule is and what its standard is.

Here then Aristotle is going to tell us what the criterion of moral excellence or rightness is. Actually his answer is incidental to his discussion of practical wisdom, and is by no means so clear as one would like. He essentially identifies practical wisdom and right principle, and writes,

> . . . it is held to be the mark of a man of practical wisdom to be able to deliberate well about what is good or beneficial for himself . . . men like Pericles are thought to have practical wisdom because they can discern what is good for themselves and for men in general. . . . Practical wisdom then is a rational disposition that grasps the truth about actions in relation to what is good or bad for human beings.[19]

These sentences tell us that practical wisdom is knowledge of the end or good to be achieved and of the means to be used, and that the criterion by which the man of practical wisdom determines what is right (the mean) is that of conduciveness to the good. In this passage, then, Aristotle appears to be a teleologist in his ethics, as he is usually thought to be. Even here, however, it remains unclear whether he is an ethical egoist or an ethical nationalist. Sometimes he sounds like an egoist, but in one passage he asserts that the good of the state is to be preferred to that of the individual, if they are not identical, and this seems to make him an ethical nationalist.[20] However, he always either assumes or insists that the good of the individual and that of his state coincide, and hence never really addresses himself to this question.

However, even if we waive the question of whether Aristotle is an ethical egoist or nationalist, we are not yet out of the woods. For Aristotle equates the good with happiness. Thus, if he is a teleologist, then he is asserting that an action is morally right or excellent if and only if it or the rule it falls under is conducive to the greatest happiness of the agent and/or of the state. But, as we saw, Aristotle presents us with two different views about happiness—one which equates happiness with contemplative or theoretical activity, and one which includes morally excellent activity as well. Now, if we follow Ross and ascribe to Aristotle the first of these views about happiness and a teleological view about the criterion of moral excellence,[21] then his position is that an action is morally right if and only if it is most conducive to the life of contemplation in the agent and/or the state. This is a clear and possible position. But, if we follow Joachim and ascribe to Aristotle the second of these views about happiness and a teleological criterion of moral excellence,[22] then his position is circular. For then he is holding that an action is morally excellent or right if and only if it is most conducive to a life of intellectually and morally excellent activity. This may be true, but it does not give us a clear way of telling which acts are morally excellent or right.

The point may be put in another way. On Ross's interpretation Aristotle is saying, (a) the good = happiness = the most excellent activity = contemplation, and (b) morally excellent activity = activity which is conducive to the most good. This is a straightforward position, which we may call Position A. On Joachim's interpretation, which we may call Position B, Aristotle is saying (a) the good = happiness = activity which is intellectually excellent + activity which is morally excellent, and (b) morally excellent activity = activity which is conducive to the most good. And this position is circular. For it involves saying that an action is morally right if it is conducive to action which is morally right, plus activity which is intellectually excellent. Then, if we ask Aristotle what the good is, the answer, in part, is that it is morally excellent action; and, if we ask him what morally excellent action is, the answer is that it is action which promotes the good, including itself.

On a deontological interpretation Aristotle would be holding either (a) that the good = happiness = contemplation—*or* (a¹) that the good = happiness = morally excellent activity + excellent intellectual activity—*and* (b) that morally excellent action is action which is seen to be right by "perception" or which conforms to certain rules whose validity rests, not on a consideration of consequences, but on intuition, tradition, or divine command. Let us call this Position C. Now, it may be that Aristotle was holding Position B; but, if we assume that he was not taking such a circular position, then we must ascribe to him either Position A, making him a highly intellectualistic teleologist (the ultimate end of moral action, education, etc., is simply contemplation), or Position C, making him a deontologist.

The main difficulties about ascribing Position C to Aristotle are the fact that he writes in the means-end idiom of the teleologist so much of the time, and the fact that he is so explicitly teleological in the account of practical wisdom quoted above. There are, however, also difficulties about ascribing Position A to him. One is the fact that he does say that morally excellent action is a form of happiness, though a secondary one. The other is the fact that he often insists that morally right action, or "doing," is good or excellent in itself, and not merely because of its consequences. These facts point to a deontological interpretation.

It seems to me, therefore, that Aristotle's reply to our final question is not so clear as it has often been thought to be. Even so, I am inclined to agree with Ross in interpreting him as taking Position A, partly because of a passage at the end of the *Eudemian Ethics*.

Here Aristotle begins much as he does in Book VI of the *Nicomachean Ethics*. He says that, as the doctor has a standard of health, so the good man must have a standard for determining the mean. This standard is 'right principle,' but to say this is not very helpful. Then he writes,

> . . . God . . . is the end with a view to which practical wisdom issues its commands. . . . That choice then . . . which will most promote the contemplation of God is most excellent; this is the noblest standard. But any that through deficiency or excess hinders one from the contemplation and service of God is bad. . . .

This passage may have been written in Aristotle's earlier and more Platonic days, as Werner Jaeger has contended,[23] but it is in accord with Aristotle's fixed view that everything aspires toward God and that God's life is one of contemplation. If we may take it as indicative of Aristotle's final position, then he is after all a teleologist about moral rightness and wrongness. He is saying that an action is morally right if and only if it is most conducive to the life of contemplation (the intellectual life) for oneself and/or one's state.

With some doubts and difficulties, we thus arrive at the conclusion that Aristotle takes the promotion of excellent intellectual activity as the end of all human action and as the criterion of moral excellence. Then acting according to the mean turns out to be acting in such a way as to advance the life of the intellect for oneself and/or others. One addition must be made here: Aristotle does not regard an action as morally excellent merely because it does the right thing.

> The agent must also be in a certain condition when he does [it]; in the first place, he must act with knowledge, in the second, he must deliberately choose to do [it] and choose to do [it] for [its] own sake, and, in the third, his action must be the fruit of a firm and lasting disposition of character. . . . although actions are called just and temperate when they are such acts as just and temperate men do, the agent is not just and temperate merely because he does such acts, but only when he does them in the way in which just and temperate men do them.[24]

To be morally excellent an action must not only be right (by whatever criterion); it must be knowingly done and express a fixed disposition to do what is right or noble because it is right or noble. The job of the moral educator then is not just to foster those dispositions that will in fact produce right action or inhibit wrong action (though he must do at least this); he must, wherever possible, cultivate a disposition to do what is right because of its intrinsic nobility, or, as Aristotle also puts it, a disposition to find pleasure in doing what is right or noble as such.

> Hence the importance, pointed out by Plato, of having been brought up so as to like or dislike the right things; for this is the right kind of education.[25]

Only if a man exhibits this disposition in all areas of choice and action are he and his actions fully virtuous or good. For Aristotle, men and their actions are not morally excellent merely because they habitually try to do what is right as such—as they are for Kant; they must also be doing what is in fact the right thing to do. Knowledge as well as good will is required. Here Aristotle's view is similar to Dewey's, as we shall see.

We have now seen, in answer to the questions raised earlier, (a) that Aristotle regards various sorts of activities as desirable, excellent, or right, but holds only two of them to be right or valuable in themselves (noble)— viz. morally excellent action and intellectually excellent activity; (b) that he ranks the first of these below the second, (c) that his view about their relation to happiness or the good life is ambiguous: sometimes he identifies happiness with contemplation but sometimes he allows moral and political action to be a form of happiness too. We have also seen that Aristotle's view of the standard of morally excellent action is not very clear, but is probably a teleological one of some sort, egoistic or nationalistic. Now we must try to see what his criterion of excellence is in the case of intellectual activities, for they too can be well or badly performed.

THE CRITERION OF INTELLECTUAL EXCELLENCE

We saw that Aristotle distinguishes two main kinds of activity on the part of the intellect as such—that of "scientific" enquiry and that of "deliberative" thinking. But he divides the latter in turn into two kinds—"practical" thinking or knowing and "productive" thinking or knowing. Thus in effect he recognizes three kinds of intellectual activity or thinking that may be excellently or badly done. What is his view of the criterion for telling when they are excellently done? He begins by saying, of course, that excellent activity of the intellect is that in which it is performing its function well. Yes, but when is it performing its function well? Aristotle's reply is that the intellect in all of its various kinds of activity is a cognitive faculty, that is, its end is truth or knowing the truth (not only dispositionally but actually). Truth-attaining thought is the intellect's function, and it is performing well when and only when it is actively engaged in thinking that is known to be true. For Aristotle it is not enough that our thinking be lively, free, critical, sincere, sensitive, open-minded, intelligent, or what have you, as Dewey appears to hold; to be excellent it must be true. As one of Aristotle's followers puts it, "It is not by the gymnastics of its faculties, it is by the truth that [the human mind] is set free, when truth is really known. . . ."[26]

Theoretical thinking is excellent or well done when it attains the truth about what is so and what is not so, without any regard to the guidance of human action or to the satisfaction of human desire. Practical thinking is excellent or well done when it attains the truth that corresponds to right desire or the truth about action in relation to what is good or bad for human beings—that is, when it achieves knowledge of the right end, or the good, and of the means for realizing it, or, more simply, when it attains knowledge of what is morally right. Productive thinking is excellent or well done when it has the truth about making, that is, about how to make something beautiful, desirable, or useful. Roughly speaking, then, excellent theoretical thinking is "knowing *that* so and so is the case," excellent practical thinking is "knowing *what* to do," and excellent productive thinking is "knowing *how* to make something." In theoretical thinking the end is simply knowing truth for its own sake; in practical thinking it is knowing truth with an eye to moral and political action; in productive thinking it is knowing truth with a view to making something. Excellent intellectual activity of the first two kinds are desirable in themselves, but that of practical thinking is also desirable because of its effects; excellent thinking of the productive kind Aristotle seems to regard as desirable only as a means.

It would be logical to ask here what the criteria are for determining the truth in each of these three areas, but this question would carry us further into Aristotle's theory of knowledge than would be useful for our purposes. Anyway, the question of the criterion of truth in practical thinking is essentially the same as that of the criterion of what is morally right, with which we have already dealt. We should perhaps notice, however, that Aristotle holds that when the mind is actually knowing something, it is identical with its object; it somehow itself takes on the form or nature of the object it is knowing, though without the object's matter. In doing so, the mind, or a part of it that Aristotle calls "the passive intellect," is in a sense passive or receptive, but another part of it, which he calls "the active intellect" (and sometimes seems to regard as immortal and even divine), must be active—discriminating, comparing, intuiting, etc. Thus, although he does not think that knowing involves any physical action, as Dewey does, Aristotle believes that knowing is an actualization and an activity of the mind—indeed, such mental activity is for him the very paradigm of activity. To think of him as holding a "spectator" theory of knowing, as both Kant and Dewey do, is still partly correct, but it is not the whole story.

SUMMARY

We now know, as far as they can be determined, the main points in Aristotle's philosophy of life. They are: (1) that the good life = the life that will satisfy us = the happy life = the life of intrinsically excellent activities (intellectual, or intellectual *and* moral, depending on our interpretation), (2) that excellent intellectual activities are those in which truth is attained or contemplated, (3) that morally excellent activity is that which hits the mean as determined by practical wisdom, or, on a teleological interpretation of Aristotle, that which most promotes happiness in the agent and/or the state, (4) that excellent intellectual activity is superior to morally excellent activity and constitutes a higher kind of happiness, and (5) that all other kinds of activities are excellent if and only if they are conducive to the moral life and/or the intellectual life. At this point we must see how education comes into Aristotle's story.

THE ROLE AND AIM OF EDUCATION

He brings education in by asking how happiness—a life of intrinsically excellent activities—is acquired. How do or may we come to be in a position to carry on such excellent activities if and when we choose to? Are we in this position by nature (by birth), by teaching, by habituation, by some other kind of training, by divine gift, or by fortune? (a) Clearly not by nature, Aristotle argues, though not against nature; all that nature provides is the basic capacities or powers required—and it does not give all of us all of these in the same amount or degree. (b) Not by divine gift; if anything is a gift of the gods, Aristotle says, it is reasonable to suppose that happiness is, but, in his metaphysics, as we have seen, God (and the gods) cannot literally be thought of as literally "doing" or giving anything— He (they) only sets a pattern or ideal for us to strive toward and even here the impetus must come from us (*the impetus* is in us by nature). (c) Good fortune, as we have also seen, is required, but our conclusion must be (d) that happiness is achieved "by excellence and by some kind of study or training"—in short, by education. I take Aristotle to mean that we put ourselves in the position of being prepared to engage in excellent practical and intellectual activity by acquiring certain dispositions or excellences by some kind of education. This is essentially what I argued for in Chapter I and need not be further spelled out here.

We may, then, summarize Aristotle's conception of the aims of education as follows. The *ultimate* aim of education, as of life, is the attainment by the individual and/or the state of the highest possible happiness, that is, the performance of intrinsically excellent activities of the highest possible kind or kinds. Education's part in the attainment of this end, and hence its *proximate* aim, is to cultivate the dispositions that will make people able, ready, and willing to perform the intrinsically excellent activities that constitute happiness and/or the other activities that are necessary or useful as means to or conditions of such intrinsically excellent ones. This is why Aristotle can say, in a passage already quoted, that, since the end of politics is the good life, its principal care must be to foster in the citizens the dispositions to do what is excellent.

With this conception of the central role of education in life and society, Aristotle in the *Politics* criticizes Plato, somewhat unfairly, for relying too much on legislation and dictation and too little on education and the dispositions it may produce. Conceivably a ruler might get his people to think the truth and to do the right by telling them at each moment what to think or what to do and by each time making some dire threat or promising some moving reward; then he would be making a minimal use of education and putting a minimal reliance on the cultivation of dispositions. This is not what Aristotle envisages (or Plato either). He clearly thinks that, ideally at least, individuals who have the necessary capacities should be educated into the required dispositions and then left to carry on pretty much under their own steam—in a kind of autonomy motivated by a desire to do what is excellent for its own sake.

THE DISPOSITIONS TO BE CULTIVATED

In principle Aristotle's answer to the question, "What dispositions or excellences are we to try to cultivate?" is already clear, at least as far as the *Ethics* is concerned (the *Politics* introduces a complication, as we shall see). We must cultivate all of the dispositions that underlie and condition our being in a position to lead the good life (with an assist from fortune), that is, to engage more or less freely in the various kinds of intrinsically excellent activities, and to do what is necessary as a means to engaging in these activities. For we must remember that it is not only the activities which are included in happiness, or which are intrinsically excellent, that are to be engaged in; those that are good only as means (making, working, etc.) must also be carried on, at least by some of us, if not by all. Even if morally excellent actions are good only as a means and are no part of happiness (as a teleological interpretation of Aristotle would hold), they are still of crucial importance and the dispositions to carry them out must still be cultivated.

MORAL VIRTUES

Although Aristotle's answer is clear in principle, we must still see how he fills it out. Let us begin by asking what dispositions he regards as morally excellent. They will, of course, be dispositions to do what is right or morally excellent, but which dispositions are these? Aristotle has a rather long list of them, which he may not regard as complete: courage, temperance, justice, liberality, magnificence, greatness of soul, good temper, truthfulness, wittiness, friendliness, righteous indignation, and others—most of which he discusses at some length. Each of them he conceives as a habitual disposition to choose the morally right action (i.e. the mean) in a certain general type of situation as determined by the criterion of moral action (whatever his view of this is), and to choose the action because it is right. Thus temperance is a disposition to do the right thing about pleasures and pains because it is right, that is, to do *what* the temperate man does and to do it *as* the temperate man does it. Liberality and magnificence are virtues relating to the use of money, the former on the part of the man who deals in small amounts of it, the latter on the part of one who can deal in large amounts. Some of Aristotle's moral excellences, it must be admitted, sound a bit strange to our ears. Most interesting, perhaps, is greatness of soul or lofty pride. The great-souled man seems almost to be Aristotle's ideal, for he regards greatness of soul as "a sort of crown of the virtues" since it enhances their excellence and cannot exist without them. He describes it in part as follows:

> . . . a man is thought to have greatness of soul if he claims much and is worthy of it. . . . [He] is an extreme in respect of the greatness of his claims, but a mean in respect of the rightness of them, for he claims what he deserves. . . . honor is his object and is what he claims and deserves. . . . the truly great-souled man must be a good man; greatness in each virtue must belong to him. It would not become him to run from danger or to act dishonestly . . . it is hard to be truly great-souled. . . . the great-souled man will be moderately pleased to receive honor from good men, feeling that he is only getting what is coming to him . . . but honor given by common people or on trivial grounds he will despise. . . . he will also bear himself with measure in respect to

> wealth, power, and good or evil fortune, not rejoicing too
> much at prosperity or grieving too much in adversity. . . .
> he . . . does not seek danger, because there are few things
> he values very much, but he will face great dangers . . . he
> confers benefits, but is ashamed to receive them. . . . he is
> haughty toward men of high position but courteous to those
> of moderate station, for . . . it is vulgar to lord it over those
> below one. He does not compete for the usual objects of
> ambition, and he is . . . slow to act except when great honor
> and achievement are at stake. . . . he is open in speech and
> action because he is contemptuous of others and cares more
> for truth than for what people think. . . . He is not given to
> admiration, . . . he does not bear a grudge, . . . he is not
> a gossip. . . .[27]

Further, says Aristotle, he will walk with a slow step and speak in
a deep and even voice. There is a certain nobility in this ideal, but
a modern reader can hardly help feeling that it represents the kind
of pride that goeth before a fall.

These, in general outline, are "the virtues [or moral excellences]
of the good man," as Aristotle calls them in the *Politics*. The fully
virtuous man, the knight in full moral armor, will have them all in
their ideal or perfect form; he will habitually but deliberately choose
the right course in all kinds of situations for its own sake (or because
it is noble, which comes to the same thing). But, of course, Aristotle
does not think that everyone is called upon to achieve all of these
virtues in their most perfect forms. He does believe that human nature
is the same in all men and hence that the moral ideal is the same
for all; we must all achieve these virtues to the degree to which
fortune and our natural capacities make it possible for us to do so.
But, although the essence of human nature is in all of us, its ingredients are not present in all of us to the same extent; hence our
capacities differ and the forms and degrees of the moral excellences
that may be expected of us will differ accordingly.

> All persons share in the different parts of the soul, but in
> different ways. The slave is entirely without the faculty of
> deliberation; the woman does possess it, but in an unauthori-
> tative form; and if children also have it, it is only in an
> immature form.

Aristotle goes on to say here that the required virtue is relative,
not only to one's native capacities, but to one's social function or role.

> . . . all must share in [moral excellence], but not in the same

way—each sharing only to the extent required by his function. The ruler must therefore have it in its perfect form . . . but others require only so much of it as is proper to each.[28]

This seems to mean that the virtues of temperance, justice, etc., take different forms depending on whether one's role is that of a ruler, a household head, a slave, a woman, a worker, or a child— that is, that the duties of one's station determine to some extent which virtues one is required to have and in what sorts of actions they are to be displayed. However, since Aristotle holds that one's social function is determined by his capacities (or rather should be), this comes to the same thing as saying that we must achieve the moral virtues to the extent and only to the extent to which nature and fortune make us capable of them. The ideal remains the same for all of us.

PIETY

One of the traditional Greek virtues was piety, but it is strikingly absent from Aristotle's list. Why? One suspects it is because Aristotle's God is not the kind of God whose existence and relation to the world calls for anything like piety in the usual sense, though he tactfully avoids saying this, and in the *Politics* even provides for religious services. We must remember, however, that, in his view, all things are striving to be like God, each by coming to perform the most excellent activity of which it is capable. Perhaps this is what Aristotle would mean by piety, but, if so, it is a "natural piety" that all things have and that does not need to be cultivated but only brought to consciousness and lighted on its way. In this sense piety is not a moral excellence; it is simply the desire for excellence that is the presupposition of Aristotle's thought.

VICE

Two undesirable moral dispositions or traits of character discussed by Aristotle must be mentioned. The first is vice, the opposite of virtue. It consists of a fixed disposition to choose, not the mean, but excess or deficiency—that is, to choose a wrong course of action. Vicious action is voluntary, according to Aristotle, just as virtuous action is, and is as blameworthy as virtuous action is praiseworthy. But, although the vicious man acts voluntarily, he acts as he does at least partly because of ignorance; he does not know the true end or the right principles of action and so acts on mistaken views of the good and the right. He takes pleasure and avoidance of pain as the end of life and action. It must be the main task of moral education to prevent this sort of practical ignorance and wrongness of purpose.

The other undesirable disposition of character is *akrasia*, variously translated as "incontinence," "unrestraint," and "weakness of will." It is different from vice. The incontinent man frequently and voluntarily does what is wrong but (a) he knows that what he is doing is wrong in a sense in which the vicious man does not, and (b) he has not settled down into a fixed disposition to do what is wrong, as the vicious man has. He does not deliberately choose to do what is wrong; his passions keep him from doing what he in some sense knows is right. He has a kind of knowledge of the true end and of the right principles of action, and his purpose is good, and so, Aristotle says, he is only half wicked. His education, like that of the wicked man, has failed, but not so much by leaving him in moral ignorance as by leaving him without self-control. Actually, he too does in a way act wrongly because of ignorance, for Aristotle believes that, if a man has *full active* or *operative* knowledge of the principles of action and of his circumstances at the moment of acting, he cannot voluntarily fail to act rightly. But the incontinent man's passions are so strong and so uncontrolled that they keep his knowledge from operating or keep him from getting the knowledge he needs. His action remains voluntary and blameworthy because he might have taken or might still take steps to get his passions under control. He has his moments of insight and good will in a way in which the vicious man does not, but he cannot live by them in any steady way. In contrast, the vicious man may have his passions under much better control and may live steadily enough, but by the wrong principles and to a bad end.

> . . . the incontinent man is like a state that passes all the right decrees and has good laws, but does not live by them . . . whereas the bad man is like a state that keeps its laws but has bad ones.[29]

Or again, incontinence is like a recurrent curable disease, while vice is like a constant incurable one.

This brings us to the topic of the intellectual excellences. Which dispositions of the intellect does Aristotle regard as desirable? Those that attain truth, of course, but which ones are these? It will help here if we first have a general picture of our intellectual life as Aristotle sees it. Intellectual life begins with a knowledge of particular things through the senses, for we have no innate knowledge. We do, however, have innately a perfected sensory ability—this is the one excellence Aristotle believes us to be born with, and so he does not speak of educating the senses, as some later educators do, including Kant. This basic sensory grasp of particulars involves a perception or intuition. With the aid of memory and imagination perception is developed into a crude but important kind of knowledge that Aristotle calls "experience" (which he is always saying the young do not yet have).

> . . . out of sense-perception comes what we call memory, and out of frequently repeated memories of the same thing comes experience. . . . From experience again—from the universal now established in the soul, the one thing that is the same in the various presentations of the particular—originate the skill of the craftsman and the knowledge of the man of science. . . . It is like a rout in battle stopped by first one man making a stand and then another, until the original formation has been restored. The soul is so constituted as to be capable of doing this. . . . When one of a number of logically similar particulars has made a stand, the first universal is present in the soul, for though the act of sense-perception is of the particular, its content is universal (man, not just Callias). A fresh stand is made among these rudimentary universals, and the process goes on until . . . the true universals are established, e.g. the concept of such and such a species of animal is a step toward that of the genus animal, which by the same process is a step towards a further generalization.[30]

By a process of induction (plus some comparison and abstraction) we may come to an intuition of universals and of connections between universals—for example, the basic concepts and premises of geometry. But this induction-cum-intuition is only one source of first principles or major premises for our thinking.

> First principles are grasped, some by induction, some by perception, some by a kind of habituation, and some in other ways.[31]

Once grasped they may serve as a basis for reasoning to further conclusions—for practical or theoretical inferences or deductions. But, finally, if and when any application is to be made, some kind of perception or intuition of the particular must come in again—of this man, this triangle, etc.

This general account holds in some form for all our thinking. But, as we have seen, Aristotle distinguishes three kinds of thinking: theoretical, practical, and productive. It follows that there are three main intellectual excellences: (1) the disposition of excellent theoretical thinking, (2) that of excellent practical thinking, and (3) that of excellent productive thinking. The first Aristotle calls *sophia* or theoretical wisdom, the second *phronesis* or practical wisdom, the third *techne* or art. These are the three inclusive dispositions of the mind that put it in the position of being able to see the truth or to judge truly.

(1) Theoretical wisdom, Aristotle says, is a combination of two other intellectual excellences, intuition and science. By intuition he means here the ability to grasp basic concepts and premises, by science "the ability to demonstrate," that is, to deduce valid conclusions from the basic premises apprehended by intuition. By this combination of intuition and deductive reasoning the mind is able to develop systems of completely certain knowledge in several fields. The subject matter of theoretical wisdom Aristotle usually describes as that which is eternal, necessary, or invariable, as compared with that which is changing, contingent, or variable. He especially insists that theoretical wisdom is not concerned either with how man should act or with anything that can be affected by or applied to man's action. When theoretical wisdom is not concerned with what is eternal, it is still seeking generalizations about what is changing— generalizations that are true necessarily, always or at least "for the most part"—laws of behavior that are invariable or at least natural. Such theoretical wisdom has three divisions: physics (which includes biology and psychology, as well as astronomy, "physics," etc.), mathematics, and metaphysics. Physics deals with things that have a separate existence but are not unchangeable, mathematics with things that are unchangeable but have no separate existence (numbers, triangles, etc.), metaphysics with things that have a separate existence and are unchangeable (e.g. God). Each of these disciplines involves a use of both intuition and science.

Looking at the matter in one way, we may say that there are three excellences of the scientific intellect: theoretical intuition, science, and theoretical wisdom (which is a combination of the others). But Aristotle would also call a knowledge of mathematics or an ability to do mathematics an intellectual excellence, and, looking at the matter in this way, we may distinguish three other excellences of the theoretical intellect: physics, mathematics, and metaphysics. When he says that happiness is contemplation or that the highest happiness is contemplation he means by contemplation the exercise of theoretical wisdom in these three fields.

(2) We have already discussed practical wisdom to some extent.

Like all thought, practical thinking begins with some kind of perception or intuition of particulars, in this case particular actions. Then somehow it arrives at a conception of the end or good to be pursued in life, or at a knowledge of the first principle(s) of action. Just how practical thinking arrives at the correct basic premises of moral and political action Aristotle does not make very clear, with the result that his conception of moral and political education also remains unclear. He seems to think that some kind of induction is involved, and insists that a process of right habituation is likewise presupposed; but does he also hold that, given this induction and this habituation, we may then grasp the first premise(s) of practical reasoning by a process of intuition like that involved in mathematics? On the whole it would seem that he does not. Perhaps his real answer to the question of how we may acquire our practical first principles is simply that we must follow the line of thought he lays out for us in the *Ethics*, especially Book I. In any case, he does mean to include under practical wisdom some kind of ability to grasp the basic premises of action. Also, though he gives us no name for this, he does find in practical wisdom something corresponding to science. For he thinks of practical wisdom as proceeding from its basic principles to conclusions for action by way of one or more "practical syllogisms," as he calls them. On the purely teleological interpretation of Aristotle's view of the moral criterion which we mentioned earlier, this process of reasoning must ultimately have as its first major premise the proposition that the end or the good or happiness is contemplation. Then, to adapt one of Aristotle's examples, it might go on as follows:[32]

A
1. The good is contemplation.
2. Health is conducive to contemplation.
3. ∴ Health is desirable for man.

B
1. Health is desirable for man.
2. Dry food is conducive to health in all men.
3. ∴ Dry food is good for all men.

C
1. Dry food is good for all men.
2. I am a man.
3. ∴ Dry food is good for me.

D
1. Dry food is good for me.
2. This bread is dry.
3. ∴ This bread is good for me.

Actually Aristotle says that the last conclusion of a piece of practical reasoning is not a proposition like D3 but an action like eating. But the main thing for us to notice is that he conceives of practical reason (a) as providing by intuition or some other method the basic normative premise; (b) as providing also all of the *factual* statements which serve as minor premises, viz. A2, B2, C2, and D2; and (c) as correctly drawing conclusions A3, B3, C3, and D3. Since a grasp of particulars is involved in minor premises C2 and D2 and in the final conclusion, Aristotle holds that practical wisdom also involves a use of a kind of intuition; in fact, in this use, intuition is simply the "perception" which he sometimes says we must appeal to in determining the mean or the right—it certainly is not the kind of intuition involved in theoretical wisdom. As for factual premises A2 and B2, which tell us what will bring about certain results, these are supplied by what Aristotle calls cleverness, which is the ability to know what to do in order to achieve a certain result and is only part of practical wisdom when it is associated with a commitment to the right end or basic principle.

Thus practical wisdom is a combination of perceptual intuition, induction, practical syllogizing, cleverness, and ability to know the first principles of action—all preceded by right habituation. The subject matter of practical wisdom consists (a) of normative judgments pertaining to action and (b) of factual judgments about what is variable and affected by human action, about what is a means to what, about the results of our actions, and about the facts of our particular situations. Aristotle sometimes talks as if practical wisdom is identical with politics, but at other times he distinguishes it into three parts: politics, which relates to the state; economics, which relates to the family or household; and ethics, which relates to the life of the individual.

(3) Productive thinking is concerned to tell us how to produce something. Hence, like practical thinking, it is concerned with the variable and contingent and with what can be affected by human action. Its excellence is art or *techne*, which Aristotle defines as a disposition to think truly about making or bringing something into existence. As indicated above, it comes to man through experience.

> . . . art arises when from many notions gained by experience one universal judgment about a class of objects is produced. For to have judgment that when Callias was ill of this disease this did him good, and similarly in the case of Socrates and in many individual cases, is a matter of experience; but to judge that it has done good to all persons of a certain constitution, marked off in one class, when they were ill of this

disease, e.g. to phlegmatic or bilious people when burning with fever—this is a matter of art.[33]

We may call art "productive wisdom," and it seems clear that, like practical wisdom, it involves perceptual intuition of particulars, induction, and cleverness, and perhaps a kind of practical syllogizing as well—all accompanied by practice. The main difference between it and practical wisdom is that its end is not doing but making, not action for its own sake, but action for the sake of bringing something into existence—health, a building, or a statue—something which may be in turn a means to activity that is valuable for its own sake. There are a number of arts or productive excellences: medicine is one of them, as the last quotation shows, others are the various crafts, and still others are the different fine arts.

When we ask Aristotle for a list of the intellectual excellences, he lists five dispositions: art, science, intuition, theoretical wisdom, and practical wisdom. In view of our discussion it would perhaps be better to say that there are seven: (1) perceptual intuition, (2) theoretical intuition, (3) science or excellent theoretical reasoning, (4) excellent practical reasoning, (5) cleverness, (6) induction, plus (7) whatever it is that grasps basic premises for action. Then theoretical wisdom would be a combination of (2) and (3), preceded by (1) and (6); practical wisdom would be a combination of (4), (5), (7), and (1), also preceded by (1) and (6); and art or productive wisdom would be a combination of (4), (5), and (1), preceded by (1) and (6). But we must remember that we could also draw up a list on a different basis: (a) excellent dispositions of the scientific intellect: geometry, astronomy, physics, biology, metaphysics, etc.; (b) excellent dispositions of the deliberative intellect concerned with doing: economics, politics, and ethics; (c) excellent dispositions of the deliberative intellect concerned with making: medicine, architecture, carpentry, shoe-making, sculpture, etc. An emphasis on the first list would mean a stress on "method" in education, while an emphasis on the second would mean a stress on "subject matter." As far as I can see, Aristotle can be read either way.

In general, then, Aristotle distinguishes three main intellectual excellences: theoretical wisdom, practical wisdom, and productive wisdom. Of these he ranks the first above the second, presumably because theoretical wisdom is more purely intellectual; practical wisdom has as its end, not knowing itself, but action. He also ranks the second above the third because, though both have action as their end, the action aimed at by practical wisdom is good in itself, whereas that aimed at by productive wisdom is good only for what it makes or produces.

PRACTICAL WISDOM AND MORAL VIRTUE

Although Aristotle lists practical wisdom as an intellectual excellence, he thinks of it as having a very intimate connection with moral excellence. (1) He insists that if our choice is to be right and our action morally excellent, then we must be committed to the right end or principle and our knowledge of facts and means must be accurate. But, he points out, moral excellence ensures our being committed to the right end or principle, while practical wisdom provides us with the necessary knowledge of facts and means, as well as with the knowledge of the right end or principle itself. (2) Aristotle also contends that we cannot be morally good unless we have practical wisdom. We can do the right thing pretty consistently without practical wisdom, either because we are naturally inclined to do the same actions that the virtuous man does or because someone conditions us to do such actions. As we have seen, however, we are not fully virtuous unless we not only do what the virtuous man does, but also do it as the virtuous man does it, viz. because it is right. This means that being virtuous involves seeing that what you are doing is right, and this requires the possession of practical wisdom.

> Moral excellence is not merely a disposition to conform to right principle, it is a disposition to cooperate with right principle.[34]

(3) Aristotle maintains that we cannot have practical wisdom unless we are morally good. If we are not committed to the right end or first principle of action, our knowledge of facts and means remains mere cleverness; it is not yet practical wisdom. To amount to practical wisdom it must be accompanied by a knowledge of the right end or first principle, and one can only know this if one is a morally good man.

> . . . the supreme good appears good only to the morally good man; vice perverts the mind and causes it to hold false views about the first principles of conduct. Hence we cannot have practical wisdom without being morally good.[35]

It looks here as if Aristotle reasons in a circle in his conception of the relation of practical wisdom and moral excellence, since he says that each presupposes the other. We must return to this point when we study Aristotle's views on moral and practical education. Just now we must notice that he maintains (4) that if a man has the intellectual excellence of practical wisdom he will be morally virtuous—he will in fact have all the moral excellences, for it is not possible to fully have one of these without having the others. Thus, while he insists against Socrates that theoretical knowledge is neither a necessary nor a sufficient condition of moral excellence, he does agree that practical knowledge is both a necessary and a sufficient condition of such excellence. But in saying this we must remember that, for him, moral excellence is also a necessary condition of practical wisdom.

It follows from these considerations that, in Aristotle's view, the intellectual excellence of practical wisdom and the moral excellences all together make up a single state of character, at least in their ideal forms—a single complex excellence which has two aspects, one a cognition of the proper ends, principles, and means of practical action, the other a fixed disposition to act accordingly for its own sake. To this extent he agrees with Socrates that excellence is one— but only to this extent, since he holds that there are excellences not included in this complex—namely, theoretical wisdom and the arts.

ART

We should also understand that what Aristotle calls a "technical" excellence is an art like shipbuilding or sculpture, taken as a whole—not as a purely intellectual affair, but as a union of know-how with a disposition to skillful action of a certain sort. In other words, both the moral and the technical excellences are really fusions of an excellence of the deliberative part of the intellect with an excellence of the appetitive part of the soul.

OTHER DISPOSITIONS

Are there any other dispositions to be cultivated besides the intellectual, moral, and technical excellences we have been discussing? There are useful skills and subjects like those involved in battle or in what Aristotle calls work, e.g. fighting in armor or plowing, which do not seem to be covered by the above list. Someone must have such skills in any society; indeed, Aristotle seems to think that we must all have at least some of them in some degree or other, though he might not be willing to call them all excellences. Certainly he would insist that we do not all need to acquire all of them, and presumably he would also say this of the arts or productive excellences. The other intellectual excellences and the moral ones, however, we are all to acquire to the extent to which we are capable of them, for, on his view, we achieve happiness—our aim in life— only insofar as we engage in excellent intellectual or moral activity. The end and ideal, according to Aristotle, is the same for all of us, since we all have the same basic nature, and we must all come as close to attaining it as possible. All of us are to be measured on the same scale of excellence, and if any of us fall short on this scale, either because of incapacity or because of ignorance, vice, weakness, or lack of effort, we must remain to that extent frustrated, unfulfilled, and unhappy, whether we know it or not.

FRIENDSHIP

There is one more disposition Aristotle treats at length—friendship. In Books II and IV of the *Ethics* he describes a kind of agreeableness or friendliness as a moral excellence, and as a mean between obsequiousness and surliness, but distinguishes this from friendship because it does not involve the element of special affection that friendship does. Friendship he takes up separately in Books VIII and IX, saying (a) that it is an excellence or involves excellence and (b) that it is most necessary for life, excellence, and happiness. Two men are friends when each has a fixed disposition of liking and goodwill toward the other and both are aware that this is the case. There are three kinds of friendship: in the first, two persons are friends because they are pleasing to one another; in the second, because they are useful to one another; in the third, because they are both good and may help each other toward excellence. Of these the last is the highest kind, the second the lowest. Friendship of all kinds is the cement that should hold society together, and in the ideal state the friendship of citizens should be that of the highest kind.

THE TASK OF EDUCATION

These, then (except for vice and incontinence), are the dispositions education is to foster, according to Aristotle, because they are required for the performance of activities that are parts of or means to the best life or highest happiness of the individual and/or the state, and because, except for sensory excellence, they are not innate or given by God; thus education is the only way man can acquire them—other than by mere chance. We must all come to possess these dispositions insofar as we can if we are to be as happy as possible—if we are to come as close as possible to achieving what we aim at in life, namely, excellence of activity—and education must help us to acquire them. Nature does make a contribution— namely, our natural endowment, and so does fortune; but, as Aristotle puts it, "the rest is the task of education."

THE EXCELLENCES OF THE GOOD MAN OR THOSE OF THE CITIZEN?

The above account of the dispositions to be fostered by education is, however, based on the *Ethics*, and, as has been indicated, the *Politics* introduces a complication. Here Aristotle asks whether a system of education is actually to cultivate the excellences of the good man (i.e. those of the *Ethics*, just reviewed); the question is startling, for one naturally assumes that this is precisely what education is for—to foster the dispositions that are most excellent in the abstract. However, Aristotle maintains that this is not obviously true. Even in the *Ethics* he writes, apparently contradicting what he had said earlier about the principal care of political science:

> As for the education of the individual as such, which makes a man a good man simply, whether this is the business of political science or of some other must be determined later; for it may be that the good man and the good citizen are not always the same.[36]

This passage seems to imply that political science and the statesman are to promote the excellences of the good man only if these are the same as those of the good citizen. The later discussion referred to is, of course, the *Politics*, where Aristotle implicitly or explicitly advances the following theses:

(a) The educational system of a people is relative to the constitution prevailing in their country. "The citizens of a state should always be educated to suit the constitution of their state."[37] In other words, the education in a country must first of all cultivate the virtues of the good citizen as these are defined by its constitution. It must foster those dispositions required for the maintenance and implementation of the prevailing constitution and its ends or principles—democratic dispositions if the constitution is democratic, etc. Education may not seek to bring about any social reform except such as is compatible with realizing more fully the ends and principles embodied in the existing constitution. Hence it may concern itself with promoting the excellences of the good man as defined in the *Ethics* only if and insofar as doing so is compatible with the constitution under which it operates, or only if and insofar as the excellences coincide with those of the good citizen as defined by that constitution.

(b) *Are* the excellences of the good man identical or compatible with those of the good citizen? Aristotle answers that they are not always compatible. Their compatibility depends on the requirements of the constitution, and the dispositions required by different constitutions vary greatly; they certainly are not always those described in the *Ethics*. Those in the *Ethics* are, in fact, he thinks, excellences that go with a certain kind of aristocratic constitution, and are incompatible with the dispositions required of a faithful citizen of a thoroughgoing democracy. But even in the ideal state, which is for him a certain kind of aristocracy, the two kinds of excellence will not always coincide. Even here there will and must be classes of people (slaves, workers, women, etc.) whose excellences as determined by the constitution are not those of the good man; it is only for the full citizens who rule the state together or in rotation that the two sets of excellences are the same (it would not be the ideal state if they were not the same).

I take these theses of Aristotle to imply that the excellences of the good man may be cultivated without question only where his ideal constitution is already in effect—or perhaps also where no constitution is yet in effect (if there can be such a place), and where the people have the required intelligence, spirit, and economic circumstances. Otherwise the excellences of the good man may be cultivated only insofar as their cultivation and exercise is compatible with the existing constitution. In short, an educator who has read the *Ethics* must stop and look, before he proceeds to apply what it tells him—and even before he proceeds to apply what the chapters on education in the *Politics* tell him.

This need not mean that Aristotle believes one should be a good citizen before one should be a good man; though he does not seem to recognize any right of revolution where these turn out to be inconsistent, he may have held that Socrates was right in refusing to obey the state when it forbade him to teach. But this does mean that education—including certainly public and perhaps also private education—must be loyal first of all to the constitution under which it serves, if not to every law that is passed. It also means that Aristotle's theory of education is not immediately and unqualifiedly relevant in all countries. We may assume, however, that he did believe it should be followed everywhere *insofar as* doing so is compatible with the constitution; thus, the theory remains after all a kind of pattern for all to use as they can.

METHODS AND CURRICULUM

TWO METHODS

We have seen why Aristotle believes that education is necessary, what dispositions it must foster, at least in the citizens of the ideal state, and why it should foster them. We must now ask what methods it is to use. In his answer Aristotle always distinguishes two methods, though he does not always do so in the same words: (a) habituation or practice, (b) instruction or verbal formulation.

> . . . all powers and abilities are either innate like that of the senses, or acquired by practice like that of playing the flute, or acquired by learning like that of the arts. . . .[38]

Or again,

> . . . men learn some things by habituation and some by instruction.[39]

In emphasizing the first of these two methods Aristotle is stressing a possibility neglected by Socrates, as we shall see; he is also in a sense anticipating the Deweyan stress on "learning by doing." For he is saying that the acquisition of certain excellences takes place, at least in part, by a repeated doing of actions like those the excellences are intended to produce. In talking of the second method, however, he appears to be advocating precisely what Dewey opposes, for he seems to mean by it the method of telling or explaining in words; in one place he even equates it with learning by listening. Sometimes he mentions that this method involves the use of and appeal to reason (*logos*), but, at any rate, he does not think of it as involving any physical activity (except maybe listening).

This does not mean, however, that the child is purely passive even in the second kind of education or learning. We must remember that Aristotle regards thinking and contemplation as activities. In any case, he carefully points out that when one person is teaching another, the first is not merely acting on the second or the second merely being acted on by the first, as when a moving lifeless object strikes a stationary one.[40] For in both persons there is desire, reason, and choice, at least in an incipient form. We ought not say, therefore, that the one is being acted on or altered by the other; or, rather, since we cannot help saying this, we must recognize that a special kind of interaction or alteration is going on. This is shown among other things, Aristotle thinks, by the fact that, if two things with reason interact, contrary outcomes are both possible, while, if two things without reason interact, only one outcome can be forthcoming. What determines the outcome in the former case is desire, or choice, on the part of the one "acted on" (say, the child) as well as on the part of the one "acting" (say, the teacher). To this extent, at least, Aristotle is recognizing the importance of activity and interest in education.

However this may be, having distinguished the two methods by which excellences may be taught and learned, Aristotle says, in a famous passage, that

> . . . intellectual excellence is for the most part both produced and increased by instruction, and therefore requires experience and time, but moral excellence is the product of habit. . . .

Aristotle does not expand at all on the acquisition of the intellectual excellences, but about that of the moral ones he goes on to write:

> . . . we become just by doing just acts, temperate by doing temperate acts, brave by doing brave acts. . . . states of character are formed by doing the corresponding acts. That is why we must control the nature of our actions. . . . It makes no small difference . . . whether we form habits of one kind or another in our youth; it makes a very great, or rather *all* the difference.[41]

In this passage, Aristotle appears to say that the moral virtues are acquired entirely by the method of practice or habituation, and that the method of verbal instruction is not at all necessary or applicable. It is doubtful, however, that this is what he really means. For one thing, he used the lecture method himself in teaching ethics; for another, he held that practical wisdom is presupposed by moral virtue (and vice versa), and so, if he regards instruction as necessary in teaching practical wisdom, as he seems to, he must also be regarding it as necessary in teaching moral virtue.

Perhaps then Aristotle's point is that practice or habituation is a necessary, and even the most important, factor in moral education. He certainly holds that the method of instruction does not suffice here, as Socrates seemed to imply when he said that virtue is knowledge. Except for a few gifted natures, says Aristotle, the young and the masses are mostly led about by their passions; with them, as with the incontinent man, verbal instruction by itself is virtually impotent.

> . . . living as they do by passion, they pursue the pleasures akin to their nature . . . and avoid the opposite pains . . . how then can reasoning reform them? To dislodge their habits by argument is difficult, if not impossible. . . . argument and instruction are not effective in all cases; the soul of the pupil must first have been prepared by the cultivation of habits . . . just as the soil must be prepared for the seed. For he who lives at the dictates of passion will neither hear nor understand the reasoning used to instruct him.[42]

That is why it makes all the difference "whether we are trained from childhood in one set of habits or another." But to say all this does not imply that the method of instruction has no role whatsoever in the formation of the moral virtues.

Aristotle says about the intellectual excellences that they are "for the most part" transmitted and acquired by instruction. Is he thinking, then, that practice, or habituation, also plays a part in intellectual education, though a smaller one? He includes the arts among the intellectual excellences, at least in part, and he says that practice is involved in learning them; he also lists practical wisdom as an intellectual excellence, but insists that right habituation is a prerequisite to its acquisition. He does hold, therefore, that the excellences of the deliberative intellect are partly "learned by doing." But what about the excellences of the scientific or theoretical intellect? Does Aristotle believe that, besides hearing instruction in mathematics, physics, and metaphysics, we must somehow practice or "do" them if we are to learn them? He does not give an explicit answer, but he may well have thought that, if one is to learn geometry, one must do geometrical exercises. This is suggested by what he goes on to say following the passage quoted not long ago from the *Metaphysics:* having said that all powers and abilities are either innate, acquired by practice, or acquired by instruction, he adds that "those which come by practice or by rational formula must be acquired by previous exercise." His example here of these latter abilities is the arts, but this statement seems to imply that some "previous exercise" is required even in the learning of the theoretical excellences. This appears also to be implied by a passage in the *Politics*:

> Moreover, in the case of every power and art, some previous education and habituation is necessary for its proper exercise. . . .[43]

In any case, Aristotle would surely have thought that one cannot be passive even in listening to instruction in the theoretical disciplines and still learn anything significant; one must at least *think* while one is listening, and for him to think is to be active.

THE ARTS

What about education in the arts? In one of the quoted passages Aristotle writes as if the arts are acquired wholly by practice and not at all by instruction; but he cannot mean this. He must have thought that masters not only show their apprentices how but also give them verbal instructions. Indeed, in another of the passages quoted, he writes as if the arts are acquired by a kind of learning different from practice, and in the *Poetics* he was himself giving instruction to writers of tragedy—instructions that were very influential in the history of drama. His full view, then, must have been that the arts or productive excellences are to be taught and acquired by a combination of the two methods of education. In fact, if what I have been saying about the other excellences is correct, it looks as if he really believes that both methods are or should be involved in *all* education, though in different proportions. Then an element of learning by doing is involved in the acquisition of any excellence, but some learning by listening is also. In the case of the moral and productive excellences the "doing" or "previous exercise" will involve actual overt action, but, in the case of the theoretical excellences at least, Aristotle would probably conceive of "doing" as involving only thinking and no physical action (unless listening, paying attention, etc., are counted as physical actions).

THE MENO

It is now clear how Aristotle answers the problem of Plato's *Meno*. There Socrates asks whether excellence is acquired by teaching, by practice, by nature, or by divine gift, argues that it is not innate and cannot be taught, and concludes, regretfully, that excellence comes, if at all, by the grace of the gods. Aristotle's reply is, in effect, that we can solve the problem only by breaking it up. We must distinguish intellectual, moral, and productive excellences. Of these, intellectual excellence is teachable by the method of instruction, though only by one who himself has it and perhaps not to everyone. The other two kinds of excellence are, indeed, not teachable by the method of instruction alone even by those who have them —on this point Socrates is right—but they *are* teachable by the method Socrates mentions and does not really consider—namely, that of habituation or practice—though perhaps only in conjunction with instruction. Moral virtue, in particular, is not just a matter of knowing what is right, as Socrates thought; it presupposes also a long period of habituation in right action. But given this, and some luck in the matter of native endowment (i.e. Greek blood), moral virtue can be taught with reasonable chance of success.

MORAL EDUCATION

This is a good place to say something more about Aristotle's views on moral education. Moral education has two aspects or parts: (a) the acquisition of the intellectual excellence of practical wisdom, that is, of the ability to see what one should do, as explained earlier, and (b) the acquisition of the moral (appetitive) excellence of moral virtue, that is, of the disposition to choose the mean or the right as determined by practical wisdom. Complete moral education will include both; in fact, as we saw, each presupposes the other. The first, practical wisdom, is taught and acquired mainly by instruction —"the direct method," as it is called. The second, moral virtue, is taught and acquired by habituation or practice—a kind of "indirect method." Aristotle does not explain just what these two kinds or parts of moral education involve, but it is not hard to guess what the first is like, and I shall here try to give only a picture of the second. Aristotle says that habituation must precede instruction in moral training, and that it consists in seeing that the child always does certain things in certain kinds of situations—for example, that he always does what is just. We must suppose that this method consists, for some time at least, in parents, teachers, and legislators having certain rules in mind and perhaps even laying them down, and in their producing conduct in conformity with these rules through the use of various motives or sanctions—that is, through the use of praise and blame, punishment and reward, legal penalties, emulation, exhortation, etc. In short, it consists in what Kant calls "discipline" (plus, as we shall see, association with good people, censorship, certain kinds of music, etc.). Aristotle explicitly rules out, however, the use of lies and trickery such as Plato condones in the *Republic*. Aristotle seems to think that his own program can bring the child to form a habit of doing what is right and avoiding what is wrong, and a liking for the former and a dislike for the latter— these being the prerequisites of any further moral development.

For at this point the child is not yet fully virtuous. He is virtuous in a sense, but in an incomplete sense; he does *what* the virtuous man does but he does not yet do it *as* the virtuous man does it— knowing that it is excellent or right and doing it *because* it is excellent or right. To achieve virtue in this full sense the child must first gain practical wisdom, which requires instruction in addition to habituation. Aristotle is not, then, reasoning in a circle when he says that moral virtue and practical wisdom presuppose each other. There is no circle, because two senses or stages of virtue are involved. The child's attainment of practical wisdom presupposes his having virtue in its *incomplete* form, and is, in turn, presupposed for his development of virtue in its *fuller* form. Actually, there is a sense in which his having virtue even in its incomplete form presupposes practical wisdom too—not on his part, however, but on that of his teacher (if valid, a point worth noticing in connection with teacher training).

Some people, of course, never go beyond the stage of incomplete virtue. In the case of those who do, however, Aristotle seems to be thinking, implicitly at least, that they move (in David Riesman's terms) from a stage of tradition-directedness to one of inner-directedness by some process of "internalizing" or "identifying with" the rules of the older generation. Perhaps Aristotle is even thinking that they, or at least some of them, go on to achieve something like what Riesman calls "autonomy" or genuinely intelligent self-direction.[44] But Aristotle does not put nearly the value on autonomy and freedom that Kant and Dewey do, though he himself achieved it to a very considerable degree. He may have felt that only a happy few can achieve autonomy in any such degree and that the others must look to such "men of practical wisdom" in order to know what the mean is—as Joachim and A. E. Taylor both suggest.[45]

In fact, one may even doubt— and I think both Kant and Dewey would doubt—that such a rigorous program of habituation as Aristotle appears to have in mind would or even could produce characters capable of very much in the way of reflective self-direction—as distinct from mere inner-directedness—except by default. Aristotle seems to put off the introduction of reflection by the child until relatively late, and by that time the child may have formed habits that preclude him from developing any real autonomy of mind and action. Aristotle's notion, as I see it, was that we all have an innate desire to do what is excellent for its own sake, and that this desire will take over the controls in our lives when and only when we have acquired the proper habits and have been properly instructed. Thus, he keeps saying that the virtuous man's motive is to do what is beautiful or noble. Such motivation by a love of the excellent is what he means by autonomy. But, while what Aristotle says reminds one of Kant's insistence that we must act out of respect for the moral law and not merely in accordance with it, one wonders if Aristotle's program is likely to generate an ability or inclination to revise one's conceptions of what is excellent as the world changes.

ADMINISTRATION

Aristotle contends, next, that a program of habituation such as is needed for education (directly for moral and indirectly for intellectual education) cannot be set up by an individual parent; a system of rules and laws is required that applies to adults as well as to children and is enforced by adequate sanctions. In other words, a state is required for any satisfactory program of education—and the state must be concerned about education: ". . . it is best that there should be a public and proper concern for such matters."[46] However, if his state does not concern itself about education a father must educate his child privately—and private education does have an advantage over public in that it is better adapted to the individual pupil. In such a state the father must himself first study the science of politics in the wider sense, including ethics and the philosophy of education. On the other hand, where the state does take a hand in education, this science must be studied by the statesman. This is how Aristotle moves from ethics to politics in the narrower sense; ethics tells us what dispositions are to be cultivated and why they are to be cultivated, but politics is needed to tell us how to set up a program of education for cultivating them.

Aristotle goes further, however, than merely to claim that the state should set up a system of law and legal sanctions that will buttress private education. He argues, first, that the state should at least regulate education in something like the way in which our states regulate even private education, and, second, that the state should take complete charge of it—in other words, that education should be wholly public. For this pair of theses he gives the following arguments. (1) The state must make sure that its citizens have the dispositions required for the maintenance and implementation of its constitution. (2) ". . . the whole state has a single end, and therefore education must be one and the same for all . . . ," or at least for all of the citizens of the state.

> (3) We must not think of a citizen as belonging to himself; we must regard every citizen as belonging to the state. For each is a part of the state and the care of each part must naturally have an eye to the care of the whole.[47]

These arguments may not convince those who believe in private education, and would be rejected by many who believe in public education, but they show that Aristotle identifies society and the state, subordinates all other associations to the state, and cannot conceive of the individual as belonging to any institution, such as a church, that in any way transcends the state or carries on any education that is not a concern of the state. They therefore show, not only why all education of citizens should be public (after the age of seven), but also why all education must be relative to the constitution of the state in question.

THE IDEAL STATE

Since Aristotle presents his more concrete proposals about education in the context of his theory of the best practicable state, we must have some notion of his conception of such a state. He begins by saying that man is a political animal and by his very nature must be a member of a state. This means that a human being can come as close as possible to attaining his end, happiness, only if he is a member of a state. At the same time, the state

> . . . comes into existence for the sake of life, and continues in existence for the sake of the good life. . . . The good life is the chief end, both for the community as a whole and for the individual.[48]

Hence, the best constitution or state is one which enables all of the people to live the best lives of which they are capable—one which not only provides favorable external circumstances but also develops, as far as they are capable of them, all of the moral and intellectual excellences that make possible the living of the good or happy life, that is, the life of intrinsically worthwhile activity.

> . . . the best constitution is that under which the state is best organized, and that state is best organized that is most conducive to happiness.[49]

What will this best state be like? Aristotle assumes that it will be relatively small: a city-state, big enough to be self-sufficient but not too big for people to know one another. It will be geographically so situated and economically so circumstanced as to provide a considerable leisure for those who are endowed with the capacities to engage in excellent activities, and it will have people who are so endowed—people with intelligence and spirit in a relatively high degree—in considerable numbers. But it will also have enough people who are not so endowed to perform the tasks that are not intrinsically excellent but are necessary to maintain activities that are. Among these people are: (1) all women, (2) those who are naturally slaves, and (3) those who are naturally workers. All of them are so truncated in their capacities, especially in intelligence and spirit, that they are unfit for war, government, intellectually excellent activity, or even citizenship—in fact, Aristotle regards them as incapable of happiness and as *means* to the life of the state, not *parts* of it. Only the well-endowed are to be citizens, and they must in their turn be warriors, rulers, and priests—and presumably teachers and educators. They must have private property in sufficient amount to permit them to engage in excellent activity, practical and intellectual. And, of course, they must be educated in all the excellences of the good man.

Aristotle maintains that the best state will be governed and guided by certain principles in all that it does: (a) that war is for the sake of peace, (b) that work, business, and action are for the sake of leisure, (c) that leisure is to be filled with intrinsically excellent activity, (d) that theoretical or contemplative activity is higher than practical or productive activity. He also believes (e) that the state will assign offices and duties in accordance with native capacity and developed disposition, so that each individual will find the best life of which he is capable in performing the activities assigned to him— even those who are slaves or work under others. However, he does not provide any plan for determining which children will become slaves, which workers, and which citizens. His view implies that this is a matter of native ability, not birth, color, etc., and it would seem, therefore, that he should have all children start in equally on the same program of education and continue in it until their incapacity to go further becomes obvious. In fact, he does not propose anything of the sort, even though he admits that those who are actually slaves or workers by birth or conquest are not always those who ought to be slaves or workers; he seems to be willing to leave such decisions to the usual devices, except for insisting that Greeks should not enslave Greeks. Finally, (f) the best state, according to Aristotle, will frame its legislation in such a way that the external goods in its control will be distributed as much as possible, not equally, but in accordance with merit. His principle of justice in such matters is: from each according to his ability, to each according to his excellence.

SOME PRINCIPLES OF EDUCATION

Coming to the more concrete rules and practices of teaching, Aristotle begins with a description of "the great debate" in education, which holds as well today as it did then.

> At present opinion is divided about the subjects of education. People do not all take the same position about what should be learned by the young, either with a view to excellence or with a view to the best life; nor is it clear whether their studies should be directed mainly to the intellect or to moral character. If we look at actual practice, the picture is also confusing; and it is not clear whether the proper studies to be pursued are those that are useful in life, those that make for excellence, or those that are non-essential. Each kind of study gets some support. Even about those that make for excellence there is no agreement, for men do not all honor the same excellence, and so naturally they differ about the proper training for it.[50]

Aristotle believes, however, that he can lay down a number of principles for the guidance of educators and legislators in the ideal state. Some of these he states explicitly, but others are only implicit in what he says. (1) Citizens and non-citizens should receive different educations, since their capacities and functions are different; as far as possible the education of citizens should be liberal, while that of non-citizens must be vocational. In other words, the education of citizens should be aimed as wholly as possible at the formation of the excellences of the good man as defined in the *Nicomachean Ethics*, while that of non-citizens must be aimed at preparing them for their work. (2) Citizens must be trained to both obey and rule, since they will have to take their turns at ruling and being ruled; non-citizens must be taught to obey, but with a somewhat different kind of obedience.

(3) Education must prepare citizens for both action and leisure. By action Aristotle means all forms of doing as defined earlier, including especially moral, military, and political action. By leisure (*schole*) he means, not free time filled with amusement, recreation, or inactivity, but free time filled with intellectually excellent activity, especially contemplation. In effect, leisure is happiness of what is called, in the *Ethics*, the highest kind. The citizen must be provided with the knowledge, abilities, and skills needed for action, but since action is for the sake of leisure, he must be even more prepared for leisure. (4) Similarly, the citizen should be equipped with the dispositions and skills needed for war, but, since war is for the sake of peace, he must be even more equipped for peace.

Aristotle thinks Sparta made the mistake of preparing its people only for war and empire. Being unprepared for peace or leisure, she was safe only when fighting, and, when finally defeated, had nothing for her pains. She simply missed the point. She missed it because, like most of the rest of the world, she identified happiness with external goods, and thought that the way to achieve it is to cultivate a single excellence, military courage. But it is the whole of excellence that ought to be cultivated, and it ought to be cultivated simply for the sake of being able to engage in excellent activities, especially intellectual ones.

(5) In general, education must prefer the higher to the lower and the end to the means, remembering in this connection that the lower is always a means to the higher, which is its end. So education must cultivate the lower for the sake of the higher—the body for the sake of the soul, the irrational part of the soul for the sake of the rational, the practical intellect for the sake of the theoretical. (6) But, in the order of time, the matter is reversed—the cultivation of the body precedes that of the soul, the cultivation of the irrational that of the rational part of the soul, and, presumably—though Aristotle does not say this—the cultivation of the practical intellect that of the theoretical.

(7) Education must prepare men to do what is necessary, what is useful, and what is noble or excellent in itself, but it must prefer the excellent and consider the necessary and the useful only as means to it. Most of what is necessary or useful is to be assigned to non-citizens, and the young who are to be citizens should not be trained in all of the useful arts, but only (a) in those that are necessary to them, for example, tying sandals, reading, and fighting in armor, and (b) in those that are liberal and fit for freemen, that is, those that do not render the body or soul unfit for any kind of intrinsically

excellent activity, moral or intellectual. The young citizen, insofar as this is possible, should not acquire any kind of disposition that will make him illiberally minded or unfit for leisure as defined in (3)—for example, a disposition to work for pay or simply at the command of another.

In this connection, Aristotle makes two interesting remarks, which are still quoted today; in fact, they are approved by both Dewey and his Aristotelian critics. One is that even "liberal subjects" may be pursued to such an extent or in such a way that the effect is illiberal. One may attend to such a subject too constantly, or be too concerned about completeness, or pursue it in a professional or even mercenary spirit.

> Much depends on the purpose for which something is done or studied. If it is for one's own sake, for a friend's sake, or for the sake of excellence, it is not illiberal; but the same thing, if done simply at the behest of others, may be menial and servile.[51]

There is, of course, a good point to this, but Aristotle almost makes one feel that one can be too wrapt up in physics, mathematics, and metaphysics—even though such contemplation is the highest happiness, and even though God does nothing else. In the opening of *On the Parts of Animals* he writes,

> Every systematic science, the humblest and the noblest alike, seems to admit of two distinct kinds of proficiency; one of which may be properly called scientific knowledge of the subject, while the other is a kind of educational acquaintance with it. For an educated man should be able to form a fair off-hand judgment as to the goodness or badness of the method used by a professor in his exposition. To be educated is in fact to be able to do this; and even the man of universal education we deem to be such in virtue of his having this ability . . . in all or nearly all branches of knowledge, and not . . . merely in some special subject.

This reminds one of a passage quoted earlier from the *Ethics*, and one feels a certain agreement with it, but, if Aristotle means to imply that the aim of education is to give us only such an educational acquaintance with a subject and not a scientific knowledge of it, even if we are capable of the latter, then he seems here to be flying in the face of his entire philosophy. Even if he is thinking that some men, like himself, should be given a scientific knowledge of the theoretical sciences, he is still being inconsistent, for his philosophy requires that all men seek and, if possible, achieve the highest excellence they are capable of. Moderation in the pursuit of moral excellence is not a virtue, and extremism in the pursuit of intellectual excellence is not a vice.

The second remark is that even the "illiberal arts" may be so pursued as to be liberal or at least not illiberal in effect. Citizens must be prepared to do some of the same work that slaves do, and so must acquire some of the same arts.

> Some of their duties differ, not in the nature of the work involved, but in their object. Hence a good deal of the work that is thought to be menial may be honorably performed by young freemen. It is not the inherent nature of actions, but the end or object for which they are done, that makes them honorable or dishonorable.[52]

The end must not be mere utility in the acquisition of external goods. "To aim at utility everywhere is entirely unbecoming to men who are great-souled and free."[53] Citizens should be prepared for their vocation as citizens but none of their education is to be vocational in the narrow sense, or at least no more than is absolutely necessary.

(8) Amusement is no part of happiness or leisure, as Aristotle sees it; although it is desirable in itself, it is also and mainly valuable as a means of recreation and restoration. It belongs, not to leisure, but to the life of work (*ascholia*); it is a foil to work and a means to more work. It has, therefore, no place in education as such, though it has a place in life (especially in the life of the non-citizen), and must be provided for.

> It is clear that amusement is *not* the object with a view to which children should be educated. For learning and play do not go together. Learning is accompanied by pain.[54]

As we shall see, Kant would endorse this passage completely, while Dewey would agree with the first sentence, qualify the second, and reject the third.

Two principles are more specific. (9) The two methods of education, habituation and instruction, must both be used, and they must be made to cooperate harmoniously, but, in general, the use of the first should precede the use of the second; hence moral education should precede intellectual education. (10) Mind and body should not be made to work hard at the same time, for the two kinds of exertion produce opposite effects, bodily toil impeding the mind and mental toil impeding the body.

Against the background of these principles, and his general position as so far expounded, Aristotle proceeds to deal with the stages of education and with the curriculum, though his discussion of both topics remains incomplete. He begins, as Plato did, with some remarks about eugenics and the regulation of marriage, arguing that the legislator must try to produce the best possible stock. Then he divides education into five periods, which he regards as set by nature itself. The *first* is that of infancy and involves what Kant calls nurture. Diet is important for health and growth; the more milk and the less wine the better. Physical movements of all kinds should be encouraged, and artificial means of keeping the body straight should not be used. The child should be inured to cold, in the interests of both health and military service. In general, the process of forming good habits should be inaugurated, making allowance for the child's capacities and concentrating at first on bodily ones.

In the *second* stage, which lasts until the age of five, there should be no study lessons or compulsory tasks, for fear of hindering growth. Again there should be much practice in physical movement. Games should be introduced, but only such as befit freemen, not such as are laborious or undisciplined; it is well, however, if they strain the lungs and develop the child's abilities and strength. Even crying contributes to growth and ought not to be prevented, as some think. All such activities should prepare the way for later pursuits; hence most children's games should be imitations of what will later be in earnest. Also the tales and stories told to children should be regulated "by those officials called children's tutors," as well as the music, drama, and art with which they may come into contact. In fact, Aristotle believes that the government must prohibit all art that portrays indecent actions, except as it is used in the service of certain gods. The tutors must see that children pass very little time in the company of slaves or of anyone with vulgar habits of language or conduct, and that they do not attend comedies or vulgar satires until they are older and their education has made them immune.

Aristotle's mention here of official tutors suggests that special public officers take part in the education of children even in the second stage, but, since he goes on to say that their education must be in the home until they are seven, he must mean only that the state should exercise a kind of supervision over home education or perhaps that it should provide families with tutors.

In the *third* period, from five to seven, all of this still holds, except that now the children must be prepared for the next stages by watching others at the lessons they will afterwards have to learn themselves. They learn, not by *listening* to a teacher, as in traditional education, nor by doing, as in Deweyan education, but by *watching* (as some of us did in the old days when a more advanced class "recited" in the front of the room while ours studied in the back). One wonders how they can do this, however, if they are not yet attending school.

The fourth period lasts from seven to the age of puberty, and the fifth from puberty to twenty-one. During these two periods education is to be fully public, for reasons indicated before, not merely subject to state regulation, and I take this to mean that it is to be carried on in public schools and training grounds. During the *fourth* period Aristotle seems to think the child will be occupied mainly with gymnastics or physical education, with an eye to health, strength, stature, athletic prowess, and manly beauty, though he may think, as some interpreters say, that the child will also begin the study of the subjects listed below. This would be possible without violating principle (10), because the physical training of this period would not be arduous.

> . . . the exercises should be light, and there should be no rigorous dieting or violent exertion, so that growth may not be hindered. The bad effects of excessive early training are obvious from the fact that in the list of Olympic victors there are only two or three cases in which a person who won as a boy won again later as a man.[55]

The Spartans, in their concern for military courage and prowess, Aristotle reminds us again, overdid things, and could count few victors in the Olympics, besides missing out on other excellences.

For the first three years of the *fifth* period the youth is to concentrate on what Aristotle calls his "other studies," by which he presumably means those to be listed shortly. Then comes a period of more serious gymnastics—hard exercise, strict diet, and probably military training. Apparently this lasts until twenty-one. How strenuous is it to be? Certainly Aristotle held that it should be such as to produce a considerable athletic and military prowess. But just as certainly he held that it should not be overdone, for, in writing about the question which parents are likely to produce the best stock, he says,

> The athlete's habit of body is not best for the purposes of political life, nor for health, nor for procreation. Neither is the habit of the valetudinarian or the man unfit for exertion. The best habit is one that falls between these two. It must involve hard exercise but not exertion which is violent or specialized, as in the case of the athlete, for it must suit the pursuits of free men.[56]

In particular, it must not impede the later life of the intellect. It looks as if Aristotle, like so many educators, both wants and does not want to produce Olympic victors. At any rate, he does not wish to see any citizen become a professional athlete, though a slave or a worker may do so.

Aristotle does not say, but he probably thought that there should be a *sixth* and higher stage of education such as he himself sought to provide—for the study of physics, mathematics, logic, metaphysics, ethics, politics, and perhaps poetics and rhetoric (on which he also lectured) and medicine (to which he often refers). In saying this I am assuming that Aristotle believed that what he was doing should be done even in the ideal state.

Aristotle lists four subjects as constituting his curriculum for the education of citizens: *grammata* (reading and writing), gymnastics, music, and drawing (including painting). The first three were usual or traditional in his day and drawing was sometimes added. He includes gymnastics because it is both necessary and useful for health, military prowess, and the virtue of courage, as well as physical beauty; and because it is not illiberal if it is not pursued to extremes or for illiberal ends. He includes reading and writing because they are useful for many purposes, some not liberal, like business and household management, but some liberal, like political life and the pursuit of knowledge and intellectual excellence. But why drawing? Aristotle's answer is cryptic, but interesting. Drawing is useful in helping one to form correct judgments of art objects and furniture, and so to avoid making mistakes in buying and selling them; but it should be studied, not (or not only) for this reason, but because it makes one perceptive (*theoretikon*) about beauty of form and figure. This is interesting because it seems to imply that the recognition of physical beauty is an intrinsically excellent intellectual activity, and perhaps a form of knowing, which is something Aristotle did not say when he talked about art in the *Ethics*.

Something similar is suggested by the *Poetics*.[57] In it Aristotle says that drawing and painting use color and form to imitate or portray things in nature, and that man takes a natural delight in imitating and in seeing imitations: ". . . though the objects themselves may be painful to see, we delight to view the most realistic representations of them in art." The explanation of our delight in making and seeing such representations, Aristotle suggests, is the fact that in doing so we are learning something, and "learning something is the greatest of pleasures not only to the philosopher but also to the rest of mankind, however small their capacity for it."

We are "learning—gathering the meaning of things, e.g. that the man there is so-and-so." Aristotle does not explain this further, but, at any rate, he appears here to regard drawing as providing a kind of knowledge, just as he goes on to say poetry does. He may, of course, also be thinking that the perception of beauty (*to kalon*) of color and form is somehow conducive to a liking for nobility (*to kalon*) of action and character. In either case, drawing would be a liberal study in his sense, as well as a useful one, provided one does not pursue it beyond a certain point. And, in any case, of course, Aristotle would hold that we learn to draw by practice or "doing" (in Dewey's sense, not his own) since that is how any art (*techne*) is learned.

Aristotle does not explain what reading and writing consist in; but they usually included the study of Homer and other Greek literature, and some acting out of dramatic parts (i.e. some "doing" in Dewey's sense). Possibly he also thought of them as including some history in the form of a study of Herodotus; he does not mention history (or geography) as a school subject, but he did know and put some store in history (as well as geography), and sometimes refers to Herodotus. In the *Poetics*, as was just indicated, he maintains that poetry communicates a knowledge of universal truths.[58] It does not describe what has been or provide us with particular statements, as history does; it is more philosophical and tells us "what such and such a kind of man will probably or necessarily say or do," even when it affixes proper names to its characters. It may also produce delight, or have a cathartic effect, according to Aristotle; but its educative value lies, for him, primarily in the fact that it gives us such knowledge of character, and he must have held this knowledge to be important in moral education, though he does not say so.

ARITHMETIC

One misses from Aristotle's list of school subjects the third of our three R's—arithmetic. Did he mean then that it is no part of the curriculum, except perhaps in the period after twenty-one (or in the training of certain slaves or workers)? He does not mention it, and he did not have quite the same love of and regard for mathematics that Plato had, but he must have considered arithmetic, along with reading and writing, as one of the subjects that are not only useful in life but also basic to the pursuit of further knowledge of various sorts. Just possibly he is including it under reading and writing when he speaks of their usefulness in business and household management. Plato put arithmetic under music in his scheme of education, and one might think that Aristotle means to do likewise, except that he always seems to mean by music quite strictly what we mean by it. However this may be, Greek elementary education had long included some arithmetic, and it is hard to believe that Aristotle meant to leave it out of the education of his citizens. He could hardly have meant the arithmetic needed in society to be left to slaves or workers, for he held a very low opinion of the intellectual ability of any natural slave or worker (and held it wrong to enslave men with more ability). And he could hardly have meant to leave all mathematics until after twenty-one, for in the *Ethics* he remarks that, although the young cannot attain to practical wisdom, or become physicists or metaphysicians, since they lack experience, they can become experts in mathematics and similar branches of knowledge that deal with abstractions easily understood without much experience.[59] It is likely, therefore, that arithmetic and geometry are among the "other subjects" studied just after puberty in Aristotle's scheme, and arithmetic may even belong to the previous period. It may even be that he would include logic and rhetoric among the "similar branches of knowledge" which he finds young men can be expert in.

MUSIC

It happens that the only school subject that Aristotle deals with in any detail is music, though he intended to take up others also, as well as other topics relating to the practice of education. Music was central in Greek education in a way in which it is not in ours (according to H. I. Marrou[60] it lost its place in education during the Hellenistic Age), and Aristotle discusses it at some length, while Kant and Dewey barely refer to it, Kant referring to it disparagingly. Probably the main reason for this is that Aristotle and the Greeks believed music to be very helpful in moral education, whereas we no longer believe this so deeply as they did (possibly because our music is very different)—even if we do sometimes wonder about the moral impact of some of the noises our teen-agers listen to. Perhaps, too, we give moral education itself less attention in our schools and other educational media than they did, though here we must remember that Aristotle himself ranks intellectual excellences above moral ones.

Why should music be one of the main factors in the education of citizens in the ideal state? Ultimately Aristotle's answer must be, "Because it is conducive to the excellences of the good man, moral or intellectual." Actually his discussion is rather confusing, and we can hardly disentangle it all here, but some interesting points get made in it that we must notice. He begins by announcing that music is neither necessary nor useful to the citizen, though it may be useful as a means of service or livelihood to a slave or worker, and is useful to all such non-citizens as a means of relaxation and restoration. "We are left with its value as an activity of the mind in leisure." Now, music is pleasing in itself, and so may be cultivated simply as an amusement or form of entertainment. Aristotle does regard this as one of the values of music; but, he argues that, although "most people now participate in it for the sake of pleasure," this cannot be the real reason for its being made a subject of education.

> . . . the real reason why it was originally included in educa-
> tion is that . . . nature itself seeks to be able, not only to
> engage rightly in occupation, but also to occupy leisure nobly,
> for, to say it yet again, this is the end of all things.[61]

We cannot pass our leisure in play, for play is not the end of life, but something to be used, in connection with occupation, as a rest from work and a restoration for further work. Play, then, is not a proper part of leisure; only activities that are excellent in themselves, not as means, are. Hence, music cannot be made a part of education merely because it is pleasant—though its pleasantness is one of its values, even in the life of a citizen.

Aristotle also mentions the cathartic effect of certain kinds of music, that is, their effect in releasing emotion in harmless ways, but, though he accepts this as a reason for having such music about, especially for slaves and workers—young, old, or teen-aged—he does not admit its cathartic effect as a reason for making music a part of the education of a citizen. Experiences are not educative merely because they are good in some way or other, but only if they are good in certain ways—only if they are conducive to knowledge or to moral virtue.

As was indicated, Aristotle is convinced that music is conducive to moral virtue, and he offers a line of thought to show this. He first contends that music can affect the character of the soul. It can, for example, directly excite or inspire ("send") us through its rhythm or tune; and it can also "imitate" or express emotion and cause us to feel the same emotion sympathetically, even apart from its rhythm or tune. He then argues that, since virtue has to do with liking and disliking the right things, we must learn habitually to judge rightly about, and to feel delight in, virtuous actions and characters. Here he is recalling a point made in the *Ethics*, namely, that the right moral education will bring us up in such a way that we feel pleasure and pain in the right things, since we tend to perform pleasurable activities and avoid painful ones. But, Aristotle continues, rhythms and tunes may contain actual imitations or representations of emotions and qualities of character—images of anger or calm, of courage and temperance or their opposites—and at the same time make us feel pleasure or pain at these representations. And, if one comes to feel pleasure or pain habitually at these representations, one will come to feel them habitually at the corresponding real actions or characters. In this way music, or rather some kinds of music, may make a very real contribution to moral education, according to Aristotle. It follows that, on his view, practice is not the only way of becoming perfect in morality. Practice is an indispensable way, but it has an important ally in music—a particularly effective ally in the case of children because of its pleasant sweetness.

In the course of this discussion Aristotle mentions the visual arts, drawing and sculpture, and indicates that they may also contain representations of states of character, and so also have a bearing on moral education. He insists that these representations are not very adequate and that the visual arts are much inferior to music as allies of morality, but he takes them seriously enough to conclude that the young should look at the works of Polygnotus and not at those of Pauson. We must, then, add this point to what was said about drawing earlier.

However, even if music helps to foster the moral excellences in this way, it does not follow, for Aristotle, that playing and listening to music are proper parts of happiness or leisure. Since music is not a form of morally excellent activity, it cannot even be a part of secondary happiness. To be a proper part of happiness or leisure musical activity must be a form of contemplation, a way of knowing. Is it? Aristotle raises the question, but does not answer it, though he keeps suggesting that music does contribute to the life of the mind. He may have thought that music makes one perceptive of beauty of sound and pattern of sound, as drawing makes one perceptive of beauty of color and form. He may also have thought, as he did of drawing and poetry, that musical imitations of action, feeling, and character give us a kind of knowledge that is desirable for its own sake. The fact that he makes neither of these claims for music proves nothing one way or the other. To parody Wittgenstein, a recent non-Aristotelian philosopher—whereof one does not speak, thereof one is simply silent.

Thus Aristotle makes a case for music, not only as a part of life, but as a part of the education of citizens. He holds, moreover, that citizens should learn to sing and play an instrument, as well as to appreciate music; they should learn to do as well as to listen, and, in fact, will learn better if they learn by doing and not by only listening.

It is obvious that it makes a great difference in the acquisition of an aptitude whether one performs the corresponding actions or not; for it is difficult, if not impossible, to become a good judge of performances, if one has never taken part in them oneself.[62]

So far, at least, Aristotle is ready to go along with Dewey. Besides, he says, children must have something to keep them occupied. A rattle keeps very young children from breaking furniture; with older children music serves a similar purpose: ". . . education is their rattle," says Aristotle in one of his few bits of humor.

Aristotle goes on to emphasize, however, that since the purpose of learning to sing or play is merely to make the young citizen a good judge of music, participation must stop when good musical judgment has been achieved. The citizen must remain an intelligent amateur; more training would be illiberal, and might make a youth unfit for military service, civic duty, or the pursuit of knowledge. The citizen's exercise in music must stop well short of that needed by a professional, and must therefore not include taking part in strenuous musical competitions. It follows, Aristotle infers, that he should not learn to play the flute, the harp, or any other instrument that requires professional skill. Aristotle is especially hard on the flute: it is not educational, but only cathartic, for it produces enthusiasm but cannot represent states of character. Besides, it keeps the player from using his voice. In his anti-professionalism, Aristotle objects to a citizen's playing for the *pleasure* of others as illiberal and vulgarizing. His playing should be for his own *improvement*. But why should one not also play for the *improvement* of others, one wonders, especially *friends*? Apparently Aristotle intended to leave such private performances, as well as professional ones, to slaves or workers. Did he mean then, that even the teacher of music was to be only an intelligent amateur?

The kinds of music to be used in education are the ethical ones, rather than those which are cathartic, activating, enthusiastic, or merely pleasing, though these may all find a place in life as a whole insofar as they are compatible with the achievement of moral and intellectual excellence (unlike Plato, Aristotle does not ban all non-educational music from the state). By ethical melodies I take Aristotle to mean those that imitate or express actions, emotions, or states of character, and cause us to feel pleasure at the representation of good or right ones and pain at the representation of bad or wrong ones. Which melodies these are we must learn, Aristotle says, from those who study philosophy and are engaged in musical education. He himself thinks that music in the Dorian mode is the best for educational purposes, as Plato does, but criticizes Plato for ruling out music in all other modes except the Phrygian. Here, one may perhaps say that Aristotle is a bit of an experimentalist.

SUMMARY ON THE EDUCATION OF CITIZENS

In Aristotle's scheme of education, then, if I am right, all future citizens take gymnastics during the fourth period and again during the second part of the fifth. They study reading and writing, music, drawing, and some kind of mathematics during the first three years after puberty, and perhaps earlier. After twenty-one they take more mathematics, physics (including biology and psychology), and philosophy—theoretical and practical—presumably by listening to lectures such as Aristotle is supposed to have given peripatetically (while walking) and as are recorded in his writings, but possibly also by taking part in research on natural history, the constitutions of different states, etc., as Aristotle's students are supposed to have done in the Lyceum (allegedly with some help from Alexander). All citizens receive exactly the same educations, for they all have the same, or closely similar, natures, capacities, and functions, and must all achieve the same moral and intellectual excellences. Since they do not have to work for a living, they do not need any strictly vocational or technical training; all their training, except for certain necessary arts or skills, can and must be liberal, conducive to moral or intellectual excellence, or at least not incompatible with it. The end of this education is leisure or contemplation, but throughout there is a heavy emphasis on moral training, consisting mainly of constant practice or habituation in doing just acts, temperate acts, courageous acts, etc., together with the use of music and literature to provide representations of right and wrong actions or good and bad characters and to produce a liking for the good and a dislike for the bad—and with some censorship of art and of the company kept. For moral virtue is an indispensable condition of or means to intellectual excellence and its exercise constitutes a secondary kind of happiness; and it consists in a habit of choosing the right because it is right, of doing *what* the good man does and doing it *as* the good man does it—with choice and with delight in it for its own sake. Except for moral virtue the citizens must not pursue anything to extremes; they must not seek professional proficiency but only educational acquaintance or the ability to make intelligent judgments in each field, whether it be an art or a science. But here, I have suggested, Aristotle runs athwart his own basic axiom that the end is always the highest excellence possible, whether the subject be moral or intellectual.

THE EDUCATION OF NON-CITIZENS

All this is about the education of citizens in the ideal state (in actual states education must follow the constitution). But this state also includes non-citizens: women, workers, and slaves. In Aristotle's scheme girls, young workers, and young slaves do not receive the education sketched above. They must, of course, have a kind of moral education, for they are required to be temperate, just, etc., insofar as they can be and in a form appropriate to their stations in life. For the rest their education is vocational, to prepare them for their household duties or their crafts, and apparently it is to take place in the home in the case of girls and young slaves, and in some kind of apprenticeship in the case of young artisans or workers—all, of course, under some kind of state regulation. About the training of slaves—remember that in his ideal state only those people will be slaves who are "naturally" so, i.e. who have a bare minimum of intellect. Aristotle writes,

> It is clear that the master must produce in the slave the kind of [moral] excellence we have been discussing, though not in the manner of a master giving him instructions about his tasks.[63]

Apparently he thought that instructions in tasks could be put in the form of commands or delegated to another, but that the slave's moral training should be put in the form of admonition, since he has *some* reason, and cannot be delegated. "Admonition," he says, "is more properly used with slaves than it is with children." This seems to imply, incidentally, that, in Aristotle's opinion, commands are properly used with children.

About the education of women Aristotle promises to write further. For, as he puts it, women make up half of the free population even in the ideal state, and hence it must make a difference whether they are good or not. He does not, however, keep his promise, possibly because he felt it did not make that much difference. "A modest silence is a woman's crown," he quotes from Sophocles; but, though he asserts that the same is not true for a man, he remains modestly silent about women. To parody Wittgenstein again—of that which should be silent, thereof one need not speak.

About artisans or workers Aristotle is even more silent. They constitute a vaguely defined and little-considered class in his ideal state; they choose their own arts and crafts and presumably learn them through practice and the instruction of older workers. They have a kind of freedom, but are generally under the control of the citizens for whom they work. They too are supposed to be men (or women) of little intellect, but nevertheless they appear to include, not only shoemakers and shipbuilders, but also professional athletes and artists, and all who have a really thorough expertness in any art or science—for example, physicians, schoolteachers, and professional philosophers! This situation is one of the outcomes of Aristotle's paradoxical insistence that citizens are to remain intelligent amateurs. He would have done better if he had set up a fourth class of super-citizens, people of considerable intellect who go so far in music, poetry, science, mathematics, or philosophy as to be unfit for military action or government, and who are free to spend their lives in leisure or contemplation—excepting, of course, those who take up medicine or teaching.

UNIFORMITY OF EDUCATION

It is clear from what has been said that Aristotle did not believe, as Robert M. Hutchins and other recent Aristotelians do, that all men should have the same education or that "education should be everywhere the same."[64] For one thing, Aristotle maintains that education must be relative to the constitution and hence will vary from country to country. Even in the ideal state, not everyone receives the same education, though all citizens do. All members of this state are expected to achieve the moral and intellectual excellences of the good man to the extent to which they can and in the form called for by their stations, but their capacities and hence their stations differ greatly, and so their educations must also. Thus Aristotle is closer to Dewey on this point than he is to Hutchins; the difference between Aristotle and Dewey is that he connects his belief in diversity of educations with a belief in aristocracy while Dewey connects it with a belief in democratic equality—a belief that Hutchins also shares. We can get an interesting comparison of the different positions if we take the two beliefs, (a) belief in the uniformity of education, (b) belief in the equality of all human beings. Aristotle denies both, Dewey accepts the second but denies the first (in a sense to be explained later), and Hutchins accepts both. As for Kant—like Dewey he accepts the second belief and denies the first (all *men* should receive the same education, but women get a different one). One might, of course, also accept the first belief and deny the second—this is what Plato does in the *Republic*, where he has everyone start in on the same program of education and stay on it as long as he is able to.

DISTRIBUTION OF EDUCATIONAL OPPORTUNITY

Actually, Aristotle ought to have adopted a plan more like that of Plato. For, as we saw before, he provides no system for determining who are natural slaves or who are to be workers. He confesses that there is no sure physical mark by which potential freemen can be distinguished from natural slaves or workers, though he does suggest that natural slaves will usually look more or less like Edwin Markham's man with a hoe: "bowed by the weight of centuries," "stolid and stunned, a brother to the ox," a "monstrous thing distorted and soul-quenched." Even in the case of girls, where there is a distinguishing physical mark, it never occurs to Aristotle (or to Kant), as it did to Plato, that some of them might have the intellect required for moral and intellectual excellence, and that they should be tested by a program of education to see how far they can go. There remains, therefore, a basic injustice in his educational and social scheme, even by his own best standard—that each individual should, as far as possible, be given the opportunity to achieve all the excellence of which he is capable. Educational opportunity cannot be distributed in proportion to excellence (a formula of justice that Aristotle also suggests), since the achievement of excellence presupposes education; it must be distributed according to capacity for excellence, but such capacity can be determined only by education—hence it must be distributed equally. If education is a rattle, everyone should be given a chance to shake it for all he is worth.

•

CHAPTER THREE

Kant's Philosophy

of

Education

•

APPROACH TO KANT'S THOUGHT

SETTING

From the fourth century B.C. to the eighteenth century A.D. is a long time, and the world of Immanuel Kant was very different from that of Aristotle. The Hellenistic Age and the Roman Empire were followed by Christianity, scholastic philosophy (itself largely influenced by Aristotle), the Papacy, and the Holy Roman Empire; and these in turn were succeeded by the Renaissance, the Reformation, nationalism, absolute government, and by modern science and philosophy (both strongly anti-Aristotelian). The works of Descartes, Locke, Leibniz, Newton, and others had ushered in the Enlightenment—of which Kant himself was one of the last luminaries. Against the background of all these changes the eighteenth century was as concerned with education as were the Greeks; new thoughts on education were sent into the world, especially by Jean-Jacques Rousseau (1712–1778), and new schemes for reforming education were launched, particularly by such followers of Rousseau as J.B. Basedow (1723–1790) and the "philanthropinists," and by J. H. Pestalozzi (1746–1827).

Reading, thinking, and writing in such a period, Kant frequently gave thought to education, feeling that a turning point was at hand. The art of education was still far from perfect, but

> It is only now that something can be done [toward improving education and perfecting mankind], since for the first time people have begun to judge rightly, and understand clearly, what actually belongs to a good education.[1]

Kant was thinking here, no doubt, of Rousseau and Basedow, by whom (along with Montaigne) his reflections on education were chiefly influenced. He supported Basedow's Institute at Dessau in words such as Dewey might have used about his experimental school-for-tomorrow at Chicago, he often adverted to education in his writings, and he took his turns at lecturing on pedagogy. He did not systematically try to reconstruct the philosophy of education as he had the more central parts of philosophy in his three *Critiques*, but he did leave us his views about "what actually belongs to a good education."

Kant's theories of education were much discussed in Germany, and played an important role in the history of educational philosophy there, and, as a consequence, also in Latin America and Japan. His successor, J. P. Herbart (1776–1841), who was very influential in the history of education, was critical of Kant's transcendentalism, especially his notion of transcendental freedom, but he adopted Kant's view that the primary aim of education is to make good men—men who will rightly—though he worked it out differently in detail. In general, however, we must admit that Kant's influence through what he said about education was not great, not so great as that of Rousseau, Pestalozzi, Herbart, or Froebel. Yet, through the impact of his thought in general, it was tremendous, not only in ethics and philosophy (including philosophy of education), but also in psychology (including the psychology of education). In this country this impact came twice, once in the period of transcendentalism and again in that of Hegelian idealism. In the second period, it helped mold the thought of W. T. Harris, a United States Commissioner of Education, and of John Dewey , as well as of many other educators, the most recent of whom is the "liberal Christian idealist"—and Kantian—philosopher of education, T. M. Greene. Even if this had not been true, however, it may be claimed, I think, that, for intrinsic quality, Kant's philosophy of education must be ranked as one of the great ones. Kant remains one of the few really outstanding philosophers who have put their minds to the theory of education in any detail.

What we have from Kant on education, apart from frequent passages in his other writings, is a separate little book, *Über Pädagogik*, published in 1803. It is much more popular and practical than his other works, and much less adequate from a philosophical point of view. It consists of his lecture notes and was edited by Theodor Rink, a student and friend. Other editions, somewhat differently arranged, have appeared since.[2] Though more complete than Aristotle's two chapters, it is not a finished work, and is rather loosely and illogically arranged. Kant's dearly loved architectonic is not very clear in this book, some classificatory and organizational passages being inconsistent with others, possibly because they were written at different times. This creates problems of interpretation, as we shall see on occasion.

In reconstructing Kant's philosophy of education one cannot, however, confine himself to Kant's explicit discussions of education, either in his little book or elsewhere. One must try to build it by using materials from his larger philosophical structure. In doing this, and in keeping with my general approach, I shall relate Kant's thought about education primarily, not to what he says in his *Critiques of Pure Reason* and *Judgment*, but to what he says in his ethical and political works, just as I did in the case of Aristotle. But Aristotle's discussion of education comes as the end of a systematic line of thought consisting of the *Ethics* and the *Politics*, while Kant's comes as a more or less complete separate book. Our treatment of Kant will therefore be somewhat different. It will, of course, center on the three questions distinguished in the first chapter, but it will take them up in a different order.

VIEWS ON PHILOSOPHY OF EDUCATION

NATURE OF EDUCATIONAL THEORY

Before we take up our three questions, however, we should notice what Kant himself says about the philosophy or theory of education. Like Aristotle, Kant distinguishes between theoretical reason and theoretical philosophy (including mathematics and science), on the one hand, and practical reason and practical philosophy, on the other—though he regards them as simply two different employments of the same faculty. Pretty clearly he too would put the philosophy of education under practical philosophy. In fact, as we shall see, it looks as if he would put it under the heading of applied ethics. In his terms, a normative philosophy of education consists essentially of *imperatives,* statements or rules about what ought to be done by parents, teachers, school administrators, and children. Kant distinguishes three kinds of imperatives. A *technical* imperative or *rule of skill* tells us what we should do if we desire to bring about a certain end or result, e.g. to use fertilizer in gardening or an *orbis pictus* (an illustrated globe or book) in teaching natural history. A *pragmatic* imperative or *counsel of prudence* is a precept about what to do in order to be happy, e.g. to cultivate friends or an ability to influence people. A *moral* imperative or *law of morality* is simply a moral principle like "Be honest" or "Treat people as ends and not as means." Technical and pragmatic imperatives Kant calls *hypothetical* imperatives because they hold only if one desires a certain end or result (fine flowers, knowledge of natural history, happiness, etc.); moral imperatives he calls *categorical* because, on his view, they hold regardless of what we desire—there are "no ifs, ands, or buts" about them. Now, Kant sometimes talks as if any art or science that involves imperatives of any of these three kinds is practical rather than theoretical. But in one place he argues that an art or science which contains only technical and pragmatic imperatives cannot be counted as practical philosophy, since such imperatives are really only corollaries to propositions in theoretical philosophy, e.g. "Use fertilizer in gardening" is a corollary to "Using fertilizer in gardening produces finer flowers, etc." Thus, he here regards housekeeping, farming, statesmanship, dietetics, etc., as theoretical rather than practical. It might then seem that he should take the same view of pedagogy, but actually he thinks of it as including or resting on moral principles, at least in part, and so he must reckon it as practical, not theoretical.

Kant does recognize, however, that a theory of pedagogy and its methods must also rest in part on theoretical propositions, based on experience, about what procedures produce what results, e.g. that the use of an *orbis pictus* will facilitate a learning of natural history. Since the theory and practice of education rest in this way on beliefs about the results of one method as compared with another, Kant maintains that we must see to it that these beliefs are as scientific as possible. The art of education must not be "mechanical," relying on uncritical and unorganized experience; it must become a scientific discipline, an art which is based on principles and science, ". . . otherwise we can hope for nothing from it, and the miseducated will educate the others."[3]

EXPERIMENTAL SCHOOLS

Kant even went so far as to advocate establishing experimental schools to help build an educational science.

People commonly imagine . . . that experiments in education are unnecessary, and that we can tell by reason whether something is good or not. In this they err greatly. Experience teaches us that the results of our efforts are often the opposite of those we expect.[4]

He then cites the Dessau Philanthropinum as having made a beginning in clearing the way; at least it showed that further experiments were needed, and that ". . . no generation can draw up a final plan of education." Kant is not an empiricist or experimentalist about the moral principles involved in education, but, for the rest, what he says here about the theory of education is a strong anticipation of Dewey. There is nothing like it in Aristotle. Kant's conception could be adopted by an Aristotelian, but Aristotle himself lacked both of the ideas involved in it—that of progress and that of an experimentally minded and scientifically organized empirical knowledge.

DISPOSITIONS TO BE FOSTERED

FIVE JOBS OF EDUCATION

Kant usually uses "education" to mean the first of the four things distinguished in chapter one, i.e. the activity of educating carried on by teachers and tutors (or even by oneself). Now and then he uses it to refer to the fourth of them, viz. the art or discipline of education, though he generally calls this "pedagogy." It is clear that, in the former usage, he thinks of education as concerned with the development of what I am calling dispositions or excellences— though he does not say so in so many words. This is implied when he says that education must develop human nature and its talents. For him, as for Aristotle, "Man is the only being who needs education" and "can only become man by education. He is merely what education makes of him."[5] Now, as we saw earlier, the crucial part of a normative philosophy of education is its list of the dispositions (abilities, traits, etc.) to be fostered by the individual and society. What then is Kant's list?

For all of Kant's love of system, it is not easy to make up a systematic list of the dispositions to be cultivated by education— although he indicates explicitly or implicitly that a large number of them should be cultivated. He does not, for example, actually divide them into intellectual and moral dispositions, as Aristotle did, except by implication. Combining two passages, however, we may take Kant to say that education must do five things:[6]

1. It must *nurture* man.
2. It must *discipline* him.
3. It must *cultivate* him, make him cultivated or cultured.
4. It must make him *prudent* or sagacious (the German word is *klug*), give him worldly wisdom (*klugheit*), or civilize him.
5. It must *moralize* him, make him moral.

Actually Kant says elsewhere that it must also:[7]

6. Give him *guidance*, direct him in putting what he has been taught into practice.

However, we need not deal separately with (6) because, for Kant, it comes under (4). It is not clear that all of the dispositions Kant has in mind can be thought of as coming under these headings, but he seems to be thinking that they can.

NURTURE

This is the job of the kind of education that is mainly to be carried out by parents during infancy. By nurture Kant seems to mean such things as nursing, feeding, caring for, and protecting the young, and especially the care and attention parents must give their children to keep them from making harmful use of their powers. Its purpose is to maintain life, foster health, and promote bodily growth. In one passage Kant equates it with physical education proper, and perhaps we should extend what he says and think of nurture as the whole process by which one builds up health and strength and acquires a good regimen for maintaining them, a process that enabled Kant to keep up his relatively frail constitution until he was eighty. In his discussion of this kind of education Kant is especially concerned to warn parents against indulgence and over-protectiveness; the child must not be permitted to become effeminate, lazy, dependent, impatient, or to become a slave to any bodily habits. Within limits he must be made tough, adaptable, and self-reliant, and he must be kept free from bad habits. Kant is so insistent on this last point that he seems to say that the child must not be permitted to acquire any habits, good or bad.

> The more habits a man allows himself to form, the less free and independent he becomes. . . . Children, therefore, must be prevented from forming any habits, nor should habits be fostered in them.[8]

Thus he also talks as if physical education of the kind in question is essentially negative. Here he seems to take too narrow a view of the nature of habits; as Dewey has shown, they need not be rigid, enslaving routines, or addictions. In any case, even this purely physical education cannot be purely negative; health, adaptability, independence, etc., are dispositions, if not habits, that have a positive as well as a negative side, and probably Kant does not really mean to deny this. Being free does not entail having no dispositions whatsoever.

DISCIPLINE

This brings us to (2), for the line between what Kant says about it and what he says about (1) is a thin one. By education, he says, a man must be disciplined. Now, when we think of a "disciplined" man, we think of a man with dispositions of a certain sort. But here again Kant usually strikes a negative note. The role of discipline, he says, is merely to correct faults, to prevent bad habits, to restrain unruliness (what is now sometimes called "anomie"), to free the will from the despotism of desires, to keep man's animality from interfering with his attainment of humanity. This makes it look as if the function of discipline in education, for Kant, is not to foster any dispositions, but simply to clear the way for the development of good dispositions by removing bad ones or preventing their formation. And, no doubt, discipline has this negative aspect; the formation of good dispositions does entail the exclusion of bad ones—but again one is tempted to comment that even discipline cannot be merely negative; it is bound as such to produce certain dispositions like being "disciplined," obedient, or slavish. Actually, Kant does sometimes strike this positive note: ". . . the child must learn submission and passive obedience."[9] He must also learn not to interfere with the liberty of others. More generally, the child must acquire self-mastery. Kant discusses this disposition in his *Lectures on Ethics*, but it is not a purely moral one, being required both on prudential and moral grounds. It is the disposition and ability to control one's inclinations and powers.

> It consists in the ability to subject all our principles and faculties to our free will. This can be done in two ways: by the rule of prudence, or by the rule of morality.[10]

What is more, Kant thinks of it here as the product of discipline. We may, therefore, take self-mastery as the positive ideal outcome of education as discipline.

Thus, even in connection with nurture and discipline we find that there are dispositions to be *fostered*; they should not be regarded as purely negative, as Kant regards them much but not all of the time. Even if they were purely negative for him, however, he would still give us a long list of dispositions to be *prevented* by them: weakness, dependence, unadaptability, effeminacy, laziness, disobedience, inconsiderateness, willfulness, unruliness, alcoholism, intemperance, impatience, untruthfulness, etc., etc.

CULTURE

We come now to (3). Kant's use of the term "culture" is somewhat confusing. Sometimes it includes discipline and sometimes not; sometimes it includes prudence and sometimes not. He always conceives of it, however, as the acquisition of dispositions of a certain sort—of what he calls abilities or *skills* (in German *Geschicklichkeit*). "Culture is the acquisition of skill." Abilities or skills are not dispositions of the sort that come under prudence or morality, though they may and ideally should be used for prudential or moral purposes. "Skill is the possession of an ability to accomplish any given end"—an acquired ability, of course. Culture is the possession of the abilities involved in making a skilled use of our various powers. The purposes to which these skills can be put are various in kind and almost endless in number. "Some [skills]," Kant remarks, "are useful in all cases, e.g. reading and writing; others only for certain purposes, e.g. music. . . ."[11]

KINDS OF SKILLS

What are the main sorts of skills Kant would list among the dispositions to be fostered by education? (a) He mentions various *bodily* skills, some relating to the use of voluntary movements, others to the use of our sense organs. Among the former are strength, quickness, confidence of movement, running, jumping, throwing, swimming, crossing a narrow plank, and the like; among the latter, skill in the use of the eye and the ear, e.g. in measuring distance, size, and direction, skill in the use of spatial imagination and memory, etc. Here Kant seems to be allowing for a kind of education of the senses, whereas Aristotle regarded sensory excellence as innate. Possibly this difference between them goes with the fact that Kant, as a part of his "Copernican revolution in philosophy," held the mind to be active in knowledge and perception in a sense in which Aristotle held it to be passive. In view of his general philosophy Kant might have gone even further, and found a place for an education of the senses and imagination that would somehow enhance a child's skill at perceiving substances, causal connections, and so on. But he does not suggest this, and I doubt that he believed education could perform such a role—though, of course, even if he did, he might have refrained from trying to explain this role in a relatively popular lecture course.

(b) Kant also mentions some closely associated dispositions. "What is wanted [in the use of voluntary movements] is that the child should always help himself."[12] He must also learn to put off or deny a present desire in view of achieving some other object or of acquiring a skill, and to accustom himself to endeavors that take some length of time. Finally, he must learn thoroughness. This disposition must be made part of one's character and accompany all one's skills, Kant says.

MENTAL SKILLS

(c) Another group of skills to be cultivated are those of the *mental* faculties. Here it is important to notice that Kant, like Aristotle and Dewey, thinks of the mental excellences primarily as skills of the mind, rather than bodies of knowledge or subjects.

> The general culture of the mental faculties . . . aims at skill and perfection, not at informing the child on some matter, but at strengthening his mental powers.[13]

Incidentally, in these words, as well as elsewhere, Kant appears to subscribe to the doctrine of education as "formal training," so much criticized by Dewey and others—namely, the conception of mental powers as muscles to be developed by appropriate exercise (but at least he is not thinking of them simply as boxes to be filled with information). Even in talking about what he calls "the cultivation of particular mental faculties," he thinks in terms of skills rather than knowledge (or, in Gilbert Ryle's phrasing, in terms of knowing *how* rather than knowing *that*).

Under this heading Kant does not give us as clear a list of dispositions to be cultivated as Aristotle does, though his list of mental powers is not very different from Aristotle's—except that he does not mention intuition (Kant does not believe that man is capable, except in sensation, of intuitive knowledge, either theoretical or practical, as Aristotle and the rationalists preceding Kant did). Kant distinguishes between the lower and the higher powers of the mind. The lower powers are the faculty of cognition,[14] the senses, the imagination, memory, the power of attention, and the wit; the higher: reason, understanding, and judgment (including aesthetic judgment). Presumably, then, there are skills of each of these powers that are to be achieved or passed on by education. But, though Kant gives us some views about the methods of teaching them, which we shall come to later, he does not name the methods. We shall simply have to think of them as the excellences of the various faculties in question. In general, Kant has less to say about intellectual than about moral education. So, in fact, does Aristotle, but in the case of Kant this is probably a reflection of his general position, which gives practical reason and will primacy over pure or theoretical reason and understanding, and morality and virtue primacy over knowledge and science; Aristotle does not so emphasize the practical faculties.

In line with his conception of the intellectual excellences as skills rather than bodies of knowledge, Kant is often scornful of mere learning. For Kant, "learning" is a word properly applied only to historical knowledge, since this is something that must be taught and cannot be discovered by one's own reason, as mathematics and philosophy can (he regarded all knowledge as either historical or rational); but Kant is scornful of such historical knowledge only if it is accompanied by stupidity or deficiency of judgment—inability to apply or relate the general to the particular. He was himself no mere "machine for the instruction of others," but he did possess a good deal of learning.

Probably Kant did not think that a man can be cultured and not have knowledge (in Ryle's sense of knowing *that*). One cannot come to possess the intellectual skills in question without also acquiring knowledge, historical or rational, e.g. one cannot learn to do mathematics well without knowing at least some mathematical truths; but Kant certainly does not emphasize this point, though he saw it in the case of mathematics. At any rate, he does believe that a child must be provided with knowledge of various kinds as part of his education; this is shown by what he says about memory, geography, etc., as well as by his own lectures in anthropology. Hence a knowledge of various subjects must be included in Kant's list of dispositions to be cultivated, even though he puts a premium on skills.

Kant's discussion of the higher mental powers in his book on education is very superficial compared with what he says about them in his three *Critiques,* perhaps because in this book he is being quite untechnical and is not including university education in his purview. For this reason it will be worthwhile to bring in some of what he writes elsewhere about understanding, judgment, and reason. Understanding is for him the faculty that forms concepts and formulates rules and generalizations. It is therefore capable of being taught or instructed, since concepts, rules, and generalizations are eminently communicable; but judgment is another matter. Judgment is the faculty of subsuming the particular under the general or of applying the general to the particular, and for this there can be no rules. If a second rule were proposed, telling us how to apply a general rule to a particular, we would need a third rule telling us how to apply the second rule, and so on *ad infinitum*.

> And thus it appears that, though understanding is capable of being instructed, and of being equipped with rules, judgment is a peculiar talent which can be practised only, and cannot be taught.[15]

A kind of education of judgment is in fact possible by practice and example, Kant thinks, but not by instruction in terms of concepts and rules.

AESTHETIC CULTURE

Since aesthetic appreciation and creation involve judgment in Kant's view, this point about education by practice carries over to aesthetic education, about which he says almost nothing in his book on education (there he mentions taste, condemns the reading of novels, and says we pursue music in order to make ourselves liked!); but he does say something in the *Critique of Judgment*. Artistic genius is a desirable human skill, but

> . . . genius is a *talent* for producing that for which no definite rule can be given; it is not a mere aptitude for what can be learned by a rule. Hence *originality* must be its first property . . . its products must be models, i.e., *exemplary* . . . genius is entirely opposed to the *spirit of imitation*. Now since learning is nothing but imitation, it follows that the greatest ability and teachableness . . . cannot avail for genius. . . . we can readily learn all that *Newton* has set forth . . . but we cannot learn to write spirited poetry, however express may be the precepts of the art and however excellent its models. . . . artistic skill cannot be communicated; it is imparted to every artist immediately by the hand of nature. . . . There is therefore for beautiful art only a *manner* (modus), not a *method* of teaching (methodus). The master must show what the pupil is to do and how he is to do it; and the universal rules, under which at last he brings his procedure, serve rather for bringing the main points back to his remembrance when the occasion requires, than for prescribing them to him. Nevertheless regard must be had here to a certain ideal, which art must have before its eyes, although it cannot be completely attained in practice.[16]

What holds for artistic creation holds, of course, also for the development of aesthetic taste; it is innate and not communicable, and while it can be developed by a kind of education, it is only by an education through example and practice, not by instruction.

SPECULATIVE THOUGHT

The education of practical reason belongs mainly under (4) and (5)—to which we shall come—but there is one point about the education of theoretical reason that we must notice here. For Aristotle its education includes not only mathematics and physics, but also metaphysics or speculative philosophy. Kant in his book on education purposely does not deal with speculative reason, and there is a reason for this apart from the fact that he is talking only about elementary education. Reason is, for Kant, the faculty of inference or reasoning, as understanding is the faculty of conceiving and judgment that of judging. As such, reason is naturally driven to speculate about the universe as a whole, its origin, its destiny—in short, to do metaphysics; but it is a central point of the *Critique of Pure Reason* that metaphysics is impossible. According to Kant, we cannot prove or disprove the existence of God, the freedom of the will, the immortality of the soul, or any of the other interesting propositions of metaphysics or natural theology. We cannot know anything either by reasoning or intuition about what is real, about what he calls *noumena* or things-in-themselves. We can know—in mathematics, physics, history, etc., and in ordinary experience—only *phenomena* or things-as-they-appear in space and time, i.e. the realm of nature. Of these our experience and science provide us a perfectly reliable knowledge, and we need not be Humean sceptics about them; but about reality as such we can know nothing, much as reason is tempted to try. There is such a reality but it is inaccessible to our cognitive faculties, though, as we shall see, we may in the interests of morality have to make certain postulates about it.

It does not follow for Kant that philosophy should not be taught, but it does follow that metaphysics and natural theology of the kind Aristotle, Aquinas, and the rationalists had in mind should not be. The appropriate excellence or skill for the faculty of reason does not lie in this direction, as they thought; in fact, reason must be *disciplined* not to attempt to go that way. Reason still has an important function and must be cultivated, in Kant's view, but its wings must be clipped. Speculative soaring is not part of the disposition to be fostered in reason. It may even stretch its wings so far as to think that nature is a teleological system, but it must not actually take off from the ground.

VOCATIONAL SKILLS

(d) To return to more mundane matters, we may ask whether

Kant includes vocational skills among the dispositions to be cultivated in the ordinary program of education. The answer is not at all clear. He says that "men need schooling or instruction to equip them with the skill needed to achieve all their ends. It gives him a value as an individual."[17] This may be taken to mean that the ordinary schools should develop specifically vocational skills, but it does not say this, and Kant does not elaborate. He may have thought that an ordinary school education would provide sufficiently for the skills needed in most vocations, without introducing any specifically vocational training, or he may have thought that special schools should be used to furnish such training. He simply does not discuss the subject explicitly. He nowhere excludes vocational training from general (or liberal) education, but he does not explicitly include it either. He complains that parents are usually interested only in preparing their children to adapt themselves to their world and to make their way in it, insisting that they ought to educate their children for humanity; and this complaint implies that he has a primarily liberal conception of education, but it does not imply his having no vocational concern at all.

PRUDENCE

(4) Kant's next main point is that education must see to it that men acquire prudence.[18] Here he uses "prudence" as a label for a variety of dispositions: those required for fitting into society, being liked, having influence, being citizens, profiting by contact with our fellowmen, etc. "Prudence is the ability to turn one's skills to account." This is the concern of what Kant calls pragmatic education. We must, I think, conceive of prudence as the art of being happy in the world, the art of using our skills and knowledge [acquired as part of (3)] in such a way as to be happy in the long run as individuals. Sometimes Kant speaks of the promotion of skill as the work of the schoolteacher and of the promotion of prudence as that of the tutor or *guide* (today's guidance counselor?). Prudence as Kant thinks of it, then, is identical with what Aristotle calls practical wisdom in some of his more egoistic passages.

For acquiring prudence, Kant says, several things are necessary. The child must "learn to disguise his feelings and to be reserved, while at the same time he learns to read the character of others." He must learn to control his temper and other passions without being apathetic, to be brave without being violent, to be cheerful, good-natured, and open-hearted, and to be sociable. He must also acquire "the art of external seeming"—refinement, manners, courtesy—"and a kind of worldly wisdom which will enable him to use all men for his own ends." The last comment is surprising, coming from a man who also says that we should treat others as ends and not as means, but we must remember that he is talking here about prudence, not morality. Even so, Kant really means by prudence, not just the ability to use others for one's own purposes, but the wisdom to combine all of one's purposes for one's own lasting benefit, and he recognizes that a man may have the ability without the wisdom.

Perhaps we may analyze what Kant calls prudence into two parts: (a) a knowledge of what to do in order to be happy in the long run, and (b) a disposition to look to the long run rather than to the moment. Under this heading, then, he would be thinking that education should give a child both the knowledge needed for happiness, and the will to use it even in the face of temptations to do otherwise.

MORALIZATION

(5) Kant introduces this topic by saying:

> Education . . . must see to the moralization of man. He is to acquire not merely the skills needed for all sorts of ends, but also the disposition to choose only good ends.[19]

Morality is perhaps Kant's favorite subject—certainly man's moralization is his chief concern in education—and in his writings on ethics and education he goes into considerable detail in listing and describing a number of relevant dispositions to be formed by education. (a) Some of them are not so much moral virtues as dispositions preliminary to and essential in morality as Kant conceives it: sense of individuality, self-reliance and independence, thinking for oneself, capacity to exercise free will and make one's own decisions, autonomy, a disposition to act on maxims reflectively arrived at. For Kant freedom and reflective autonomy lie at the heart both of morality and of human perfection (not tradition-directedness and other-directedness, of which we hear so much today) and he insists that the dispositions pertaining to them be promoted, not prevented, by education.

> *Practical* or *moral* education is that through which a man is so formed as to be able to live as a free being. . . . It is education for personality, education of a free being who is able to maintain himself and to be a member of society while keeping a sense of his own personal value.[20]

Kant is as insistent on autonomy, freedom, and individuality as Dewey is or as even the existentialists are—or as any critics of recent American education are. This emphasis on autonomy in what he writes about education and ethics is one of the most obvious differences between Kant and Aristotle. Although there is an important truth in the frequent statement that the Greeks prized freedom, and although Aristotle does provide for a considerable freedom in his *Politics,* there is little explicit provision for it in his system of education. He does, in his *Ethics,* stress the fact that a fully virtuous man will do what is right because he sees that it is right, but his emphasis on habituation in moral education makes it hard to see just how the child or youth can achieve even this much autonomy.

CHARACTER

Kant also mentions character in this connection. Now by "character" we often mean "good character," and sometimes Kant does too, for example, when he says that obedience and truthfulness are essential features in the character of a child. In this sense character is identical with what he calls good will or virtue. But sometimes he uses the term to mean a disposition that is essential to morality but may belong to a merely prudent or even to a bad man (but not to what Aristotle calls a weak or incontinent man). Thus he writes in his *Anthropology*:

> Character as such is the disposition of the will by which a person binds himself to certain practical principles [maxims] which he sets permanently before himself by his own reason.[21]

Accordingly he says in another passage:

> First form character, then a good character. The former is done by practice in a firm intention in the espousal of certain maxims after reflection.[22]

How the latter is done we shall see hereafter. Incidentally, this quotation shows how similar Kant's view of moral education is to Aristotle's —and also how different.

It should also be observed here, in view of Kant's insistence on thinking and using one's reason to arrive at maxims for one's life, that he is also regarding the cultivation of the intellectual faculties as an important condition of morality and as part of moral, as well as of intellectual education. The moral life, for him as for Dewey (but not for Aristotle), must be within the capacity of the common man, but it does require him to think out his maxims, and hence education must help him to think them out as well as he can. This means that he must be given the necessary intellectual skills (discussed earlier) and also the relevant knowledge of life and the world.

(b) Of the more purely moral dispositions, there is one which is general and includes the others. Kant calls it "good will," "virtue," or "good character"—and sometimes "morality." This is "the disposition to choose only good ends" or, as Kant also puts it, the disposition to act not merely in accordance with duty but from a sense of duty, not merely in accordance with the moral law but out of respect for the moral law. "Virtue . . . is self-constraint . . . by the mere thought of one's duty in accordance with its formal law." This disposition, Kant says, is "the true goal of all moral cultivation." So far Aristotle would agree. But, as we might expect, Kant does not define virtue merely as "a long standing *habit* of morally good actions, acquired by practice," as Aristotle does; he insists, rather, that it must result "from considered, firm, and continually purified principles" if it is to be armed for all situations and adequately ensured against new temptations. He also rejects "the celebrated principle (Aristotle's) which locates virtue in the mean between two vices." Virtue, he argues, is not a matter of the *degree* to which one follows certain maxims, it is a matter of the *kind* of maxims one has.[23]

To be moral, then, one must have this disposition to do what is right because it is right at all times, whatever the temptations to do otherwise. This does not mean that what one thinks is right is always right—we shall see shortly what Kant's criterion is for determining what we ought to do—but it does mean that one is not morally virtuous and one's acts are not morally good (though they may be right in the sense of conforming to the moral law) unless one acts from a sense of duty or out of respect for the moral law. One must become moral in this sense. Does this mean that one must suppress all desires and dispositions other than this one of trying to do one's duty, and never act out of sheer love for others but always only because one feels morally obliged to? Kant does sometimes seem to be taking such an extremely moralistic or rigoristic view, though he never goes so far as to suggest we should despise our fellows or do our duty with distaste (in fact he thinks, as Aristotle did, that the virtuous man will take pleasure, or rather *joy*, in doing his duty, though, of course, he will not do his duty in order to gain this pleasure). In his book on religion,[24] for instance, he takes the position that if a man is moved to an action which is in fact in accordance with the moral law (e.g. it keeps a promise), not by respect for the moral law but by some other motive (e.g. sheer love for others), then he is morally bad, not good, and not even morally indifferent. Kant's real point seems to be, however, not that one is to extirpate all other desires and dispositions, but that one is to cultivate a good will so assiduously that it is always operative and so strong as to be *able* always to determine one's actions.

Other desires and dispositions may also operate, but they must do so within the framework of a prevailing will to do one's duty. Actions motivated wholly by other motives are without moral value even if they are in fact right or beneficent, and they may, of course, be morally bad. If one's moral will is not strong enough to move him to do his duty, if other considerations are *needed* to get him to do it, then he is bad or at least morally imperfect. The importance of all this for moral education is clear. Natural inclinations need not be extirpated—even in his book on religion Kant says they are good and should not be extirpated, since only what is opposed to the moral law must be eradicated—but a disposition to do our duty must be made dominant over them in our lives. We must strive "with all [our] might to make the thought of duty for its own sake the sufficient motive of every dutiful action."[25]

OTHER GENERAL DISPOSITIONS

(c) There are other rather general dispositions which Kant mentions and which belong rather to the moral life as a whole than to one sector of it. Self-mastery must be listed here again. "The first step towards the formation of a good character is to put our passions [to] one side,"[26] and to control our desires and inclinations. This entails learning renunciation, endurance, and fortitude. We must also learn patience, not in the sense of giving up hope, but in that of having courage to go on. Moral courage itself might also be mentioned here, but Kant puts more stress on humility. He condemns all forms of servility, even in children. Every individual for him has an absolute worth equal to that of every other. No man need humble himself before another—though, of course, pride is a vice. There is also a false humility which Kant condemns—this consists in disavowing or underrating one's moral worth in the belief that by doing so one acquires more worth; but there is a true humility that one should feel when he compares himself with the moral law and with what it requires him to be. It would be interesting to compare what Kant says here with Aristotle's description of the great-souled man.

While Kant thus recognizes a certain kind of humility, he does not believe that a child should be taught shame, except in the case of lying. The natural role of shame, he thinks, is to cause one to betray himself after lying, but to cry "Shame!" in other cases only produces timidity and deception unnecessarily.

The other disposition to be mentioned here is respect for humanity, a sense of the dignity of human nature, whether in one's own person or another's, and the sense of the equality of all men that goes with it. This sense is in a way the backdrop of morality as Kant conceives it, and he himself teaches it repeatedly in his writings.

Kant attributes his own perception of the dignity of humanity to the influence of Rousseau. At forty, shortly after reading *Emile*, he said in a famous fragment:

> I am myself by inclination a seeker after truth. I feel a consuming thirst for knowledge and a restless passion to advance in it, as well as satisfaction in every forward step. There was a time when I thought that this alone could constitute the honor of mankind, and I despised the common man who knows nothing. Rousseau set me right. This blind prejudice vanished; I learned to respect human nature, and I should consider myself far more useless than the ordinary working-man if I did not believe that this view could give worth to all others to establish the rights of man.[27]

In effect Kant tells us here that there was a time when he believed what is essentially Aristotle's position and that he was converted by reading Rousseau to the position which controls his later ethical and educational theories. From the view which gives the prize to knowledge and truth he moved to the view which gives it to individuality, character, and humanity.

TWO PROBLEMS OF MORAL EDUCATION

For the rest, the problem of moral education is twofold: "we must place before [our children] the duties they have to perform," i.e. teach them what their duties are, and we must foster in them the dispositions to perform these duties from a sense of duty, i.e. cultivate the corresponding virtues, which, summed up, constitute virtue or good will. For Kant it is not enough to teach children what their duties are, since he, unlike Socrates, believes that one may know his duty and yet not do it. In fact, Kant is more fully convinced of this than Aristotle is. Respect for the moral law may become strong enough to overcome the inclinations and even the desire for one's own happiness, if these conflict with duty, but duty may also be overcome by them.

> . . . one does not, merely by the theory of how one should behave in keeping with the concept of virtue, acquire the strength to put the rule into practice.[28]

LIST OF DUTIES

(d) In order, then, to see what more specific moral dispositions are to be cultivated, we must find out what our duties are. In his main works Kant deals in detail only with the duties of men as men to other men as men. There are also duties which depend on their particular circumstances and relations to one another, e.g. those of a parent to his child or a teacher to his pupil, but Kant does not regard these duties as belonging to what he calls "the metaphysics of morals"; they do, however, bear on questions about education, as we shall see later. As for the more general duties of men as such, they may be classified as follows on the basis of Kant's various discussions (this scheme is somewhat simplified for present purposes):[29]

A. Duties to oneself:
   1. Perfect or obligatory duties to oneself:
      a. To preserve oneself, i.e. not to commit suicide, and not to mutilate, defile, or stupefy oneself
      b. To be truthful, not to lie
      c. Not to be miserly toward oneself
      d. To respect oneself, not to be servile
   2. Imperfect or meritorious duties to oneself:
      a. To seek one's own perfection
         (1) Natural perfection
         (2) Moral perfection
B. Duties to others:
   1. Perfect or obligatory duties to others:
      a. To keep promises
      b. To be truthful, not to lie
      c. To seek to establish a system of positive (legal) laws and to obey them
      d. To respect others, even those who are immoral (this does not entail honoring or revering them)
   2. Imperfect or meritorious duties to others:
      a. To promote their happiness, to be benevolent toward them, to love them (practically, not sentimentally)
      b. To be grateful
      c. To be sympathetic
      d. To be friendly and sociable.

SOME EXPLANATIONS

We cannot study this list in detail, but a few elaborations must be made. (a) The list does not include a direct duty to seek our own happiness. Kant denies, not only the view of ethical egoism that one's own happiness is the basis for determining one's moral duties (it is only the basis for determining *prudential* imperatives), but also the more common view that the promotion of one's own happiness is one of our moral duties. He does hold that a rational being will rightly take his own happiness as an end (though not as his only end), and indeed ought to do so if he does not, but he believes that men do in fact already take it as an end, and argues that they therefore cannot be said to have an *obligation* to do so.

> Since every man (by virtue of his *natural* impulses) has his own happiness as his end, it would be contradictory to consider this an obligatory end. What we will inevitably and spontaneously does not come under the concept of *duty*, which is a necessitation to an end we adopt reluctantly.[30]

However, Kant does insist that one has an indirect duty to promote one's own prosperity and welfare insofar as this is a necessary condition for carrying out other duties.

(b) Neither does the list include a direct duty to promote the perfection of others, and this is surprising. Kant has a reason for not recognizing such a duty.

> For the *perfection* of another man, as a person, consists precisely in *his own* power to adopt his end in accordance with his own concept of duty; and it is self-contradictory to demand that I . . . make it my duty to do what only the other person can do.[31]

Kant's rejection of the perfecting of others as a positive duty is thus a part of his general insistence on freedom and autonomy. Each person's perfection is his own business, though his happiness is not. Again, however, Kant allows that, since one has a duty to promote the happiness of others, he does also have an indirect negative duty with respect to their moral perfection—he must not "give scandal," i.e. he must not help to bring it about that others do things for which they will suffer pangs of conscience.

(c) We must see somewhat more fully what Kant conceives to be contained in the duties of cultivating our own perfection and promoting other people's happiness, since this bears on our subsequent discussion. About the former Kant writes:

> When we say that man has a duty to take as his end the perfection characteristic of man as such (of humanity, really), we must locate perfection in what man can bring into being by his actions, not in the mere gifts he receives from nature. . . . This duty must therefore be the *cultivation* of one's *powers* (or natural capacities). . . . Man has a duty of striving to raise himself from . . . his animality and to realize ever more fully [his] humanity. . . .[32]

This involves, first, the cultivation of *natural* perfection, that is, the cultivation of the *skills* dealt with earlier. "Cultivate your powers of mind and body so that they are fit to realize any end you can come upon."[33] In other words, "Seek a good education." It involves, second, the pursuit of *moral* perfection, that is, of virtue or good will and all of the other moral dispositions already mentioned.

> Man's greatest moral perfection is to do his duty and this *from a motive of duty* (to make the [moral] law not merely the rule but also the motive of his actions).

This duty requires us to know ourselves.

> Know your heart—whether it is good or evil, whether the source of your actions is pure or impure. . . . Moral self-knowledge. . . . is the beginning of all human wisdom. For wisdom consists in the harmony of the will of a being with his final end. . . .[34]

(d) About the obligation to promote the happiness of others Kant says that this involves making their permissible ends one's own, that is, it requires one to help others achieve what they are after if their pursuit is not wrong.

> It is for them to decide what things they consider elements in their happiness; but I am entitled to refuse some of these things if I disagree with their judgments, so long as the other has no right to demand a thing from me as his due.[35]

We must, of course, not help a man in such a way as to humiliate him, for this is not to respect him as we ought. How far must we be prepared to go? Kant's answer is that the rule says

> . . . only that I should sacrifice a part of my well-being to others . . . it cannot assign determinate limits to the extent of this sacrifice. These limits will depend, in large part, on what a person's true needs consist of . . . and it must be left to each to decide this for himself. For a maxim of promoting another's happiness at the sacrifice of my own happiness, my true needs, would contradict itself were it made a universal law. Hence this duty . . . has in it a play-room for doing more or less.[36]

A word is also needed about another form in which Kant states this duty: "Love thy neighbor as thyself." This does not mean we have a duty to *feel* love for him—feelings cannot be commanded—but only that we should will (not merely wish for) his happiness.

These being our duties, the dispositions to be fostered are those that correspond: honesty, self-respect, fidelity, benevolence, gratitude, friendship, etc.

REMARKS

Thus we come to the end of Kant's answer to our first question. Looking back over it a few remarks come to mind. First, it may be pointed out that the headings—skill, prudence, and morality—correspond to the three kinds of imperatives distinguished by Kant. Second, we see that Kant holds that one has a moral duty to cultivate in *oneself* skills and moral dispositions, but not to cultivate prudence (except as an indirect duty). On the other hand, if we ask what dispositions it is one's duty to cultivate in *others*, Kant's answer appears to be almost the converse of this. For he seems to say that one has no duty to help cultivate either skills or moral dispositions in others, since both belong to perfection and we have no duty to contribute to another's perfection (except by refraining from interfering with it). That leaves only prudence. Kant must be thinking that one has a duty to help build up prudence in others, since this is necessary for their happiness. Actually, however, Kant also sees that skills are necessary for happiness, too, and so perhaps we should not take him to mean that we have no duty to promote another's *natural* perfection, but only that we have no duty to promote another's *moral* perfection. On the other hand, he may be thinking that whether or not we have a duty to help develop another's natural perfection (i.e. to educate him) depends on his circumstances and on our relations to him, and hence is not a question he can answer in a "metaphysics of morals." Of this more later.

Third, it is clear that Kant is not arguing that only moral dispositions are to be cultivated; skills, prudence, and knowledge are also to be fostered. It is also apparent, however, that, although Aristotle ranks the intellectual excellences highest, Kant ranks the moral ones first; and, although Aristotle distinguishes both intellectual and moral excellences from skills (*techne*), Kant seems to regard intellectual excellences as a kind of skill, though different from other kinds of skill.

PHYSICAL AND PRACTICAL EDUCATION

Two topics must be taken up here, before we pass on to Kant's answer to our second question. The first is the distinction between *physical* and *practical* education which is central to Kant's thought on education but is not made very clear. We have seen that Kant in effect assigns five jobs to education: nurture, discipline, cultivation of skills, development of prudence, and moralization. Now, sometimes Kant identifies physical education with nurture (as I did in dealing with nurture). This would put the other four jobs under practical education. But sometimes Kant puts discipline under physical education and contrasts it with practical education. Accordingly he sometimes puts the cultivation of skill, prudence, and morality under practical education, stressing their *positive* character in comparison with the *negative* character of nurture and discipline. To compound the difficulty, he also seems sometimes to identify practical with positive moral education—negative moral education comes under discipline and so under physical education—making nurture, discipline, and the cultivation of skill and prudence all parts of physical education. This is all very confusing to a reader. Kant certainly meant to extend the notion of physical education well beyond our ordinary meaning, but just how far?

What was Kant trying to do in dividing education into physical and practical as he did? Neither term means for him what it means for us. The best clue to what he has in mind lies in his connection of physical education with nature (in fact, we might well substitute the word "natural" for the word "physical" in Kant's discussion) and of practical education with freedom.

> We call anything *"practical"* which has reference to freedom. . . . We must . . . distinguish between nature and freedom. To give laws to freedom is quite another thing from cultivating nature. . . . We may, therefore, call the cultivation of the mind physical, in a certain sense, just as well as the cultivation of the body. This physical cultivation of the mind, however, must be distinguished from moral training, in that it aims only at nature, while moral training aims at freedom.[37]

Here Kant is connecting his distinction between two kinds of education with his basic distinction between the phenomenal and the noumenal worlds. We saw that he distinguishes between things as they appear and things as they really are. This is true of the human self too. It appears in time and space as a phenomenal self, but in itself it is a thing-in-itself, a noumenon, and is not in space and time. As a phenomenon the self belongs to nature and what it does is determined by previous causes according to the laws of nature. In reality, as a noumenon, however, it is free and undetermined; that this is so cannot be proved by theoretical reason, but must be postulated by practical reason on the basis of morality, for morality presupposes freedom of the will. Thus the noumenal realm is for Kant the realm of freedom, morality, and practical reason, while the phenomenal realm is that of nature, determinism, science, and theoretical reason.

Now, Kant seems to think that, as man belongs somehow to both realms, he must be subject to two kinds of education, one physical or natural, the other practical or moral, one an education of the phenomenal self for life in nature, the other an education of the noumenal self for freedom, one aiming at natural perfection and perhaps happiness, the other at moral perfection. This conception poses problems, as does the basic distinction of two worlds, or realms, and Kant does not make it very clear. However, if this is what he has in mind, then we must take him to be identifying practical with positive moral education, and to be putting nurture, discipline, cultivation of skill, and development of prudence under physical or natural education. On this interpretation one can explain the fact that he sometimes includes culture (skills) and prudence under practical education by pointing out that they too involve the learning of maxims and imperatives (hypothetical) and are needed for free and moral action, at least for its appearance in the phenomenal world.

THE GOOD MAN AND THE CITIZEN

The second topic remaining to be dealt with here has to do with Aristotle's distinction between the excellences of the good man and those of the good citizen. Aristotle held, it will be recalled, that these two sets of dispositions do not always coincide, and that insofar as they do not, education must cultivate the latter rather than the former. Now, the dispositions we have been reviewing are, for Kant, the excellences of the good man. Does he think that they are also the excellences of the good citizen? If not, which excellences does he think education should cultivate?

Kant does not consider these questions in this form, but he says something by way of answering them. He does not even raise the possibility that education should promote the excellences of the good citizen as defined by the constitution and law of one's country, thus varying from country to country in the dispositions it fosters. He simply takes it for granted as obvious that education in all countries is to promote human perfection, i.e. the dispositions indicated above, and not simply whatever dispositions their constitutions call for. Education must not simply serve parental or national purposes.

> . . . parents usually only care that their children *make their way* in the world, and [rulers] look upon their subjects merely as tools for their own purposes [elsewhere Kant writes that "all of them look ever and only to the prosperity of their own

countries"]. Parents care for the home, rulers for the state. Neither have as their aim the universal good and the perfection to which man is destined. . . . But the basis of a scheme of education must be cosmopolitan.

It must advance the whole human race towards its destiny.

> . . . children ought to be educated, not for the present, but for a possibly improved condition of man in the future. . . .[38]

How different this is from Aristotle! Aristotle's conception is a static, nationalistic, and relativistic one. Kant, in the first place, is insisting that any educational system must teach the virtues of the good man, not just those of the citizen of the country in which it operates; in the second place, he is maintaining that in doing so it must be internationalistic in its inspiration and look to the whole future of humanity.

It is obvious that Kant's philosophy of education would have very different implications for any program of aid to education in underdeveloped countries than would Aristotle's. Kant would also give a very different answer to the question, much discussed in our century, "Dare the Schools Build a New Social Order?" On Aristotle's view they dare not; they dare at most try to see that the prevailing constitution is more fully realized than it is, not to work for a new one. For Kant, however, as we shall see, they not only dare, they must help to build a new social order—an international republic of perpetual peace in which men may more and more fully attain their proper natural and moral perfections as outlined above.

At the same time Kant does say, in discussing education in prudence, that it makes of a man a citizen (*Bürger*) and equips him for civil society (*bürgerliche Gesellschaft*); he seems to mean by this that it makes him (and should make him) a good citizen of the state in which he lives. Kant is, in fact, quite insistent that one has a duty always to obey the law. In his own life, he spoke up strongly for freedom of thought and expression, but when the reactionary Prussian government of Frederick William II forbade him to go on expressing his unorthodox views on religion, he at once obeyed for the rest of the king's life (the king died in 1797). Privately he wrote that although it is wrong to deny one's beliefs, in a case like this it is the duty of a subject to remain silent; he added, "While one should never speak anything but the truth, it is not, therefore, one's duty to speak the whole truth in public." In his theory Kant also held that one must always obey, at least externally. He sympathized with the American and French revolutions, but nevertheless held that the prohibition of revolution is absolute. A man has inalienable rights that he cannot give up, including the right to make his opinion known, but these rights are not to be exercised against the sovereign. One must respect and be loyal to the constitution and laws under which he lives. This sounds much like Aristotle, but it seems clear that Kant asks only for a kind of external obedience, and thinks that the individual may and should, while giving such obedience, cultivate in himself the excellences of the good man (as he himself presumably did even under Frederick William II), and that education should help him to do so. This means that the schools in any society should have the academic freedom to cultivate the perfections of mankind in their pupils—if necessary, with a new order in mind. Kant praises the Dessau Institute because its teachers were free to work out their own plans and methods, and were in contact with all the learned men of Germany, and this is how he thought it should be in all schools. But what if the state forbids its schools to cultivate some of the perfections in question, fearing that they may lead to the rise of a new order? Then, after all, Kant's answer, like Aristotle's, seems to be that the schools must obey (and on moral grounds, not just prudential ones), trusting that nature and history will eventually bring about the new order anyway.

THE AIMS OF EDUCATION

QUESTION

We have spent a good deal of time on Kant's answer to the question of what dispositions education is to foster. Now we must take up his answer to the second question: Why should education foster these dispositions rather than others? What are the more ultimate aims of education that require their development? Or what are the basic principles that dictate their cultivation? Kant does not deal very fully or systematically with this question in his book on education, but we must try to work out his answer on the basis of what he writes there and elsewhere. In a way it is contained in the opening sentence of his *Anthropology*:

> All advances in culture, by which man educates himself, have the goal of putting these acquired knowledges and skills to use in the world, but the most important object in it to which he can apply them is *man*, for he is his own ultimate end.

However, this ringing statement of humanism is somewhat opaque and must be spelled out. Kant says sometimes that the job of education is to develop all of man's natural gifts; sometimes he says more fully that it is to develop man's natural gifts in their due proportion and in relation to their end, and thus advance the whole human race towards its destiny.[39]

But what is their due proportion, what is their end, and what is the destiny of the human race? Kant says the end is "humanity" or "the perfection of human nature," but what is this?

Generally, as we saw, Kant thinks of human perfection as consisting of the dispositions (skills and moral traits) reviewed above. Then, in saying that the aim of education and of man is the perfection of human nature, he would seem to mean that the end is the fullest possible acquisition of those dispositions. In that case, the answer to our question why we should acquire and foster those dispositions is, "for their own sakes." Is this Kant's view?

A POSSIBLE ANSWER

One might give a prudential or pragmatic line of argument to show that we should acquire the dispositions on Kant's list or that society should foster them in us. That is, one might contend that acquiring them is for one's own greatest happiness and that fostering them in us is for the greatest general happiness. Now, Kant does not entirely reject such a line of thought, which is essentially Aristotle's, at least in the case of non-moral dispositions, but he does not regard it as adequate by itself. For him no justification of action in terms of happiness is adequate unless it is advanced within a framework of moral principles. An action must at least be compatible with the moral law to be justified. Besides, according to Kant, happiness is only a conditional good. By a "good" here Kant does not mean simply something that is desired or aimed at, as Aristotle does. He agrees that we do desire or aim at happiness, but denies that this makes it good. For Kant, to say that something is good is to say that it is a suitable object of will for a rational being, that it is right or obligatory for such a being to take it as an end, not merely that it is desired. By happiness also Kant does not mean what Aristotle means. Aristotle identifies happiness with excellent activity, and maintains that it alone is unconditionally good. Kant thinks of happiness as much more like pleasure, viz. "the satisfaction of all our desires" or "general well-being and contentment with one's condition." This is essentially the way we usually think of happiness ourselves. Kant argues, then, that happiness, so conceived, is not unconditionally good, as many seem to think. It is good only if and insofar as it can be combined with good will, good character, or morality.

> . . . the sight of a being adorned with no feature of a pure
> and good will, enjoying uninterrupted prosperity, can never
> give pleasure to a rational impartial spectator.[40]

In fact, Kant proclaims in a famous sentence:

> Nothing in the world—indeed nothing even beyond the world
> —can possibly be conceived which could be called good with-
> out qualification, except a *good will*.[41]

Everything else—talents of the mind, qualities of temperament, gifts
of fortune, acquired skills, health, prudence, happiness, and freedom
—may be bad if they are combined with a bad character or will.
Even contemplation, which Aristotle finally identifies with happiness
and regards as unconditionally good, is really not so, according to
Kant. Only the strictly moral dispositions, which are summed up in
good will, are unconditionally good. They cannot become bad by
being combined with anything else; whatever happens, good will
"like a jewel, still shines by its own light."

KANT'S ANSWER

Kant must then show, by a *moral* argument, that we should
promote the dispositions listed, if he is to answer our question.
But now there are two questions, as we have already intimated,
though Kant does not distinguish them. One is the question of why
an individual (e.g. a child) should seek to acquire those dispositions
(or submit to an education by which they are fostered). The second
is the question of why others (e.g. his parents or state) should try to
cultivate those dispositions in him. In essence Kant's answer to both
must be: because if they do not do so, they will not be doing their
duty. Let us take the former question first.

It is easy to see how Kant can show that I or any individual
ought to cultivate the strictly moral dispositions—benevolence, truthfulness, etc. If they are morally good dispositions, then it is one's
duty to acquire them. All that Kant has to do here is to show that
they *are* morally good dispositions. To do this he must show that
telling the truth, promoting another's happiness, etc., are, in fact,
duties. This was taken for granted in listing them above, but now it
must be shown. Now, Kant does not think that we intuit duties like
"Tell the truth," "Help others," etc., or that they are self-evident,
as many so-called intuitionists have held. They must be shown to be
duties by being derived from "the supreme principle of morality."
What is this supreme principle? A teleologist in ethics like Mill would
reply that it is a principle like "We ought to do what will promote

a certain end (pleasure, happiness, knowledge, etc.)"; then he would argue that we ought to be truthful, benevolent, etc., because this is conducive to that end. For Kant, however, none of these ends are unconditional goods; hence they cannot serve by themselves to justify anything. Moreover, he maintains, on such a teleological theory, the rules of not lying, etc., will only be hypothetical imperatives; they will hold only for beings who desire the end in question, and so they will not be universally and necessarily valid. Moral rules, he insists, must be necessarily valid for all rational beings—they must be such that a rational being cannot disown them and still be rational, even though he may violate them. That, for him, is involved in the very notion of morality as we have come to conceive it even at the common sense level. Moral imperatives must be categorical and a priori, not dependent on experience or on what we happen to desire. Hence, Kant concludes, a teleological theory would be a subversion of morality.

THE SUPREME PRINCIPLE OF MORALITY

Kant then is a deontologist in ethics. The supreme principle of morality cannot be a command to promote a certain *end* in all that we do. It must be a *formal* principle that holds necessarily for all rational beings no matter what their desires or ends; but, again, he does not believe that such a principle is intuitive or self-evident. It must be deducible from the very concept of a rational being. Now, Kant maintains, a rational being must be *consistent* in his actions and judgments about action. That is, he must act and judge by maxims or rules, at least implicitly if not explicitly. Moreover, he must be willing to see everyone else act and judge by the same maxims or rules; he must be willing to see his maxims become universal laws of conduct. In fact, since he cannot appeal to his desires or goals to determine what he ought to do, he can only tell what is right or wrong by asking which maxims he can will to be universally acted on. This conclusion checks with common sense, Kant contends, because we regularly use it in our moral thinking; we generally think that what is right for one man to do in a certain kind of situation is right for anyone to do in the same kind of situation. Thus the supreme principle of morality—or what Kant also calls the first form of the categorical imperative—is: "Act only on maxims which you can will to be universal laws."[42] If you cannot will the maxim on which you propose to act in a certain situation to be a universal law (universally acted on by those who are in that kind of situation), then your proposed action is wrong; the opposite course of action is right, or, rather, obligatory—if the maxim involved in it can be willed to be a universal law.

To take one of Kant's examples: suppose that, in order to ex-
tricate myself from difficulty, I propose to make a promise I do not
intend to keep. Then the maxim of my action is: "When I can extri-
cate myself from difficulty only by making a lying promise I will do
so." Now suppose that I ask if it would be right for me to make
this lying promise. Then I must ask myself if I can will that everyone who finds himself in the same kind of case may also make a
lying promise. If I do this, Kant says,

> I immediately see that I could will the lie but not a universal
> law to lie. For with such a law [with such a maxim universally
> acted on by people in difficulty] there would be no promises
> at all, in as much as it would be futile to make a pretense of
> my intention in regard to future actions to those who would
> not believe this pretense or—if they overhastily did so—would
> pay me back in my own coin. Thus my maxim would neces-
> sarily destroy itself as soon as it was made a universal law.[43]

I find I cannot consistently will that my maxim be universally acted
on. This would involve my wanting it both ways. Hence making lying
promises is wrong, and keeping promises obligatory, for the maxim of
keeping promises can be willed to be a universal law.

Kant believes that he can show by similar arguments that we
ought not to commit suicide, that we have a duty to cultivate our
talents and faculties (i.e. to seek our own perfection), that we have
an obligation to help others who are in trouble (and, in general, to
promote the happiness of others)—in short, that he can establish all
of the duties listed earlier. He also believes that he can establish
another very general principle which he sometimes calls the second
form of the categorical imperative, and which is equally famous:

> Act so that you treat humanity, whether in your own person
> or in that of another, always as an end and never as a
> means only.[44]

This he derives from the first as follows:

> The first principle of the doctrine of virtue is: act according
> to a maxim of *ends* which it can be a universal law for every-
> one to have.[45]

That is, adopt those ends and only those ends which you can will that
everyone should adopt; thus, "According to this principle man is an

end, to himself as well as to others."[46] Kant believes that from this second general principle he can also deduce all of the duties listed earlier, and he sometimes prefers this second line of deduction to the first. He uses it particularly in establishing the duties of telling the truth, respecting one's own humanity, and respecting that of others.

It is easy to see now how Kant can give a moral argument to show that one should cultivate non-moral skills and quasi-moral dispositions like resolution, character, etc.: (a) one has a duty to cultivate one's talents, (b) skills are needed in order to be able to carry out one's other duties, and (c) character, etc., are necessary conditions of acquiring good will. Besides, (d) one has a duty not to be dependent on others.

THE DUTY TO EDUCATE

Why should others in one's family or society do anything to help one acquire these dispositions? Here one would expect Kant to answer, "Because they have a duty to do so." But this, as we saw earlier, is just what Kant denies; one person has no duty to promote the perfection of another (in fact, Kant almost goes so far as to suggest that it would be *wrong* to try to do so). This dictum might even be taken to imply that parents and teachers have no business cultivating dispositions in children—or in other words, that all education should be self-education. Yet, while Kant insists that the child must be active in moral or practical education (though not in physical education), he certainly writes in his book on education as if other-education is perfectly proper. In some passages he even talks as if it is a duty for one generation to educate the next.

One must, of course, point out that Kant does believe one person has a duty to promote another's happiness, and must be thinking that the parent generation has a duty to promote the perfections of the younger generation at least insofar as these include skills and other dispositions (e.g. prudence) that are necessary for its happiness. One might also point out, with some plausibility, that, when Kant says we have no duty to promote the perfection of others, he means only that we have no duty to advance their *moral* perfection, and may still be holding that we ought to advance their *natural* perfection (skills, etc.). Both of these points seem well taken, but they do nothing to show that older people should do something about the moral education of younger ones, as Kant appears to think when writing about education. He certainly is not siding with those more recent educators who advocate only guidance, non-directive counseling, and the like, and who are fearful of "imposing" their moral values on their pupils, even though he seems to do so in the dictum under discussion.

It seems to me that Kant must be holding that parents and

teachers do have a duty to do what they can, at least up to a certain point, to cultivate the perfection, moral as well as natural, of their children and pupils. He does indeed believe that *men as men* have no duty to work at each other's perfection (moral and perhaps also natural). That is the level he is writing at in the "metaphysics of morals." As has been mentioned, however, he recognizes that there are duties that do not hold of men as men, but depend on their circumstances and relations to one another—duties of men to women, of the learned to the ignorant, of the old to the young, and so on. Though he may deny that men as men have a duty to educate one another, he may still think that the older have such a duty to the younger. In fact, in his *Lectures on Ethics*, composed in 1780-81, Kant talks specifically about "duties arising from differences of age" and, in doing so, gives in four pages a brief summary of his whole philosophy of education.[47] His view seems to be that it is only after the young have reached a certain point of development that others have no duty to do anything about their perfection. Before that children need the help of others—in fact, they need discipline and even compulsion—to prevent the formation of bad habits, as well as for positive instruction. Even for this period Kant insists on a regard for the child's freedom and eventual autonomy, and he thinks that all such external aid (except the force of law) should come to an end as soon as possible. Until then it must be given—with an eye both to natural and moral perfection—preferably out of a sense of duty.

THE END OF EDUCATION

This means that, for the period during which other-education is to go on, the aim of education is not simply the happiness of the pupil but also his perfection, moral and non-moral. The educator (parent or teacher) has the duty to promote the perfection as well as the happiness of the child or pupil (and his happiness as well as his perfection). The pupil, on the other hand, has simply a duty to seek his own perfection, moral and natural; he will also aim at his own happiness, but he has no moral obligation to do so, only a prudential one, and he ought to seek it only so far as it is compatible with his being a good man. From a moral point of view, which is the one that counts for Kant, the aim of self-education is simply perfection, or humanity, that of other-education is twofold: happiness and perfection. Both sorts of education, however, should promote happiness only insofar as it is compatible with virtue and duty, since happiness is only conditionally a good, i.e. it is good only when combined with moral excellence. The same is true of non-moral dispositions like skill and prudence. They should be cultivated by both the child and his educators but only in conjunction with the cultivation of a good will, for they too are only good conditionally.

The main question for us is what Kant regards as the aims of the activity of educating (of teachers, schools, etc.). If what has been said is correct, the aim of education in this sense is a combination of moral perfection, natural perfection, and happiness—a combination in which moral perfection is the primary and indispensable ingredient and in which natural perfection and happiness are to be included, but only insofar as they are compatible with moral perfection. Such a combination of these three sorts of ingredients is what Kant calls the *summum bonum, bonum consummatum,* or highest good. It alone can be regarded, he thinks, as the whole end of man and creation. Good will is the only thing that, by itself, is unconditionally good; it is the *supremum bonum,* and the condition of other things being good. Kant even talks sometimes as if it is by itself the whole end of man and creation. He does in effect proclaim, "Seek ye first the kingdom of heaven (good will), and all other things will be added unto you," adding, of course, that good will must be sought (and duty done) for its own sake and not out of a belief that other things will be added unto one; nevertheless, he believes that other things, natural perfection and happiness, can be added unto it and that the resulting combination is the highest good—the achievement of which is "humanity," the end and destiny of man.

Here we must remember again that education is to take as its goal, not just the perfecting of man under present conditions, but the progress of the human race itself. There is in Kant a notion of an evolution of mankind to ever greater perfection (and happiness) in which education can and should play a part. In his *Lectures on Ethics,* under the heading "The Ultimate Destiny of the Human Race," he even writes as if education contains man's only hope for progress, since nothing can be expected from the governments of nations but nationalistic rivalry and war, but in other works he presents a philosophy of history in which nature itself, including history, is interpreted as working for "a senate of the nations," or international republic, and for the fullest perfection, or highest good, of mankind.[48] The goal of nature, he suggests, is the realization of humanity in an international society, and rivalry and war are not so much obstacles in the way as instruments of progress. The natural egoism and rivalry of men and nations spurs them on to develop skills, prudence, etc.; but in this development of their knowledge and insight, they come to see the necessity of a union supported by their gregariousness and moral sense, which are also natural. Thus men form societies and states, but the same dialectic can be expected to bring them finally to give up even their nationalisms and to come together in a world government and "perpetual peace." The entire course is necessary for the fullest development of man's faculties, but the happy outcome is certain to take place. In fact, Kant sometimes seems to regard it as so inevitable that education and direct effort on our part is unnecessary, except perhaps to speed up the process. On the whole, however, his view is that education can and must play a part in the process all along—that of developing the skills and the prudence that form a factor in the dialectic, and also that of developing the moral dispositions which will lead people to form republics and enable them to live in perpetual peace, promoting their own perfection and the happiness of others. Its eye, however, must always be, not on success in the strife of individuals and nations, but on the ultimate goal—"the kingdom of God on earth."

As I understand Kant, then, education has or should have an end, and this is the making of man or the achievement of humanity— the attainment by the individual and the race of the *summum bonum*, which is moral perfection plus the natural perfection and the happiness compatible with it. His argument to show this is moral and rests on "the supreme principle of morality," as stated earlier, but the end is not simply moral goodness. Kant often talks as if it is simply virtue or morality, however, partly because this is the primary element in the *summum bonum* and conditions the value of the other elements, and partly because it alone is wholly within our power— it depends entirely on our free will, while the other elements in the highest good depend at least to some extent on fortune, as Aristotle said. The highest good does, however, include these other elements, though within the limits of morality, and morality requires one to seek and to promote them—with two qualifications: one has no duty to seek one's own happiness, except indirectly, and one has no duty (or right?) to promote the perfection of others (especially moral perfection) except while they are young.

It follows from what has been said, however, not only that education has the *end* just defined, but also that there are certain *moral principles* which educators, parents, and teachers must always keep in mind in deciding about teaching methods, school policies, etc. They must themselves in their treatment of children and of each other choose the maxims of their actions in accordance with the supreme principle of morality and obey all of the duties, listed above, that may be derived from it, among them those of love and respect.

THE METHODS AND PRACTICES OF EDUCATION

FIVE METHODS

The third main question is the most practical one: how should education proceed in developing the dispositions described in answer to the first question (thus achieving the aims stated in answer to the second)? Here Kant is often surprisingly concrete, as will become apparent. In the first chapter I defined education as the use of certain methods to foster certain desirable dispositions or excellences. Aristotle distinguishes two such methods: practice or habituation and instruction or teaching. Kant begins by listing three.

> By education we understand nurture (maintenance), discipline (training), and instruction. . . .[49]

Sometimes he talks as if culture is another method, but I take it to be the cultivation of skill by means of instruction, etc. Kant does, however, mention certain other methods: punishment, which presumably comes under discipline; exercise, which is Aristotle's practice; the use of examples; argument and discussion; and catechism. Probably he means the last three to be included under instruction (which he also calls teaching). But he also mentions a method that is now popular, "guidance," saying that it is the tutor's job, while instruction is that of the schoolteacher.

> *Guidance* means directing the pupil in putting into practice what he has been taught [by the teacher]. . . . The [teacher] trains for school only, the [tutor] for life.[50]

I have above taken this to mean that guidance is involved in inculcating prudence. Instruction I take to be the imparting of information, doctrine, and rules by the use of words or examples.

THE TWO KINDS OF EDUCATION AGAIN

The main methods distinguished by Kant seem then to be five: nurture, discipline, exercise, instruction, and guidance. Now Kant, as we saw, distinguishes two main kinds of education: physical or natural education and moral or practical education. Talking about their methods he says (1) that physical education

> depends on exercise and discipline, without the child needing to learn any maxims. It is passive for the pupil, he must follow the direction of others. Others think for him.

(2) that moral education (positive)

> depends not on discipline, but on maxims. All would be lost if it were based on example, threats, punishment, etc. . . .

> Physical education is distinguished from moral by the fact that in the former the child is passive, in the latter active.[51]

Kant does not elaborate, but he seems to stress discipline and exercise (and nurture) in connection with physical education and instruction in connection with practical education. His saying that the child is passive in the former and active in the latter is interesting in view of Dewey's insistence that the child must be active in all of his education. Kant is certainly closer to the traditional view in what he says about physical or natural education, but even here he says that exercise is to be used; and if we include the cultivation of bodily and intellectual skills under physical education, as I have argued we should, then, as we shall see, it involves a good deal of a kind of activity of body and mind on the part of the child. In general, when Kant says that the child is passive in such education, he does not mean that the child is not doing anything—and even in traditional education he was always doing something, if only listening—he means that the child is not thinking for himself in the sense of making decisions about what is going on in his life, or of understanding the point of it, as he must in positive moral education. Dewey is more insistent on bringing in this element of decision and understanding into all education—though he felt that some of his followers were overdoing it—but Kant does not regard it as essential except in moral education. On this point, presumably, he would join forces with some of Dewey's critics.

It may be surprising to some readers to find Kant even so qualifiedly defending education in which the child is passive. For his "Copernican revolution in philosophy," as he called it, consisted precisely in the thesis that the mind is active in knowing and not passive even in the sense in which Aristotle thought it was. For Kant the mind actively shapes the sensory materials, which form the basis of its knowledge, through the use of the "forms" of space and time and the "categories" of causality and substance. Through this shaping, it makes up the world as we know it; that is why what we know must be only phenomena and cannot be things in themselves. Now this thesis has sometimes suggested to educators that Kant's philosophy entails a greater emphasis on activity in education, especially in the education of the intellect, but Kant draws no such conclusion, as I have already intimated, and I see no reason why he should. That the mind is active in this way is not an empirical but an epistemological thesis (in Kant's terms, a transcendental thesis), and it is nothing that education can do anything about. The forms and categories involved are, according to Kant, innate in the mind, not learned, and the mind uses them automatically in shaping its objects; it does not have to be taught how to do this. Even the intermediate "schemata" it employs in applying the categories are a priori. We do, of course, have to learn by experience and teaching what substances there are, what causes what, and so on; but we do not need to be educated to think in terms of the concepts of causality or substance. We cannot help doing so. Thus, as far as I can see, Kant's critical philosophy is entirely compatible with all that Aristotle said about education, or at least about intellectual education. Kant and Aristotle do differ on education, as we are seeing, but this is not because Aristotle believes in a passive or spectator theory of knowing and Kant does not. It is true that Kant's philosophy is part of the ancestry of Dewey's criticism of the spectator theory of knowledge and, thus, of passivity in education, but the connection is historical rather than logical. It is also true that there is in Kant's philosophy of education an emphasis on the child's activity, will, freedom, and autonomy that is not prominent in Aristotle or in educational thinking before Locke and Rousseau, but this emphasis is connected with Kant's ethical theory rather than with his epistemology, and appears mainly in what he says about practical or moral education.

GENERAL REMARKS

What Kant has to say about the practices of education consists, as it should, of recommendations or normative statements about what to do and what not to do that are in general based, on the one hand, on his answers to our first two questions (and ultimately on the basic principles of his ethics), and, on the other, on his empirical beliefs about human psychology and the effects of various practices. We shall not have space to show this in detail, but the logic involved was explained and illustrated in the first chapter, and, anyway, it will usually be obvious how the recommendations in question are related to what has been said. In a rough, general way it will also become clear that Kant stands between the two movements now often stereotyped as the "old" or "traditional" and the "new" or "progressive" educations; he puts more stress on self-help, doing, initiative, and freedom than the former, and more stress on compulsion, discipline, obedience, and work than the latter.

We must notice first that, while Kant is interested that education effectively foster the dispositions listed, he insists that all of what is done in order to foster them must itself be in accordance with the moral principles enunciated earlier. This is nicely illustrated by his saying that while children are not to be spoiled, their wishes are not to be thwarted purposely, because this is "an utterly wrong way of bringing them up"—wrong, not because it is ineffective, but because it transgresses the moral law even though it may be calculated to advance morality by producing character or obedience.

We must also observe that, for all his moralism, Kant is not entirely against nature, especially in what he says about physical but even in what he says about moral education. In fact, he repeatedly states that much of education is negative: "its aim should be simply the restraint of whatever is unnatural."

> . . . early education is only negative—that is, we have not to add anything to the provision of Nature, but merely to see that such provision is duly carried out. . . . all we have to do is not spoil the child's nature. . . .[52]

This way of speaking is due to Rousseau's influence, but it is also connected with Kant's general philosophy, in which nature is thought of as a purposive system with "humanity" as a goal. Left to itself, however, Kant thinks nature will not take us beyond animality. Discipline is needed to keep nature on its true course until humanity can begin to be achieved by other methods of education. Until then "artificial" means are to be avoided, because, in the end, the desired dispositions will be more adequately achieved, if only bad habits and "unnatural" dispositions are prevented from forming before their cultivation can be successfully begun. Even in religious education, "the way chosen must always be in accordance with Nature."

Kant is not advocating a hands-off "education according to nature" such as Rousseau sometimes seems to propose. Discipline is needed to restrain man's natural unruliness and to control his inclinations, and civilization and culture are essential to his becoming human, even if they also complicate matters. Without them he would remain both wild and raw. Yet there is a degree to which Kant is willing to take nature as a norm or at least to let it take its course in education, though only because and insofar as its course is conducive to the ends determined by the moral argument explained earlier. The true criterion of education is morality, not nature. On this point, as far as I can see, Kant's position is close to Aristotle's, and perhaps also to Dewey's, except that he does not derive his morality from nature in either of the ways they do, and is more insistent on the need of compulsion in education than Dewey is.

I shall now try to summarize Kant's views about the practices to be used by parents and educators, relating them as systematically as possible to the five headings used earlier in classifying the dispositions to be cultivated: nurture, discipline, skill (culture), prudence, and morality. In each case I shall try to indicate the methods of education Kant regards as appropriate, the period in a child's life at which it is to go on, the curriculum it involves, and the other chief points Kant tries to make.

Nurture belongs under physical education, and Kant associates it with infancy, though what he says about it extends beyond infancy. He also regards nurture as mainly negative, a point on which I have already commented. It involves for Kant especially such activities, mainly parental, as nursing, feeding, caring for, and the like. Here the proximate aim is health and the prevention of bad habits in preparation for the later stages of education. In view of this Kant argues for the use of mother's milk, cold baths, cool and hard beds, and warns against the use of spices, stimulants, too warm food or clothing, the swathing of limbs, rocking cradles, artificial devices for learning to walk, over-protectiveness, indulgence, and excessive hardening processes such as the Russians used. Babies should be given freedom of movement and allowed to learn things for them-selves. If they cry, the reason should be sought; if it is with good reason, they should be cared for, but, if not, they should be left alone. They should not be given anything just because they cry for it, but, if they need it or ask properly, "it should be given them, provided it is for their good." They should not be constantly played with or caressed. Requests should be granted unless there is a good reason to the contrary. If there is a good reason to the contrary, it should not be granted. In any case, refusal should be final. A child should not learn love of ease, timidity, ill-temper, effeminacy, choosyness, etc., or get into unnecessary routines of body or mind.

Discipline also belongs to physical education, and so in it too the child is passive. Its aim, according to Kant, is also negative: the restraint of inclination and unruliness in preparation for the culti-vation of skill and the achievement of prudence and morality. Disci-pline must precede instruction. Kant links it with childhood, rather than infancy, but says it must begin early, for neglect of discipline cannot be remedied later. It involves the use of commands and rules in order to teach submission and obedience.

> In the first period of childhood the child must learn submission and [passive] obedience. . . . Above all things, obedience is an essential feature in the character of a child. . . .[53]

Preferably the obedience should be voluntary and "arise out of con-fidence," but compulsion is, in fact, necessary as an instrument of discipline. "Discipline implies compulsion." Preferably restraint should be moral as much as possible, but at first it must be mechanical. In any case, disobedience should be punished. Punishment is either moral or physical—the former when it involves withholding honor, love, or praise, or looking with contempt.

> . . . This kind of punishment is best, since it is an aid to moral training. . . . Physical punishment consists either in refusing a child's requests or in the infliction of pain. The first is akin to moral punishment. . . . The second form must be used with caution lest an *indoles servilis* [slavish disposition] should be the result. It is of no use to give children rewards; it makes them selfish and [mercenary].[54]

A look of contempt or withdrawal of respect is the only fit punishment for lying. The best kind of physical punishment is natural—the consequences the child suffers naturally from what he does, e.g. illness from overeating. Other physical punishment should be a mere supplement to the insufficiency of moral punishment. No punishment should be inflicted with signs of anger, and we should never bear children a grudge, or show preference for one child over another.

> . . . and as a general rule punishment must be inflicted on children with great caution, that they may understand that its one aim is their improvement.[55]

However, discipline must not be such as to produce slavishness. It is true that, at first, the child must obey blindly, but his will must not be broken, only bent so as to yield to natural obstacles and to respect the freedom of others. If he is stubborn the best way of dealing with him is to refuse to do anything to please him. The end is not slavishness but freedom and self-mastery, with respect for others.

CULTURE

Culture or education in *skill* Kant describes as positive. Sometimes he places it under practical education, and it does involve the learning of maxims or imperatives, namely *technical* ones about what to do or not to do to bring about a certain end, but I have argued that his real view is that it is still part of physical education because it merely cultivates nature and does not give laws to freedom. This means that, however much he works in learning skills, the child is nevertheless passive in Kant's sense in doing so. In general, culture comes after and presupposes nurture and discipline, but, of course, both must still be going on during the acquisition of skill. Though discipline comes in, the main methods of culture are exercise and instruction, the latter including not only the direct statement of information, generalizations, rules, etc., but the use of examples, discussion, and catechism. The aim is not simply to acquire skills as means to the achievement of further ends such as happiness or moral perfection; it is also partly to make the child *naturally* perfect; in other words, skill in the use of one's faculties is an end in itself, though only a conditional end in the sense explained earlier.

"What has to be done is to see that natural ability is cultivated." This means especially that children should be given opportunity for exercising their faculties, as well as instruction. Here again Kant insists that the first rule is to dispense with artificial aids as far as possible, but he advocates the early use of games which both develop bodily skill and confidence and exercise the senses and spatial imagination, especially if they also teach desirable dispositions of the kinds mentioned before. Thus it is important that games should not be mere games but have some end or object.

Preschool culture or cultivation of the mind should be largely of this "free" kind, involving play and games, but education cannot be all play, Kant contends; the suggestion of some educators that everything should be learned as if it were in play he labels "utterly preposterous." School education should consist of work, not play; it should be serious and involve restraint and compulsion.

> A child must play, . . . but he must also learn to work. . . . and where can the inclination to work be cultivated so well as at school? School is a place of compulsory culture.[56]

In work the activity is not pleasant in itself, and is undertaken for the sake of some end other than itself. Aristotle and Dewey both try to minimize the place of work in this sense in education (and life), the former by freeing citizens of the need to work, the latter by trying to dispose things in such a way that what needs to be done is at the same time worthwhile in itself. Kant, however, is convinced that work in his sense must be learned by everyone and so must be a part of education—both education for skill and education for morality. In fact, he seems to think that the most essential skills and traits of character cannot be learned without work on the child's part, and therefore not without compulsion of some kind—a point on which Aristotle would perhaps agree, but one which Dewey tries to circumvent, not by making things easy, but by seeking to connect everything with the operative interests of the child. On this last move Kant comments briefly:

> One often hears it said that we should put everything before children in such a way that they do it from *inclination*. In some

cases, . . . this is all very well, but there is much besides which we must place before them as *duty*.[57]

For throughout life one must do things which one is not inclined to do, e.g. paying taxes or performing the tasks connected with one's office or station. School then must be a place of work, both because of the requirements of life in general and because work is necessary for adequate learning.

In connection with the cultivation of the cognitive faculties, therefore, Kant finds place not only for exercise or practice, but for a certain amount of drill, memorization, and mechanical learning. He also lays down some general principles. The inferior cognitive faculties of memory and imagination should not be cultivated for their own sakes, but, as Aristotle thought, only with a view to and in connection with the cultivation of understanding, reason, and judgment. Learning and memory without judgment is of no value. Distraction is the enemy of all education and should not be permitted, least of all in school. Children must learn the difference between knowledge and mere belief or opinion. In teaching them, knowledge must always be related to application and practice, as well as to its expression in speech and writing.

Kant regards certain subjects as having educational values for the cognitive faculties. History is an excellent means of exercising the understanding in judgment, languages an excellent means of cultivating memory (though they are better learned by conversation than by memorization), mathematics is best for uniting knowledge with its application in practice. Geography and history provide information to serve as a basis of responsible thought. He also says some things about the best ways of teaching various subjects. Geography is best learned mechanically, with the help of maps. The best way of teaching history has yet to be discovered, but the mechanical method of catechizing (question and answer) has much to commend it. What is learned mechanically is best remembered. Novel reading weakens the memory. A well-constructed *orbis pictus* is useful in teaching natural history, if aided by drawing and modeling. Some of this would repel Dewey, but Kant writes in the spirit of Dewey in saying:

> The first lessons in science will most advantageously be directed to the study of geography, mathematical as well as physical. Tales of travel, illustrated by pictures and maps, will lead on to political geography. From the present condition of the earth's surface we go back to its earlier condition, and this leads us to ancient geography, ancient history, and so on.[58]

Kant does not think children should be always encouraged to argue, reason, and ask why. Their minds need development and guidance, and must not be allowed to get ahead of themselves, lest they become over-inquisitive, critical, and lack solidity. Still, children must learn to think for themselves; again Kant sounds much like Dewey.

> The best way of cultivating the mental faculties is to *do our-selves* all that we wish to accomplish; for instance, by carrying out into practice the grammatical rule which we have learnt. We understand a map best when we are able to draw it for ourselves. The best way to understand is to do. That which we learn most thoroughly and remember the best, is what we have in a way taught ourselves.[59]

Something about judgment and aesthetic education was recounted earlier. As for the cultivation of reason, Kant says,

> . . . we must proceed according to the Socratic method. . . . [Children] must not be allowed to argue about everything. . . . But on the whole we should try to draw out their own ideas, founded on reason, rather than to introduce such ideas into their minds. The Socratic method should form, then, the rule for the catechetical method.[60]

But the method is slow and hard to use with profit in classes of any size, and, in any event, there are fields in which the mechanical method of informing and catechizing is useful, e.g. revealed religion and history. One can see here that Kant would partly agree and partly disagree with Dewey. For Kant there must be compulsion and mechanical learning, but there must also be a kind of activity and thinking for oneself, and a connection with practice. There is even a suggestion of learning by doing. So far, Kant is not regarding the child as wholly passive in this part of physical education, but his recognition of the role of activity is not due to his theory of knowledge or of mind; it is due simply to his belief that experience shows that we achieve skills, even those of the intellect—and knowledge—most effectively through some kind of activity.

PRUDENCE

Education in prudence Kant does not say much about beyond what was expounded earlier. In general it presupposes the acquisition of skill and so comes later. It is, of course, positive, and in my interpretation comes under physical education, though Kant sometimes puts it under practical education. Sometimes, as was indicated, he describes it as the province of a tutor rather than a school teacher, and as using the method of guidance rather than instruction. Yet it must include at least some instruction about the facts of life—about what will lead to happiness and what will not, for as far as content is concerned, it will consist in learning pragmatic imperatives or counsels of prudence—maxims about what to do or not to do in view of one's own long-run happiness. For Kant, as we saw, this includes learning such things as manners, sociability, and citizenship —it may also include some vocational guidance, but Kant does not say so. It must also involve or presuppose some discipline of our inclinations and passions and learning to control and postpone desires in the interest of more long-run satisfaction. For education in prudence has a twofold problem: to teach and learn the relevant knowledge and imperatives and to foster and acquire the disposition to act on them (insofar as this is compatible with the cultivation of natural and moral perfection); however, since Kant believes that we all do naturally take our own happiness as an end, it seems clear that he must regard the first of these problems as the main one. He does not mention any particular parts of the school curriculum as being concerned with or useful in prudential education. In fact, he seems to think that such education must remain the province, not of the schools but of private or home education—except for training in sociability and citizenship. This training is part of education in prudence but it is best provided by the schools, for they provide, or should provide, a life with others that will prepare the child to live happily and acceptably in society later. Here Kant makes a point later generalized by Dewey.

MORALIZATION

As one would expect, Kant gives most of his attention to moral education, of which the goal is to bring it about "that actions be done not merely according to duty . . . but from duty." He thought that it was too much neglected in the education of his day. In its full positive form moral education comes last in time, except perhaps for prudential education, but in some form it must come in from the very beginning. Indeed, a large part of discipline is simply *negative* moral education; it involves the use of compulsion and punishment, especially those of a moral kind, in order to prevent the formation of bad moral dispositions and to teach obedience and submission. This kind or phase of moral education, then, has already been dealt with. *Positive* moral education is what Kant usually calls moral or practical education, as distinct from physical. It depends, he says, not upon discipline or habit, but on "maxims." In it the child is active in the sense of thinking and willing in terms of maxims; he is learning to act according to maxims or rules the reasonableness of which he can see for himself—and ultimately to formulate and act on maxims that he can will to be universal laws.

The first phase of this positive moral education is the formation of character in the sense explained before. This is done "by practice in a firm intention in the espousal of certain maxims after reflection," that is, by practice in formulating and firmly adopting rules for one's action on the basis of reflection; Parents and teachers should help to provide such practice.

> For instance, if a man makes a promise, he must keep it . . . for a man who makes a resolution and fails to keep it will have no more confidence in himself.[61]

The second phase is the formation of good character, the acquisition of morally good dispositions. The task of this part of moral education, as we saw, is twofold: teaching and learning what our duties are, and fostering in us the dispositions to do our duties from a sense of duty. The two tasks are related, of course, but they must not be confused, and Kant has something to say about each. We know what he thinks our duties are and why; the question now is (a) how he thinks children should be taught what these duties are and (b) how they may be given the good will to perform them. Kant calls the answer to (a) "ethical didactic," the answer to (b) "ethical ascetic" and places them both under "ethical methodology," i.e. moral pedagogy.

DIDACTIC

In this aspect of moral education Kant seems to advocate something more or less like what is now sometimes called "the direct method" of teaching moral principles, which Dewey opposes. Kant calls it the "erotematic" or "doctrinal" method, and says it may take either the form of *lecturing* [the "dogmatic" method]—"as when all those to whom it is directed are a mere audience," or that of *questioning*—"in which the teacher asks his pupil what he wants to teach him."

> And this method of questioning is, in turn, divided into that of *dialogue* and that of *catechism*, depending on whether the teacher addresses his questions to the pupil's *reason* or merely to his *memory*.[62]

The method of dialogue Kant also calls the Socratic method. In line with his general emphasis on the pupil's activity, freedom, and thinking for himself in positive moral education, Kant seems to prefer the questioning to the lecturing method, and dialogue to catechism. He explains and illustrates most fully the catechetical method of moral teaching, which he regards as "for the still untrained pupil the first and most essential doctrinal instrument of the theory of virtue." In it the teacher imparts moral doctrine by asking questions, letting the student answer if he can (but not letting him ask questions, since he will not know what questions to ask at this stage), underlining the answer if it is correct, and otherwise giving the correct answer himself for the pupil to memorize, adding reasons as soon as the pupil can appreciate them.

Such a catechism may be used at various levels, but Kant thinks it is most helpful if it includes some *casuistic* questions in connection with each rule or principle being taught, that is, if problem cases are presented for the children to try to solve.

> For instance, a man has a certain debt to pay to-day, but he sees another man in sore need, and, moved with pity, gives him the money which belongs of right to his creditor. Is this right or wrong?[63]

Such cases, Kant stresses, have the advantage of cultivating the pupil's reason at the same time that they provide moral instruction. He also calls attention to the fact that children are easily *interested* in discussing such cases seriously.

Kant warns, however, for reasons we shall come to, that any such moral catechism must precede and not be interwoven with or represented as following upon a religious one. He is particularly concerned to maintain the purity of moral reasoning and action. In moral didactic, therefore, the reasons given to justify a rule or regarded as acceptable by the teacher cannot consist of an appeal to what people actually do, nor to the good or bad consequences for the individual or society of acting in a certain way, nor even to the will of God. Duty stands on its own feet—whether something is a duty depends finally on whether one can consistently will it to be a universal law and on nothing else. The final object of didactic is to bring the young to see this and to be able to think out for themselves what maxims they can adopt and will for universal adoption. This takes practice and discussion.

It follows, since the basic imperative of morality is "inherent in the structure of every man's reason," that ethical didactic should not represent moral principles as resting in any way either on feeling and sentiment or on experience. So Kant sometimes attacks the use of examples—that is, the use of exemplary figures or actions—in the didactic part of moral education, on the ground that it makes it appear as if ethical principles rest on or can be proved by such cases. Actually one can only select such cases if one already knows the principles.

> Nor could anything be more fatal to morality than that we should wish to derive it from examples. For every example of it . . . must first itself be tested by principles of morality, whether it is worthy to serve . . . as a pattern. . . . Even the Holy One of the Gospels must first be compared with our ideal of moral perfection before we can recognize Him as such. . . . Imitation finds no place at all in morality, and examples serve only for encouragement, that is, they establish the possibility of [doing] what the law commands, they make visible what the practical rule expresses. . . .[64]

In other words, examples cannot serve as the basis or source of our knowledge of moral principles; they have a role in moral education, but in its ascetic, not its didactic, phase.

ASCETIC

In ethical ascetic the general aim is to foster good-will in the sense of "a frame of mind that is brave and cheerful in the observance of duty," as taught in ethical didactic, for its own sake. Fortitude and renunciation are involved, but so is a habitually cheerful heart. Hence moral ascetic, as Kant calls it, does not mean fear, penance, self-torture, or crucifixion of the flesh; these, he says, can only bring with them secret hatred of duty and virtue. At most it consists "in combatting the impulses of nature to the extent that we are able to master them when a situation comes up in which they threaten morality."[65]

On the other hand, the attempt of a parent or teacher to foster virtue in a child must not use an appeal to sanctions in terms of prudence, happiness, or a life hereafter, nor to feelings of affection or sympathy. Moral sanctions like withdrawing respect, etc., alone are appropriate, but only as long as they are needed—as part of negative moral education—and they are appropriate only because behind them is the thought that duty is to be done for its own sake. Everything must be done to keep the child from forming the notion that anything but respect for duty is of moral value or an incentive proper to morality. Other inclinations are not all bad, but they are not parts of a morally good will. Here again Kant stresses the need of keeping morality pure, shining by its own light. He thinks, in fact, that if the child can be brought to see any duty in this light, his innate moral feeling or respect for the moral law will break through and become an incentive for him to act accordingly.

Thus he thinks that such casuistic discussions as were described under didactic not only help children see their duties, but also get them interested in morality, since it is natural for man to love a subject in which he finds he can exercise himself proficiently.

> I do not know why the educators of youth have not long since made use of this propensity of reason [even in children] to enter with pleasure upon the most subtle examination of practical questions put to them. . . .[66]

Here Kant brings in the use of examples and emulation again. The teacher must, of course, be an example of virtue himself, but also, "after laying the foundation in a purely moral catechism," he should search biography and history (not novels) for examples of dutiful action of all kinds,

> . . . so that, by comparing similar actions under various circumstances, [he can] begin to exercise the moral judgment of [his] pupils in marking the greater or less moral significance of the actions.[67]

The imitation of examples is no part of mature morality, for Kant, but, as he puts it,

> . . . to the as yet unformed human being, imitation is what first determines him to embrace the maxims that he afterwards makes his own.[68]

Bad examples may also be used at this stage as *warnings*, but examples should not be presented as establishing any maxims.

> For a maxim of virtue consists precisely in the subjective autonomy of each man's practical reason, and so implies that the law itself, not the conduct of other men, serves as one's motive. Thus the teacher will not tell his pupil, "Take an example from that good (orderly, diligent) boy!" For this would only cause the pupil to hate that boy. . . . Good example . . . should not serve as a model but only as a proof that it is really possible to act in accordance with duty.[69]

Example should show what it is like to act virtuously and that it is possible, but care must be taken in their use so that what begins as imitation ends up as pure respect for moral duty.

Kant is also concerned to remind us here of the point made earlier—that the discussion of examples and casuistic cases interests children, so that frequent practice in it may be expected to leave a lasting esteem for good and contempt for bad conduct.

Besides warning teachers and parents against using other children as examples to be followed, Kant also warns them against using "examples of so-called noble (super-meritorious) actions, which so fill our sentimental writings." It is proper to extol actions "which display a great, unselfish, and sympathetic disposition and humanity" but only as examples of devotion to duty; to go further is merely to encourage a romantic longing for unattainable perfection.[70]

In outline then, Kant concludes, the method of ethical ascetic is as follows: (a) to make judging according to moral principles a natural occupation in connection with our actions as well as in our observation of those of others, sharpening these judgments by asking, first, whether the action is in accordance with a moral principle and, if so, just what this principle is, and, second, whether the action is also done *for the sake* of duty. This exercise is necessary and it does produce a certain interest in morality, as we have seen, but it is not enough to establish a real commitment to it. Hence it is also necessary (b) to display purity of will and moral disposition through vivid examples of dutiful action which reveal to the child that he can act not from inclination but from respect for moral principle, and that only then does he feel free and respect himself. This perception, Kant thinks, if it really takes hold, will lead to a resolution to practice virtue.

RELIGION

It is interesting and significant that Kant does not list piety or religion, along with nurture, discipline, culture, prudence, and morality, as one of the jobs of education. He may actually have thought of religion as a part of culture, since he mentions it along with other subjects relating to the cultivation of the mind, though not to say that it should be taught, but only to advocate the catechetical method for teaching revealed, and the Socratic method for teaching natural, religion. However, he does discuss the teaching of religion in connection with moral or practical education. He insists, as we saw, that religious education is not a part of or necessary to moral education. He seems to think that religion should be taught (in the schools?), but holds that religious education should rest on moral education, not vice versa.

> Religion . . . is morality applied to the knowledge of God.
> . . . Morality . . . must come first and theology follow; and

that is religion. Religion without moral conscientiousness is a service of superstition [and an endeavor to win favor].[71]

Kant doubts that religious ideas can be imparted to children very early, since they presuppose (or ought to presuppose) some knowledge of duty and some ability to grasp theology. In fact, he suggests that ideally children should first be taught about ends and aims and what concerns mankind, instructed about nature and the universe, and have their judgment sharpened, and only after all this has been done should they learn about God. This, however, is impossible in actual society where children very early hear God mentioned. Hence, Kant thinks, "we must give children some idea of the Supreme Being." But, he adds, ". . . these ideas must be few in number, and . . . merely negative." The main point, at least with children, is to prevent misconceptions and irreverence—and to keep them from esteeming people according to their religion, since true "religion is everywhere the same." It is acting in accordance with God's will, and we tell what He wills by discovering through reason what is right, not the other way around.

What Kant says here requires a bit of amplification on the basis of what he says in other works. He believes that religious propositions cannot be proved or disproved by reason, and that any alleged revelation must be tested by reason, but he also holds that morality requires us to "postulate," not only the freedom of the will, but also the immortality of the soul and the existence of God, the former because it is necessary for us to attain perfection, the latter because it is necessary for the existence of the *summum bonum*. Both perfection and the *summum bonum* being commanded by the moral law, they must be possible, and so we must believe, though we have no proof, that there is a God and that we are immortal. But we may believe this only because we already know that we have certain duties which we must perform for their own sake. Hence morality does not, on Kant's view, depend on religion either logically or psychologically, either for justification or for motivation, i.e. neither ethical didactic nor ethical ascetic requires any appeal to religion. Morality does necessarily lead to religion, but

> . . . it stands in need neither of the idea of another Being over [man], for him to apprehend his duty, nor of an incentive other than the [moral] law itself, for him to do his duty. . . . Hence, for its own sake morality does not need religion at all . . . by virtue of pure practical reason it is self-sufficient.[72]

Religious belief, therefore, presupposes the validity and sufficiency of morality, not vice versa. Religion, for Kant, is morality conceived as the will of God. We must learn so to conceive morality, and hence religion should be taught—Kant even believes we should institute a kind of universal ethical church to match his cosmopolitan state—but its content is simply to do our duty to ourselves and our fellow-men out of a sense of duty, not out of fear or love of God if this is anything but a sense of duty. The notion of additional duties to God Kant regards as incomprehensible to the human mind.

MAN'S INNATE NATURE

Education presupposes that perfection, natural and moral, is not natural or innate in such a way that man will become perfect simply in the natural course of events, but it also presupposes that man is not by nature inevitably imperfect or bad. In this connection Kant says in his book on education: (a) that man is equipped with all the tendencies towards the good and that the rudiments of evil are not present in his natural dispositions, (b) that man is by nature neither morally good nor morally bad, (c) that he has a natural inclination to every vice.[73] These statements, which are all important for his educational philosophy, can be clarified somewhat in the light of his book, *Religion within the Limits of Reason Alone* (1793), but they are also complicated by what he says there.[74] There Kant mentions the pessimistic view that man is by nature bad, the optimistic view that man is by nature good—which he notes has gained a following "among philosophers and, of late, especially among those interested in education"—and two compromise views, namely, that man is by nature *both* good and bad, and that he is *neither* good nor bad. He reminds us that we must distinguish between man as a sensible, or phenomenal, and determined being appearing in space and time and man as an intelligible, or noumenal, and free being who is not in space or time. As phenomenon, man has by nature three original predispositions: (1) a predisposition to *animality* or non-rational self-love, including desires to preserve self, propogate the species, and live with others, (2) a predisposition to *humanity* (natural perfection) or rational self-love, including especially a desire for equality with and superiority over others, which is nature's spur to culture, (3) a predisposition to personality, good will, or moral perfection. These are all predispositions to good but vice or evil can be "grafted" on the first two, e.g. gluttony, lasciviousness, and wild lawlessness, though not on the third. Man is by nature good then in the sense that as a phenomenal being his nature contains only predispositions to good. This does not mean, however, (as vs. Rousseau) that as such a being he automatically shows up as virtuous if nothing prevents, as a lily automatically shows up as pure white if nothing interferes. As phenomenon man needs education to become good and an absence of it to become bad. In this sense he is by nature *neither* good nor bad and may in fact become *both* by acquiring one virtue (benevolence) and not another (honesty).

All of this is about man as phenomenon, as part of nature. Back of it is man as noumenon, member of the realm of freedom. As such, Kant maintains, man must be either all good or all bad—either take the moral law as his maxim or not. If so, he is virtuous; if not, he is vicious. Whichever he is, he cannot be so by nature if this means that he is not so by free choice, for a man can be virtuous or vicious only by free choice, not by natural necessity. Well, then, which is he? Things get a bit sticky at this point, but Kant seems to think, "in view of the multitude of crying examples which experience of the actions of man puts before our eyes," that man, every man, has an "innate propensity to evil" (again, vs. Rousseau). Man has by an act of choice which we cannot fathom chosen, not virtue, but an evil character of some kind, and this character, though freely chosen, can be called "innate" in the sense that it is true of all men and prior to all experience in time. Nevertheless, we need not believe that it is irrevocable. As we saw, we have a duty to be virtuous—but "ought" implies "can"; if we ought to be virtuous, it must be possible for us to be. Hence, Kant concludes, we must be able, again by an act of free choice, to choose to be good, even if we cannot understand how this is possible. If in experience one shows up as good after a process of education, presumably he has made this choice.

A DIFFICULTY

What was just said does amplify the three statements made by Kant in his book on education, and it makes them compatible, but it raises a serious problem for his philosophy of education, for it means that one is virtuous or vicious, good or bad, by an inexplicable free and timeless choice made by his noumenal or real self—but, if this is so, what is the role of moral or practical education? It would seem that such education can go on only in space and time and can concern only man as he appears. How then can it affect a choice one makes as noumenon? If education cannot in any way affect this choice, what is the point of engaging in it? What Kant says makes it look as if he thinks that the whole temporal process which we call moral development, struggle, etc., is merely the appearance in space and time of a non-temporal act of choice made by one's real self. This seems to imply that moral education is not just phenomenal, but epiphenomenal, a kind of lantern-show reflecting what is really going on behind the scenes. We may have to engage in it, but the issue is decided elsewhere.

Kant does not face this difficulty very squarely, though he often skirts it. He seems not to want to say that moral education is simply an epiphenomenal show. Perhaps his view is that, while one is really good or bad by a timeless and free decision of his noumenal self, it takes education or miseducation to enable this choice to appear in the phenomenal world. We cannot understand how or why this should be, but, since we have a duty to educate and be educated, we must go on doing so, postulating that it all makes sense, that some kind of noumenal drama is going on to which our phenomenal endeavor corresponds and is somehow essential.

Two comments are necessary. One is that this difficulty involves only moral or practical education. Physical education, for Kant, is concerned with nature, not freedom. Natural perfection is a result of discipline and cultivation and is not a matter of choice in the same way that moral perfection is. This is what Kant finally turns out to mean by calling the kind of education involved natural or physical, and by saying that in it the child is passive, not active.

The other comment is that the difficulty in question is not peculiar to Kant's philosophy, with its distinction between the two worlds of phenomena and noumena, nature and freedom. It is present in some form in any philosophy which holds that virtue and vice are voluntary in the sense of being chosen in an act of what C. A. Campbell calls "contra-causal freedom." That is, it is present in some form for any one who rejects determinism and espouses either indeterminism or self-determinism as a theory of human action, for, on any such view, moral dispositions in their true form cannot be produced by education of any sort. They entail the making of an uncaused and free choice of character, and so cannot in the final analysis be acquired by practice or teaching. Even if one says that choices can be *influenced* though not *caused* by education, it will still be true that a step is required that is simply free. Kant's position is only the most extreme—and, he would add, logical—of a whole family of views that face the same problem. In particular, it reminds one of existentialism, which also insists that one chooses one's character by a free act of undetermined and inexplicable, even "arbitrary," choice or decision, a view which, if pushed far enough, makes any kind of moral education fruitless or impossible. Some existentialists even go so far as to say that one chooses one's own natural predispositions—as well as what one does with them—but then they are going beyond anything that Kant ever dreamed of saying.

It may be that Aristotle also faces the same general problem. He does say that virtue and vice are voluntary and chosen. On the other hand, what he says in explanation of voluntariness, weakness of will, etc., is entirely compatible with the kind of determinism which says that while all of our choices and voluntary actions are caused, they are caused by our own beliefs and desires, and not by something external. In any case, he does not emphasize the role of choice in the acquisition of moral virtue as Kant does.

In emphasizing choice as he does, Kant is stressing an alternative which Socrates and Plato did not recognize in the *Meno*, where they ask whether virtue is possessed by nature or acquired by teaching, practice, or gift of the gods. Intellectual excellence he agrees is acquired by practice and teaching. *Moral* virtue, however, though not acquired simply by nature, is not acquired simply by practice or teaching either, since a free and autonomous choice is involved. For the same reason, it cannot be a gift of God. Not even God can make a man virtuous; only a man himself can do so.

> . . . otherwise he could not be held responsible for [his virtue] and could therefore be *morally* neither good nor evil. . . . some supernatural cooperation may be necessary . . . [but] man must first make himself worthy to receive it, and must *lay hold* of this aid (which is no small matter) . . . for only then can goodness be imputed to him. . . .[75]

Virtue, to be virtue, must be chosen by an act of contra-causal freedom, and, in Kant's opinion, any theory of education must keep this point central. His own theory is outstanding because it does so. With all its problems it is the result of a resolute insistence on the autonomy and freedom of the moral agent and of the perfected man.

Roughly speaking, Kant thinks that nurture, discipline, and culture come in that order in the education of children, followed by prudence and morality, but he recognizes that all of them must go on in some form from the beginning. What he insists on, just as Dewey does, is that in all of these areas education must be geared to the age of the child. The child must be disciplined, skilled, prudent, polite, and even moral, after the manner of children, not after the manner of grown-ups. "Children should only be taught those things that are suited to their age."[76] This is one of the respects in which Kant thinks that education should follow nature. In a general way, he distinguishes three main stages of education: education for childhood, education for youth, and education for manhood. The second begins at about the age of ten, when childhood ends and the child begins to reflect; and the third should end at about sixteen

> . . . when nature has ordained that [the youth] shall be capable of guiding his own conduct; and when . . . he can become a father himself, and have to educate his own children.[77]

That is, education is to go on only until the youth has learned "how to live as a free being" and then stop. Kant is thinking here of ordinary education, of course; some few would still go to the university afterwards, to study philosophy, anthropology, etc., and possibly to prepare to teach, but for the large majority,

> After this we may still make use of some means of culture, and secretly exercise some discipline; but of education in the ordinary sense of the word we shall have no further need.[78]

Is this a charter for adult education?

PRIVATE OR PUBLIC?

Kant does not say much on this question in our sense of the terms. He does talk about "private" versus "public" education, but by the former he usually means "home" education by parent or tutor, and by the latter "school" education, whether public or private in our sense. If we take the question in our sense, his discussion is unclear, but seems to run as follows. As we have seen, he holds that the end of education is an internationalistic and futuristic one, and this, for him, seems to rule out state control and even state support; but Kant also takes a dim view of parental aims in education. He concludes therefore that the management of the schools should be in the hands of the most enlightened people, people of broad views who take an interest in the universal good and the ultimate perfection of mankind. So far his view is the opposite of Aristotle's. He seems to allow, however, that, if properly educated, rulers may themselves come to take such larger views, and that education may then be made public in one sense. Until then, he seems to think, it must rely on private support.

Taking the question in his sense, what is Kant's position on home versus school education? He believes there should be schools. School education has definite advantages over home education in training children for life in society, and even in the development of certain skills. In fact, in a passage criticizing Rousseau, Kant seems to disparage tutoring altogether as "artificial," except perhaps as a way of producing the first schoolteachers. In his lectures on education, however, he seems to keep room for home education, parental and tutorial. In fact, he says that the aim of school education is to improve home education, presumably by educating parents and tutors. Putting all of what he says together, I take his position to be that education for skill and for life in society should go on mainly in school, while nurture and prudential education should go on mainly in the home, moral education going on in both; and that, until a sufficient school system can be set up, the few schools there are can only try to improve the prevailing (in Kant's day) home education.

DISTRIBUTION

Who should be educated? Clearly every human being should be given the general sort of education described above up to some point. In his book Kant pretty definitely has only boys in view, but elsewhere he says that both sexes should be educated, suggesting that Rousseau may be right in thinking that the proper education of women would have a salutary effect on men and morals, but even there he appears to think that the proper education of women will belong to the home rather than the school and consist of guidance (including especially the formation of feeling and taste) rather than instruction. "She must know men rather than books. Honor is her greatest virtue, domesticity her merit."[79] This is more than Aristotle said, but not much more.

UNIFORMITY

Should all boys have the *same* education? In general, yes. But Kant recognizes differences in capacities and talents, and probably does not believe that everyone should cultivate all the same skills or bodies of knowledge. On the other hand, he implies in one passage that education should bring about uniformity in the sense of leading all men to act on the same principles, and in another that every boy should learn something basic in every branch of knowledge, since he cannot know which of them he will need later—both very familiar sentiments.

•

CHAPTER FOUR

Dewey's Philosophy

of

Education

•

PRELIMINARIES

APPROACHING DEWEY

As Kant's world was not that of Aristotle, so Dewey's world was not that of Kant, though less than a century separated them. Romanticism and anti-rationalism had arisen and become strong, and a whole family of idealistic philosophies had grown up, stemming from Kant and from romanticism. Science had made great strides and entered new fields, and, in particular, the theory of evolution had gained wide acceptance. The industrial and the domestic revolutions had also made great progress, effecting profound changes in society and government. The hold of Christianity on the educated mind, on the other hand, had considerably weakened. And, of course, with a tremendous effort in pioneering, America had arisen from colonial status to that of a great nation in which most of these developments had gone about as far as they had anywhere, even though the main contributions to them had been made in other places.

Dewey's philosophy of education may be thought of, in part, as a historical outgrowth of some of the developments just mentioned—

and as America's contribution to their advance. Dewey himself thinks of it, more specifically, as the expression in education of the following movements: modern experimental science (including psychology), the industrial revolution, social democracy, and the theory of evolution. In fact, one of his main arguments in its favor is a claim that it is the logical outcome in education of these four modern developments which we have already accepted.

DIFFICULTIES

However, Dewey's philosophy of education is also a philosophical construction in its own right, and it is in this aspect that we shall be concerned with it, rather than with its historical origin or consequences. Its presentation entails problems not involved in presenting those of Aristotle or Kant. In the case of both Aristotle and Kant the body of writing directly concerned with education is relatively small, and except for passages in other works, comes in one piece. Dewey, however, wrote a great deal about education over a period of sixty-five years, and, though there is comparatively little change of position in all this time, the total body of writing is immense, as well as repetitious and unsystematic. In particular it contains a number of separate versions, shorter or longer, of his philosophy of education, from "My Pedagogic Creed" (1897), through *The School and Society* (1899), *The Child and the Curriculum* (1902), *Democracy and Education* (1916), and several others, to *Experience and Education* (1938). Besides these there are a large number of articles on education, and, of course, relevant passages in other works which are not primarily about education.

Added difficulties are the fact that Dewey's style is not very clear, the fact that he seldom states his whole meaning on any given point in any one place, so that one has constantly to keep other passages in mind, and the fact that he gives very little help in the way of organization and logical presentation. What follows is an attempt to present Dewey's philosophy of education in my own way, centering as before on the three questions to be answered by any such philosophy; hopefully, it does not leave out too much or misrepresent too egregiously.

THE NATURE OF PHILOSOPHY OF EDUCATION

DEWEY ON PHILOSOPHY AND EDUCATION

Though we are primarily interested in Dewey's philosophy of education itself, we must say a little about his views on the nature of educational philosophy and theory, a subject on which he wrote a good deal. The first main point is that he rejects the distinction between theoretical and practical philosophy which is so central in Aristotle and Kant. For Dewey, in line with the theory of evolution and pragmatism, all thought is practical in function, even philosophy. Philosophy arises out of the problems of human life, especially out of those connected with social conflicts, and is, or at least should be, concerned with the solution of such problems. Philosophy should be the most general theory of practice, eventuating in .

> the projection of large generous hypotheses which, if used as plans of action, will give intelligent direction to men in search for ways to make the world more one of worth and significance.[1]

It follows that the philosophy of education is the theory of educational practice. In fact, for Dewey, all philosophy is philosophy of education. In a famous passage, he says,

> If we are willing to conceive education as the process of forming fundamental dispositions, intellectual and emotional, toward nature and fellow men, philosophy may even be defined as *the general theory of education* . . . philosophy is the theory of education as a deliberately conducted practice.[2]

Dewey's argument here may be put as follows:

(1) Education is the process of forming fundamental dispositions.
(2) Philosophy is the general theory of forming such dispositions.
(3) Therefore philosophy is the general theory of education.

He even goes so far as to say that "If a [philosophical] theory makes no difference in educational endeavor, it must be artificial." In his autobiographical statement he reasserts this view:

> . . . philosophizing should focus about education as the supreme human interest in which, moreover, other problems, cosmological, moral, logical, come to a head.[3]

Why should education take a general philosophical theory as its guide? Why, for example, should it not simply aim at the unchanged perpetuation of existing institutions or at the formation of the dispositions that are generally regarded as useful and desirable in society? Among other things, because

> the business of schooling tends to become a routine empirical affair unless its aims and methods are animated by such a broad and sympathetic survey of its place in contemporary life as it is the business of philosophy to provide.[4]

Dewey would want to add that existing institutions may be unjust, impoverishing, or restrictive, and the dispositions that are generally regarded as useful and desirable may not really be so. There may not even be any such prevailing agreement about the dispositions to be cultivated as is presupposed in the question.

EXPERIMENTALISM AND EDUCATION

The second main point is that Dewey insists that all philosophy, including the philosophy of education, must be empirical, in the sense of using the kind of experimental enquiry that is characteristic of the empirical sciences. The method of scientific intelligence and intelligent action based on the use of this method is, according to Dewey, "the sole ultimate resource of mankind in every field whatsoever."[5] That is Dewey's basic conviction and chief gospel, and is spelled out more fully in the following passage to which I shall want to refer again. He says the problems involved in improving man's estate are three: that of "controlling the occurrence or existence of consummatory experiences" or "experiences marked by intrinsic values," that of enriching such experiences "by clarifying and deepening their contained meanings," and that of "extending the range of persons and groups who enjoy such values." Then he writes,

> What is characteristic of my theory is simply the emphasis placed upon the knowledge mode of experience, defined in terms of the outcome of competent enquiry, as that which accomplishes these functions; an emphasis which goes so far as to say that intelligence, as the fruit of such knowledge, is the *only* available instrumentality for accomplishing them. The contrast is with those theories which hold that transcendent *a priori* principles, rational intuitions, revelations from on high, adherence to established authorities in state and church, inevitable social revolutions, etc., are the agencies by which experienced values are to be made more secure and more extensively enjoyed.[6]

In these words Dewey speaks out for the method of experimental enquiry as the sole basis of human belief and action, against Kant, Aristotle, Christianity, der Fuehrer, the Church, Marx, Maritain, Niebuhr, Hutchins, and all the others who deny or refuse to believe that "it is possible for experience, in becoming genuinely experimental, to develop its own regulative ideas and standards." Behind these words, as their support, of course, lies Dewey's entire philosophy, his empiricism, his pragmatism, and his naturalism— matters that we cannot go into here.

In accordance with this conviction Dewey maintains, first, that theories about teaching methods and other educational practices (for example, that the use of an *orbis pictus* and a moral catechism are the most effective ways of teaching natural history and morality, respectively) must be based on the best possible empirical evidence. This is one of his main themes in connection with educational reform, and lies behind his interest in experimental schools; education in the sense of the discipline that studies and guides the processes of education must become scientific. This is a point with which Kant would agree, as we saw. Possibly Aristotle would also agree, but he had no notion of experimental enquiry and did not seem to feel that any more empirical evidence was needed on any subject than the Greeks already had or could easily get by traveling and looking at specimens.

Dewey also contends, secondly, that *all* of the premises about the nature of man and the world which are used in determining what dispositions are to be fostered or how they are to be fostered must be empirically testable. It is to the sciences that we must go "to find out the facts of the world"; it is for them to say "what generalizations are tenable about the world," not philosophy, theology, authority, or anything else. No non-empirical premises such as metaphysicians and theologians characteristically use and insistently claim to be necessary are allowable or even available. Here Kant would disagree in principle, and perhaps Aristotle too (certainly his present-day followers do), for Kant accepts certain postulates about the world that are based, not on experience, but on morality, which is a priori, and Aristotle holds that some propositions about the world are intuitively or demonstratively certain. In practice, however, both men might agree with Dewey, for Kant does not use his postulates in determining what should be done either in morality or education, and Aristotle seems to imply that there are no necessary truths in ethics or politics (or at least that the necessary truths of theoretical philosophy have no practical consequences for action).

What about basic ethical or value premises, premises about the ends of education, etc.? Here Kant introduces a priori, non-empirical moral principles: the supreme categorical imperative and the derived duties to cultivate one's talents and to promote the happiness of others. What Aristotle does is not very clear, in view of his remark that we must not expect in ethics and politics the kind of certainty found in mathematics, but his line of thought certainly is not empirical in Dewey's sense, and the Aristotelian tradition has always held that ethical principles and basic ends are determined by reason, not by empirical enquiry of a scientific kind. This is one of the main issues between Maritain, Adler, and Hutchins, on the one hand, and the Deweyans on the other. For Dewey argues, in the third place, not only that experience is capable of developing its own regulative standards, but that all ends and ideals must be "framed in terms of the possibilities of actually experienced situations."[7] Even our most basic standards and our most ultimate ends must be regarded as hypotheses about the satisfaction of human needs and desires, or about the realization of human potentialities, and must be tested by and possibly revised in the light of subsequent experience. None of them can be taken as fixed, final, or certain a priori.

In other words, Dewey is contending that *all* of the propositions that enter into a normative philosophy of education must be grounded in reflective empirical enquiry of an experimental kind and in nothing else—whether they are normative or factual, basic or derivative. In this he differs from many of his recent critics, from Kant, and probably from Aristotle. I should point out, however, that he can disagree with them on this issue about the *nature* of normative philosophy of education and yet agree with them (or at least some of them) about its *content*. For he might find that all of their beliefs about the aims and methods of education do in fact pass the test of experimental enquiry; but, of course, the rest of what he has to say is due precisely to the fact that he finds, rightly or wrongly, that many of them do not pass this test and hence must be rejected. The views of the traditionalists in education, for Dewey, are not mistaken because they are traditional—indeed, their long acceptance shows that they have some basis in experience—but only because and insofar as they turn out to be refuted by further scientific enquiry.

THE DISPOSITIONS TO BE FORMED

A PROBLEM

I have been assuming that education, especially education in the first sense defined in Chapter I, is seeking or should seek to foster the formation in the young of certain dispositions or excellences—that this is the job or proximate goal of educative activity. Now, as was indicated in the first chapter, Dewey sometimes seems to reject this assumption, that is, he sometimes talks as if education is not concerned with the formation of dispositions at all. Thus he identifies education with living or growing, describes it as the continuous reconstruction of experience or as the enrichment of the content or meaning of experiences, and says that it goes on "in, by, and for experience"—all as if no dispositions come in. We must not, however, be misled by this mode of speech in Dewey, for he also speaks constantly of the formation of character, habits, attitudes, beliefs, etc., in education, and in the famous passage quoted a few pages ago even defines education (as I did) as "the process of forming fundamental dispositions . . . toward nature and fellow men. . . ." We must, then, conclude that Dewey's full view is that living, growing, reconstructing and enriching experience, releasing potentialities, etc., necessarily *involve* the formation of dispositions of various sorts. The formation of these dispositions is not the final or whole end of education for Dewey, as it sometimes seems to be for Kant, but it is a necessary condition of its achieving any more final or complete ends.

TWO POINTS

Well, then, if Dewey does not disown our first question, what are the attitudes, habits, beliefs, and traits that educative processes are to shape or bring about? What fundamental dispositions toward nature and fellow men is the process of education to form? In accordance with what was said earlier, and in contrast with Aristotle and Kant, Dewey holds that any answer to this question must be tentative, since it must rest on experience and may need to be revised in the light of further experience. The list of dispositions may need to be revised as we find out more and more about man and the world, and as the circumstances of human life change. Even if the items on the list remain the same, their meaning may change; they may have to be redefined as a result of changes either in our environment or in our knowledge.

Dewey also insists, again in opposition to Aristotle and Kant, that excellences cannot be divided into two separate kinds. He argues that any question about what kind of a self one is to be is a moral question, and hence that all dispositions are moral, since they enter into the being of the self. Thus he rejects Aristotle's distinction between moral and intellectual excellences and Kant's between moral and natural perfections. No dispositions are purely moral, if this means something distinctive, and all of them have a moral bearing. It follows, of course, for Dewey, that all education is moral, even if it is also scientific, and that moral education is not a separable activity or part of the curriculum.

DISPOSITIONS NOT TO BE FOSTERED

Still we want at least a tentative list of "fundamental dispositions" from Dewey; philosophy as the general theory of education must provide us with one if it is to do anything at all. Yet, though he implies that philosophy is the general theory of the formation of fundamental dispositions, it is hard to find in Dewey any systematic account of the dispositions to be formed such as we found in Kant or Aristotle. If we look at his philosophy as a whole, however, we see at once that many dispositions which they and other thinkers would include in their lists must be excluded by Dewey—namely, all attitudes and beliefs that depend in any way on a rationalistic theory of knowledge or a supernaturalistic metaphysics or on an appeal to authorities in state or church. For all such attitudes and beliefs are incompatible with his general experimentalism and naturalism; given his position he cannot approve of any disposition to rely on transcendent a priori principles, rational intuitions, revelation, authority, tradition, inevitable revolution, any belief in God as usually conceived, freedom as Kant conceived of it, the immortality of the soul, or any attitudes that rest on such beliefs.

Dewey, then, is against the fostering of many dispositions advocated as excellences by other philosophers of education, recent and classical. This is perhaps the cruelest stroke of all in the eyes of those who oppose him; it is also something that is forgotten or covered up by those who think that they can combine an acceptance of Dewey's general theory of education with a more or less traditional form of theistic faith, as many educators do. At the same time it presents public school educators with a problem. For, as I understand it, the public schools must be neutral, not only between Catholicism and Protestantism, not only between Christianity and Judaism, but also between naturalism or atheism and supernaturalism or theism. Then, while they cannot seek to inculcate religious attitudes or values of any of the traditional kinds, they also cannot try to demythologize education, to foster opposition to such religious attitudes or values, or to disparage their validity—as a true Deweyan must. The existence of this problem does not imply that Dewey's view is false, for its falsity could only be shown by careful critical argument, if at all, but it does follow, it seems to me, that public school educators must be careful about the way they apply Dewey's philosophy of education. They may be able to foster the dispositions it calls for in its positive aspect, but must avoid implementing completely its negative aspect.

REFLECTIVE INTELLIGENCE

For Dewey's positive view of the dispositions to be promoted we must look to his ethical and political works, as we did with Aristotle and Kant—especially to Part II of the second edition of *Ethics* (1932), recently reprinted as *Theory of the Moral Life*—for, according to Dewey, moral theory is the part of philosophy that is especially concerned to ask what kind of a self we are to try to realize. Dewey begins by assuming, as most philosophers do, including certainly Kant and perhaps Aristotle, that the transition from customary to

reflective morality is not only necessary once problems arise but is also a good thing in principle. Michael Oakeshott, a conservative thinker, also distinguishes these two forms of the moral life.[8] In the first, he says

> the moral life is a *habit of affection and behaviour;* not a habit of reflective *thought,* but a habit of *affection* and *conduct . . .* conduct is as nearly as possible without reflection.

In the second,

> . . . activity is determined, not by a habit of behaviour, but by *the reflective application of a moral criterion . . .* a special value is attributed to self-consciousness, individual or social; not only is the rule or ideal the product of reflective thought, but the application of the rule or the ideal to the situation is also a reflective activity. . . . its distinctive virtue is to be subjecting behaviour to a continuous corrective analysis and criticism.

Oakeshott decries the second form of moral life and hankers after a return to the first, though he sees that such a return is impossible; not so Dewey. He is an apostle of the method of reflective enquiry, as we saw, and he believes that the method is as desirable in morals as in the sciences. For him the moral life—including conduct, choice, and self-making—should be precisely "a habit of reflective thought." Affection and action there must be, of course, but *they* should not be simply habitual; what should be habitual is the *use* of *intelligence,* and affection and action should be habitual only insofar as their being so is a condition of intelligent living. As for spontaneity, there is at least as much room for it in a reflective as in a customary morality. A habit of reflective thought, as Dewey thinks of it, means a habit of using the method of reflection whenever we sense a problem and of trying to sense a problem whenever there is one; it does not mean that we must "sickly o'er with the pale cast of thought" the whole native hue of our lives, or find food for thought where there is none.

> There is no better evidence of a well formed moral character than knowledge of when to raise the moral issue and when not.[9]

Similarly, there is no better evidence of a well-formed reflective habit than knowledge of when to raise an issue and when not.

Thus Dewey insists, first of all, that we must develop a reflective disposition or habit of *intelligence*. This means acquiring a whole complex excellence which is moral as well as intellectual. It involves (a) developing a disposition to reflect, as just indicated. This in turn involves learning to put off action or to postpone desire, in other words to control impulse in order to enquire and deliberate. It also entails forming a will to know everything that is relevant to the formulation and solution of the problems one is or may be faced with. Here Dewey says that what counts morally is rather the will to know than the extent of one's actual knowledge, but he must be thinking that we should actually acquire, as far as possible, the relevant knowledge in question, since a will to know that does not set about getting knowledge is a contradiction. In other words, a habit of reflection includes a habit of getting knowledge, first-hand if possible, second-hand if necessary. It also includes (b) developing longer-range and more inclusive aims, learning to act on the basis of conclusions reached by reflection, and, in general, forming a disposition, not only to reflect on the basis of the clearest concepts and best knowledge available, but also to act accordingly—not only to think, but also to execute, intelligently. To have this complex disposition, Dewey says, is to have *character*.

> . . . character consists of an abiding identification of impulse with thought, in which impulse provides the drive while thought supplies consecutiveness, patience, and persistence, leading to a unified course of conduct.[10]

With it comes an assumption of *responsibility* for consequences. If it is accompanied by a well-reasoned and empirically tested conception of what is truly good as against what merely seems good then one also has the cardinal virtue of *wisdom*, as Dewey conceives of it, which thus turns out to be much like Kant's prudence and Aristotle's practical wisdom.

Dewey's first insistence, then, is that we should acquire the habit of reflective thinking in connection with questions of both fact and action, meaning by this that we should acquire the abilities or skills involved in doing such thinking well, the knowledge needed to bring it to sound conclusions, and the disposition to rely on it as the sole basis for action and belief. To see further what this entails we must clarify what Dewey means by reflective thinking. He does not mean just any kind of mental activity. He means

> active, persistent, and careful consideration of any belief or supposed form of knowledge in the light of the grounds that support it, and the further conclusions to which it tends,[11]

or of any proposed action in the light of its conditions and consequences. Such thinking, as he sees it, always does or at least should follow a certain pattern,[12] which he regards as characteristic of and best exemplified in modern experimental science, but which can be carried out at various levels and in various contexts and forms. Take the factual or scientific question why certain bubbles behave in a certain way. (1) There is a problem, a felt difficulty. All real thinking, according to Dewey, begins with some such problem, actually felt as a problem needing solution. (2) The problem must be clarified and defined, through the use of analysis, past experience, and relevant knowledge already attained. With the use of these same resources, plus imagination, (3) a tentative hypothesis as to the most likely solution must be formulated, and (4) its consequences and implications deduced and envisaged. (5) Finally the hypothesis must be tested by being acted on in some way to see whether it is confirmed by further experience. This is the step that is crucial in determining whether it is to be believed and used as a basis for possible further action. Only if it is adequately confirmed by subsequent experience may it be regarded as true and as a piece of knowledge, but, no matter how well confirmed it may be, it cannot be taken as absolutely certain. The worth of the whole process as a piece of thinking depends on the extent and accuracy of what is done in steps (2), (3), and (4).

Dewey claims that the same pattern of thought can and should be used in dealing with moral questions. In fact, one of his main theses is that we should put morals on the same kind of experimental basis as that on which we have already put the study of nature with such remarkable success. He does not deny that the problem "What should I do now?" is different from the question "Why do those bubbles behave as they do?" but he believes that the same general kind of experimental or scientific method is to be used to solve it.

> A moral situation is one in which judgment and choice are required antecedently to overt action. The practical meaning of the situation—that is to say the action needed to satisfy it—is not self-evident. It has to be searched for. There are conflicting desires and alternative apparent goods. What is needed is to find the right course of action, the right good. Hence, enquiry is exacted: observation of the detailed makeup of the

situation; analysis into its diverse factors; clarification of what is obscure; discounting the more insistent and vivid traits; tracing the consequences of the various modes of action that suggest themselves; regarding the decision reached as hypothetical and tentative until the anticipated or supposed consequences which led to its adoption have been squared with actual consequences. This inquiry is intelligence.[13]

ACQUISITION OF INTELLECTUAL SKILL AND KNOWLEDGE

It will be clear, and Dewey often points it out, that the habit of intelligence, whether one is dealing with factual or with moral questions, entails not only the acquisition of *knowledge*, as has been mentioned, but also the acquisition of intellectual and emotional *discipline* and the development of all of the intellectual *abilities* or *skills* needed to perform steps (2), (3), and (4) well in connection with the sorts of problems one is likely to face. In other words, the same kinds of intellectual dispositions are needed for both scientific enquiry and moral deliberation. This will be clear in the case of discipline and skills, but may not be in the case of knowledge, for, on many views, among them those of Aristotle and Kant, there are two kinds of knowledge—namely, practical or moral and scientific or theoretical—and one might suppose that scientific enquiry requires the second kind of knowledge and moral deliberation the first. On Dewey's view, however, there is only one kind of knowledge and one may call it either moral or scientific. Moral science

> is ineradicably empirical, not theological nor metaphysical nor mathematical. . . . [It] is not something with a separate province. It is physical, biological and historic knowledge placed in a human context where it will illuminate and guide the activities of men.[14]
>
> . . . there is no gulf dividing non-moral knowledge from that which is truly moral. At any moment conceptions which once seemed to belong exclusively to the biological or physical realm may asssume moral import. This will happen whenever they are discovered to have a bearing on the common good. When knowledge of bacteria and germs and their relation to the spread of disease was achieved, sanitation . . . took on a moral significance it did not have before.[15]

To this one might reply that in order to know how to use all of this physical, biological, and historic knowledge one must first know what basic principle or end our actions should subserve, so that a knowledge of a purely moral kind must be presupposed. But

Dewey thinks that even this knowledge of basic ends or principles is ineradicably empirical, and must be built up and tested by the experimental method just outlined. He does not make his claim very clear, but if he is right, then the knowledge to be learned is all of one kind, or family of kinds, not of two radically different types.

SOME TRAITS OF MIND

Dewey is also concerned to point out, however, that the habit of intelligence, whether applied in science or in morals, includes certain traits that are indisputably moral virtues. In one place he lists "wide sympathy, keen sensitiveness, persistence in the face of the disagreeable, balance of interests enabling us to undertake the work of analysis and decision intelligently"; in another "straightforwardness, flexible intellectual interest or open-minded will to learn, integrity of purpose, and acceptance of responsibility for the consequences of one's activity including thought [or as he also calls it 'intellectual thoroughness']."[16] These are dispositions of a class not much stressed by Aristotle or Kant, but which Dewey regards as indispensable in the practice of intelligence in all fields whatsoever. Thus he finds that the life of intellectual excellence itself contains a whole group of moral virtues, as well as knowledge and skill. This is one of the reasons he refuses to separate moral and intellectual excellences; it also helps clarify why Dewey can speak so hopefully of the method of intelligence as the sole resource of mankind in every field whatsoever, and why he even goes so far as to say

> . . . the prime need of every person at present is capacity to think; the power to see problems, to relate facts to them, to use and enjoy ideas. If a young man or woman comes from school with this power, all other things may be in time added to him. He will find himself intellectually and morally.[17]

It certainly does something to explain why he thinks that "making intelligence central in education" in this way need not result in a narrowly intellectual or coldly neutral attitude toward social problems but may actually generate an ardent democratic social concern. For all of the traits involved in the method of intelligence as he conceives it are essential to the democratic way of life and tend, at least to some extent, to produce it, even if something more is needed to bring it to full flower.

ANSWER TO SOME CRITICS

At the same time, the fact that Dewey insists on the habit of intelligence in the sense just explained as the one thing most needful in our culture suffices to answer the charges of anti-intellectualism, conformism, and life-adjustmentism which have been directed against him. It may be true that our schools are fostering anti-intellectualism, life-adjustmentship, and other-directedness, but, if it is, this only shows that Dewey's philosophy of education has not been adequately applied by the schools, since his main concern is to make scientific intelligence and its conclusions the basis of all our attitudes, beliefs, and actions. In fact, the theologians who accuse him of "scientism" are much more understanding of Dewey than those who make the other charges, but, of course, they beg the question in assuming that scientism is mistaken. It is true that Dewey is against certain kinds of intellectualism—for example, those of Aristotle and Kant—and that some of his doctrines would lead to anti-intellectualism if taken apart from the others, but it remains true nevertheless that what he is for is still a genuinely intellectual life.

FURTHER   DISPOSITIONS

The passage last quoted, as well as some others, suggest that Dewey may be thinking that education needs only to foster the habit of reflective thought and the dispositions that go with it. He does, however, mention other dispositions as desirable. Some of these seem still to be closely connected in his mind with the method of intelligence: *impartiality* (including justice), tolerance, objectivity, acting on principles, following the Golden Rule (or Kant's first principle), breadth of interest, and interest in objects that endure and are approved on reflection. He also mentions *courage* and *temperance,* but presents them as manifestations of, respectively, persistence in the face of obstacles and self-control, both of which have already been listed as involved in the use of intelligence. Conscientiousness he sometimes identifies with being carefully reflective, sometimes with having an "active will to discover new values and to revise former notions," and sometimes with "sensitiveness to the rights and claims of others."[18] This last he also calls faithfulness, and with it enter a group of dispositions which Dewey regards as very important, but which do not seem to be aspects of being intelligently reflective, though Dewey sometimes appears to think so: *sociability, sympathy,* and *benevolence,* love, social concern, or regard for the common good.

FAITHFULNESS

What Dewey means by faithfulness "in acknowledgment of the claims involved in [one's] relation with others" needs a little explanation, since this part of his ethics is often neglected by both his critics and his followers. He rejects, of course, all theories like Kant's that regard the right as something non-empirical. He also thinks, as teleologists in ethics do, that it is *"desirable* that acts which are deemed right should in fact be contributory to good"; but he agrees with the deontologists to the extent of holding that "*x* is right" does not simply *mean* "*x* is conducive to the good."

> . . . as an idea, "right" introduces an element which is quite outside that of the good. This element is that of *exaction, demand.* . . . The Good is that which attracts; the Right is that which asserts that we *ought* to be drawn by some object whether we are naturally attracted to it or not.[19]

Human beings, Dewey explains, stand in various intimate relations to one another—for example, those of parent and child, or friend and friend—and hence they are subject to a variety of expectations and demands (as well as rights). Often these are incorporated in rules and supported by social pressure of various sorts, even if they are not embodied in law. The existence and authority of these demands is simply a matter of empirical fact.

> For Right is only an abstract name for the multitude of concrete demands in action which others impress upon us, and of which we are obliged, if we would live, to take some account. Its authority is the exigency of their demands, the efficacy of their insistencies.[20]
> . . . Right, law, duty, arise from the relations which human beings intimately sustain to one another, and . . . their authoritative force springs from the very nature of the relation that binds people together.[21]

Now, Dewey does believe, with the utilitarians, that social institutions, relations, roles, and rules should be made intelligent, reasonable, and conducive to the welfare of all who are involved in them, and that education should play a part in making them so, but in the meantime he also believes that education should both make us aware of these realities of human association, these rights and demands of others, and foster a sense of obligation to be faithful in respecting them. In fact, it should seek to build up in each individual a disposition to take the thing exacted as his own good, even if he does not so judge it at the time. ". . . What 'should be' is that an individual should *find* the required conduct good."[22] He may, of course, examine and criticize any particular claim, but he must learn to ask in doing so what claims he is willing to make on others and to see them make on him. He must develop a mind to be fair and a concern for the common good.

In close conjunction with what he says here about the right, Dewey says that one should learn to "be solicitous, *thoughtful*, in the award of praise and blame, use of approbation and disapprobation."[23] Praise and blame, approval and disapproval, punishment and reward, etc., are acts by which we seek to influence (and educate) others. Dewey does not outlaw them, as some progressives do (except for praise and approval), but he does believe that we should use them thoughtfully or intelligently, according to a standard. We should learn to use them, not retrospectively, as retributivists do, that is, as rewards or punishments for what has been done, but prospectively, as means of directing future action—not just in some direction we happen to desire but in the direction of promoting the general welfare or common good.

In these discussions it becomes clear that Dewey does have in mind a *criterion* or *standard* for determining what claims are justified, what rules are right, and what actions are to be approved or disapproved; and that his criterion is a teleological utilitarian one: the promotion of the general welfare or happiness (though he rejects the hedonistic identification of the good or happiness with pleasure, much as Aristotle does). In his aversion to the notion of fixed principles and final ends he sometimes covers up the fact that he is himself subscribing to a basic principle or end of a sort. He does this because he is afraid that if the general welfare "were regarded as the direct end of acts [or as a rule], it might be taken to be something fixed and inflexible"; but he does not mind calling it a "standard."

> As a standard it is rather a cautionary direction, saying that when we judge an act . . . we should first consider its consequences in general, and then its special consequences with respect to whatever affects the well-being of others. . . . it provides a consistent point of view to be taken in all deliberation, but it does not pretend to determine in advance precisely what constitutes the general welfare or common good. It leaves room open for discovery of new constituents of well-being, and for varying combinations of these constituents. . . . It requires, rather than merely permits, continual advance in the conception of what constitutes happiness in the concrete.[24]

In effect Dewey in this much neglected passage is accepting a fixed basic principle or ultimate end, but rejecting all fixed conceptions of its content. On this latter point he remains an experimentalist in a way in which Aristotle, the hedonists, and many others are not, though, interestingly enough, hardly more so than Kant, who also has a rather open conception of what is involved in happiness and perfection.

Indeed, Dewey finds room for Kant's supreme principle of morality within his own. He objects to Kant's formalism and apparent disregard for consequences, but he accepts Kant's principle as a directive to be impartial in the consideration of consequences. I should imagine the results if I and others always acted on the end or maxim I propose to act on, and see whether I would then be willing to stand by it. If not, my proposed action is wrong. I must be willing to see others act toward me as I propose to act toward them; but I must also ask whether everyone's acting in that way will serve the welfare of all.

Thus, for Dewey, besides the habit of intelligence in thought and action, and all the abilities and traits pertaining to it, we should also acquire such dispositions as regard for the rights and claims of others and concern for the common good. The following passage stresses the latter:

> . . . the very problem of morals [and education] is to form an original body of impulsive tendencies into a voluntary self in which desires and affections center in the values which are common; in which interest focuses in objects that contribute to the enrichment of the lives of all.[25]

But this passage restores the balance:

> A union of benevolent impulse and intelligent reflection is the interest [disposition] most likely to result in conduct that is good. But in this union the role of thoughtful inquiry is quite as important as that of sympathetic affection.[26]

The fostering of this union is the chief proximate task of education on Dewey's view.

DEMOCRACY

So far I have not mentioned democracy. However, if there is anything that Dewey stands for, it is that we should acquire the dispositions called for by democracy as both a form of government and as a way of living with others, and that our society and education should be so set up as to foster them in us, for, unlike

Aristotle and even Kant, Dewey regards a completely democratic society as the ideal one. What are the dispositions called for by democracy? As Dewey sees them they are just those that have already been listed. It is important to notice this, but not necessary to go over them.

AESTHETIC TASTE

Two further dispositions must be mentioned, however. One is aesthetic taste. Dewey regards its development as an important part of the education of man, though he does not always make this explicit. For all his stress on science as a mode of knowledge and control of experienced objects, he does not regard science as the final thing in life. "The final thing is appreciation and use of things of direct experience,"[27] and the function of the fine arts in education is to intensify and enhance our appreciation and use of these things.

> They reveal a depth and range of meaning in experiences which otherwise might be mediocre and trivial. . . . They select and focus the elements of enjoyable worth which make any experience directly enjoyable.[28]

RELIGIOUS FAITH

The other disposition to be added is a kind of religious faith. While Dewey rules out religious faith of the traditional sort, faith in the existence and operation of supernatural beings, he does advocate an attitude toward life and the world which he thinks it appropriate to call "religious"—a devotion to an ideal end, to "ideal possibilities unified through imaginative realization and projection," and a faith that man and the universe are such that the method of intelligence and cooperative endeavor will gradually bring the ideal into being. An atheist and a naturalist can be religious in this sense, and Dewey is—he is even willing to say that the attitude described is a kind of belief in "God." In effect, however, his "common faith" is only an enhancement and intensification of the dispositions toward nature and fellow men which we have already covered, though it should be mentioned to complete the picture.[29]

THE GOOD MAN AND THE CITIZEN AGAIN

Earlier, in discussing Aristotle and Kant, we dealt with the question of the virtues of the good man vs. those of the good citizen. We saw that for Aristotle education is and should be relative to the constitution of the country and must prefer the dispositions that make for good citizenship to those of the good man, if there is any discrepancy between them. What about Dewey? There are places where he too seems to imply that education must follow the constitution—that in a democracy it must be democratic and in an aristocracy aristocratic. For example, this is what he seems to mean when he says "education will vary with the quality of life which prevails in a group."[30] Strictly speaking this is only a factual statement, but the line between factual and normative statements in Dewey is an unclear one, and he seems to be thinking not only that education does vary with the political quality of the group but that it should do so. If this is his view then his position is like that of Aristotle, except that he regards democratic dispositions as ideal, while Aristotle regards aristocratic ones as ideal. Then they would agree that democratic dispositions should be fostered by American education, aristocratic ones by Greek education, etc., and that neither the Americans nor the Greeks should try to reconstruct each other's systems of education (or those of Germany, Japan, or Russia).

On the other hand, Dewey is always stressing the fact that "As the means of the general institution of intelligent action, [education] holds the key to orderly social reconstruction."[31] In "My Pedagogic Creed" he says, "I believe that education is the fundamental method of social progress and reform."[32] He never goes as far as some recent educational philosophers (and Kant?) have in thinking that the schools may be used by educators, parents, and teachers to build a new social order, but he does talk of using education as "an instrument of realizing the better hopes of men."[33] He points out that, whatever the schools do, they are fostering certain dispositions and helping to bring about a certain social order, old or new, better or worse, and that

> accordingly, the problem is not whether the schools *should* participate in the production of a future society (since they do so anyway) but whether they should do it blindly and irresponsibly or with the maximum possible of courageous intelligence and responsibility.[34]

Dewey's answer, of course, is the latter, and I take this to mean that he thinks the schools ought to teach the dispositions described above, whatever the constitution of their country may be, and that, if and where they are forbidden to do so, educators should fight for the needed academic freedom. Their first concern should not be to realize any preconceived goal in the way of a social order but rather to promote "a union of benevolent impulse and intelligent reflection" and let come whatever social order may issue from this union.

REASONS FOR FORMING THESE DISPOSITIONS

ANOTHER PROBLEM

We have now seen that Dewey conceives of the task of education as the formation of certain dispositions, though he sometimes talks as if he does not. We have also seen which dispositions he thinks education should try to form. Next, we must look at his answer to our second question. Why must education try to form these dispositions rather than others? What principle must it obey or what end must it pursue which requires it to foster these dispositions? Here again we encounter a problem. For Dewey not only insists that no such principles or ends can be taken as fixed and final, he also talks very often as if education has no end but itself, no end but more education, and so on. He seems, that is, to disown our second question; again, however, the passages in which he does this are misleading. He certainly does reject the view that educators and pupils should pursue goals that are imposed upon them from with-out—for example, by a ruling class or a church—as well as the view that the end of education is some event, far off or near, divine or otherwise, toward which the whole educational creation moves in the sense of being merely a means. He certainly means also to deny that education is governed by any end or principle that has a fixed content; but he does not really mean that it is or should be governed by no end or principle whatsoever. Indeed, he often says or implies that it has a purpose or at least that there are criteria for determining whether it is taking place. For example, he writes that an experience is not educative merely because it is an experience, nor merely because it is immediately enjoyable, but if and only if it has a certain kind of effect.[35] Our second question really is: what kind of an effect must an educator's activity or a child's experience have to be educative? If Dewey gives us any answer to this, as he must, then he is doing the same thing Aristotle and Kant and others are doing when they ascribe an end to education. Dewey prefers, as we saw, to talk about a "standard" rather than an end or a rule, but it comes to much the same thing. Dewey does not really disown our question, he only disowns some ways of answering it. What then is his answer?

A POSSIBLE VIEW

He might reply that an activity or experience is educative if it is conducive to the formation of the dispositions listed above, and that those dispositions are to be cultivated for their own sakes. Then he would be saying that the end of education and life is simply to acquire and possess those dispositions, or, in other words, to become a certain kind of a self. (On this view, persons, like poems, must not mean, but be.) However, Dewey discusses this view, which he ascribes to Kant, and rejects it.

> Some theories hold that the self, apart from what it does, is the supreme and exclusive moral end. This view is contained in Kant's assertion that the Good will, aside from the consequences of acts performed, is the only Moral Good.[36]

It is true, Dewey argues, that selfhood, or character, or the acquisition and possession of excellences is not "a *mere* means, an external instrument, of attaining certain ends"; but neither are actions and their consequences mere means "for maintaining the good self." There is in this, as Aristotle recognizes, a circular arrangement; but this at least means that the end of education is not merely the formation of certain dispositions, which Aristotle reminds us we can possess even when we are asleep, but also the performance of certain activities and the production of certain consequences—in this sense education as the formation of dispositions does have an end beyond itself, if only in this sense. What sorts of activities and consequences are to be promoted?

TWO ANSWERS

I find the following passage helpful in interpreting Dewey at this point.[37] He is describing "the effect of the present absolutistic logic upon the method and aims of education" and writes:

> Even when the processes of education do not aim at the unchanged perpetuation of existing institutions, it is assumed that there must be a mental picture of some desired end, personal and social, which is to be attained, and that this conception of a fixed and determinate end ought to control educative processes. Reformers share this conviction with conservatives. The disciples of Lenin and Mussolini vie with the captains of capitalistic society in endeavoring to bring about a formation of dispositions and ideas which will conduce to a preconceived goal. . . . An experimental social method would probably manifest itself first of all in surrender to this notion. Every care would be taken to surround the young with the physical and social conditions which best conduce, as far as freed knowledge extends, to release of personal potentialities. The habits thus formed would have entrusted to them the meeting of future social requirements and the devel-

opment of the future state of society. Then and only then would all social agencies that are available operate as resources in behalf of a bettered community life.

In a way, Dewey's answer is all here. Dewey rejects as usual the notion that the processes of education have any preconceived or fixed and determinate end, conservative or radical; but he does not deny, in fact he takes for granted, that the processes of education are and should be intended to bring about the formation of dispositions, ideas, or habits, *and* that the formation of such dispositions, ideas, or habits is and should be intended to have certain results—that is, education has an end or standard, though not a "fixed" or "preconceived" one. He also affirms his faith in freed or experimental knowledge as a guide in pursuing this end or standard.

I take this all to support what I have been saying, but what interests me just now is that Dewey tells us here what his end or standard of education is. In fact, he seems to give us two answers: (1) "to release personal potentialities" and (2) to bring about "the development of the future state of society" or "a bettered community life." It is also interesting to note that, at least verbally, Kant and Aristotle give both of the same answers, except that the latter does not stress the future in the same way. The second answer is familiar to us, since we have already seen that Dewey's moral standard (if not "end") is the general welfare, the common good, or the improvement of man's estate. The first, however, is the answer that is usually associated with his views on education, for he is always saying that growth is the end, that education aims at growth, or that education is growing, and I take this to be the same as saying that "the purpose [of education] is to set free and to develop the capacities of human individuals."[38]

I say that Dewey seems here (and elsewhere) to give us two ends or standards for education because the two are not necessarily compatible—for Johnny's personal potentialities might be such that if his education frees and develops them, it will be doing what is not for the common good. Whether promoting his growth and advancing the general welfare coincide depends on what his potentialities are.

THE NATURE OF GROWTH

We shall come back to this point again, but just now we must notice that the notion of growth or self-realization is basic, not only in the first, but also in the second standard—for what is meant by promoting the common good or the general welfare? According to Dewey this just means promoting "the all-around growth of every member of society," at least as far as possible.[39] The two standards may conflict if Johnny's all-around growth is inconsistent with that of others, but the conception of growth is central in both of them. Either way education is "to surround the young with the physical and social conditions which best conduce, as far as freed knowledge extends, to release of personal potentialities." But what does this mean? What is growth? An experience is educative if and only if it contributes to growth; but what is the criterion of growth? This is the crucial question of Dewey's philosophy of education, the one which his critics have raised most insistently and which he and his followers have answered least satisfactorily. Sometimes their answer seems to come to this: an experience is educative if it is conducive to growth and it is conducive to growth if it produces another experience which is conducive to more growth and this experience is conducive to more growth if it produces a third experience which is conducive to still more growth, etc., etc.—but this will hardly do.

Actually I believe that, if we put what Dewey says about education as growth together with what he says about the good, we can find what is at least a more satisfactory answer to our question. Let us begin with some things he says in his educational writings. When he talks about growth as the end or essence of life and education he sometimes says things like the following:[40]

> . . . it is the chief business of life at every point to make living thus contribute to an enrichment of its own perceptible meaning,
> . . . education is not a means to living, but is identical with the operation of living a life which is fruitful and inherently significant,
> . . . education . . . is that reconstruction or reorganization of experience which adds to the meaning of experience, and which increases ability to direct the course of subsequent experience. (1) The increment of meaning corresponds to the increased perception of the connections and continuities of the activities in which we are engaged. . . . An activity which brings education . . . with it makes one aware of some of the connections which had been imperceptible. . . . (2) The other side of an educative experience is an added power of subsequent direction or control. To say that one knows what he is about . . . is to say . . . that he can better anticipate what is going to happen; that he can, therefore, get ready . . . in advance so as to secure beneficial consequences and avert undesirable ones. A genuinely educative experience, then, [is] one in which instruction is conveyed and ability increased. . . . It is [the educator's] business to arrange for the kind of experiences which, while they do not repel the student, but

rather engage his activities, are, nevertheless, more than immediately enjoyable since they promote having desirable [or
'worthwhile'] future experiences.

These passages are not very clear but they tell us a good deal.
They tell us that, for Dewey, an experience contributes to growth
or is educative if it contributes to the formation of dispositions (for,
as we saw, dispositions must figure in the process even though Dewey
does not always mention them) that increase the desirability or value
of one's experiences and give him the ability to secure good experiences or avert bad ones. This gives us a criterion (if not an
"end") of growth; we are growing if and only if our lives are becoming better or richer.

THE GOOD

What we need to know now is which experiences are desirable,
good, or worthwhile. What, according to Dewey, is the good? For
his answer we must go to his works on ethics and the theory of
value. He begins by rejecting hedonism, the view that pleasure is
the end or the good. Pleasure and satisfaction, he argues, are not
the object of desire as hedonists think; the objects of desire are things
like food or fame or even the happiness of others, and, while we may
get pleasure or satisfaction when we achieve these objects, we don't
always, and even if we do the pleasure or satisfaction is not our
object—it comes because we have achieved our object. Psychological
hedonism puts the cart before the horse—a point which Aristotle
saw but which, interestingly enough, Kant did not. Anyway, Dewey
continues, a thing is not good just because it is desired or liked, for
what is desired or liked may turn out to be disappointing or bad.
Even pleasures are not all good when they are considered along
with their conditions and consequences. Besides, there is a kind of
paradox involved in making pleasure the direct end or object of our
pursuit. If we go about being interested only in pleasure and not in
people and objects for their own sake, we have nothing to take pleasure in. The way to attain pleasure is not seek for it but to pursue
other things, among them the welfare of others.

Dewey also contends, as Aristotle does (but again not Kant),
that the hedonist is wrong in identifying happiness or well-being with
pleasure. Happiness is "the satisfaction of the whole self" while
pleasure is "the satisfaction of a single and independent appetite."
Pleasure is more temporary than happiness and more dependent on
external things.

Happiness . . . is a stable condition, because it is dependent not upon what transiently happens to us but upon the standing disposition of the self. One may find happiness in the midst of annoyances; be contented and cheerful in spite of a succession of disagreeable experiences, if one has braveness and equanimity of soul. Agreeableness depends upon the way a particular event touches us. . . . Happiness is a matter of the disposition we actively bring with us to meet situations. . . . Even so it is not directly an *end* of desire and effort, in the sense of an end-in-view purposely sought for, but is rather an end-product, a necessary accompaniment, of the character which is interested in objects that are enduring and intrinsically related to an outgoing and expansive nature . . . true happiness . . . issues from objects which are enjoyable in themselves but which also reënforce and enlarge the other desires and tendencies which are sources of happiness; in a pleasure there is no such harmonizing and expanding tendency.[41]

This account of happiness is similar in different ways to those of Aristotle and Kant, but Kant does not use his analysis to distinguish happiness and pleasure, and both Kant and Aristotle seem to think that happiness as they define it is the direct end of desire and effort, rather than a by-product. This passage also tells us that happiness presupposes the possession, by nature or by education, of certain kinds of disposition—courage, equanimity, and interests in objects that are enduring, expanding, and harmonizing, or, as Dewey also puts it, in goods that are approved upon reflection after wide examination of their relations. The main point for present purposes, however, is that for Dewey pleasure is not the good or the criterion of educativeness or growth, though his critics sometimes take Deweyan educators to think that it is—perhaps with justice in some instances.

Some of Dewey's critics (for example, Bertrand Russell) also take him to be advocating, in effect at least, "the doctrine of 'success,' understood in the sense of enlightened self-interest." Dewey does think that there is something to be said for this "success" view of life and of the aims of education.

. . . when one considers the amount of harm done by sheer ignorance, folly, carelessness, by surrender to momentary whim and impulse [or by "good intentions"], one may safely conclude that the state of things would be better than it is if more persons were moved by intelligent interest in external achievement. . . . Moreover, there are comparatively few who can afford to despise reference to success in achievement.[42]

So Dewey, like Kant, finds a place for prudence. Nevertheless he rejects the doctrine of success as the end, just as much as his critics (most of whom also find a place for it) do, and on much the same grounds. It keeps too much to the external aspects of life, encourages too much the idea of "getting on," and accepts too unquestioningly the current estimates of what this consists in.

At the same time Dewey also criticizes asceticism, which he interprets as taking discipline, exercise, and self-denial to be the end or good. Again, he finds a place for it—for more of it than his critics and even some of his followers recognize. As we saw, the method of reflection and consideration of consequences requires us to learn to postpone or even to deny present impulses. Besides,

> Ends contemplated only in thought are weak in comparison with the urgencies of passion. Our reflective judgment of the good needs an ally outside of reflection. Habit is such an ally. And habits are not maintained save by exercise. They are produced only by a course which is persisted in. . . . [and] it is a fact that some degree of unpleasantness is almost sure to attend the first performance of deeds that are done for the sake of forming a strong habit. "Discipline" is proverbially hard to undergo.[43]

Some discipline is necessary; it is, however, necessary and desirable only as a factor in the construction of a larger good or more inclusive interest and is in fact normally achieved as a part of the construction of such goods and interests. It is necessary as a condition of the good life, and valuable only as a condition of such a life (this life, not one hereafter), not as an end in itself. Even those who regard this life simply as a proving ground for one hereafter, are really considering discipline and self-denial only as means and not as ends. For Dewey they are not mere means to the good life; they are or should be parts of it that contribute to its all-around goodness.

What is the good life? In stating his views Dewey always distinguishes between the desir*ed* and the desir*able*, the satisfy*ing* and the satis*factory*, the enjoy*ed* and the enjoy*able*—between what is apparently or naturally good and what is really or morally good. What is really good is attractive, desired, satisfying, but what is attractive, desired, satisfying is not necessarily good. The term "values" is often used, unfortunately I think, to stand for things that are desired or *thought* to be good, but Dewey uses it to mean things that *are* good. Goods or values for him are things or experiences that are good all things considered, good in the light of experience and scientific knowledge of their connections, their conditions and their consequences. To quote some of his sentences:[44]

> [Values are not] enjoyments that happen anyhow, but . . .
> enjoyments which are the consequences of intelligent action
> . . . enjoyment becomes a value when we discover the rela-
> tions upon which its presence depends. . . . To say that some-
> thing satisfies is to report something as an isolated finality.
> To assert that it is satis*factory* [good] is to define it in its
> connections and interactions. . . . To declare something
> satis*factory* is to assert that it meets specifiable conditions.
> It is, in effect, a judgment that the thing "will do." It in-
> volves a prediction; it contemplates a future in which the
> thing will continue to serve. . . . Values . . . may be con-
> nected inherently with liking, and yet not with *every* liking
> but only with those that judgment has approved after exami-
> nation of the relation upon which the object liked depends.
> . . . There is no value except where there is a satisfaction,
> but there have to be certain conditions fulfilled to transform
> a satisfaction into a value. . . . values [are] identical with
> goods that are the fruit of intelligently directed activity. . . .

The good life, then, according to Dewey, is a harmonious whole consisting of good experiences or values—experiences that are achieved
through intelligent action, that are approved after reflection in the
light of full knowledge of their conditions and consequences, and that
are enjoyed *as* being so achieved and so approved. Such enjoyments
are what Dewey sometimes calls "consummatory experiences" and he
insists that they differ in kind from other enjoyments.

> Enjoyments that issue from conduct directed by insight into
> relations have a meaning and a validity due to the way in
> which they are experienced. Such enjoyments are not repented
> of . . . there is a sense of validity, of authorization, which
> intensifies the enjoyment. . . . To find a thing enjoy*able* is,
> so to say, a *plus* enjoyment.[45]

Such consummatory experiences, it must also be noticed, are good
for their own sakes, even if they are good only in their relations;
they have value as means, but they also have value in themselves.
They are, to use a phrase quoted earlier, "the final thing." For all
his pragmatism and instrumentalism Dewey does not hold that
"good" always means "good for." "Some goods," he says, "are not
good *for* anything; they are just goods," and his argument for this
is precisely the one his opponents sometimes use against him.

> . . . it is not [always] necessary to ask what [a thing] is
> good for. This is a question which can be asked only about

> instrumental values. . . . [But] we cannot stop asking the
> question about an instrumental good, one whose value lies in
> its being good *for* something, unless there is at some point
> something intrinsically good, good for itself.[46]

It is true that Dewey is often so concerned to criticize others who
distinguish means and ends, extrinsic and intrinsic values, that he
misleads both friend and foe—and even himself—into forgetting this
passage; but there it is—and it is central to his whole philosophy
of education. It is the main basis for his belief that the child's school
years must be made good in themselves and not taken as mere means
to later years or to another life.

The end of education, according to Dewey, is then not just
growth and further growth. It is growth, but growth has a criterion
and a direction. To grow is to develop a self capable of living a life
that is good or enjoyable in the special way just indicated. It is to
form "dispositions which conduce to an elevated and pure happiness."[47] An experience is educative, then, if and only if it contributes to the realization of such a self and so to a good or better
life, a life which is satis*factory*, a life which is found good by one
who lives it and has full knowledge of its meaning. Education is not
just a "reconstruction of experience," as Dewey keeps saying, as if
it were simply a constant creation of new experiences and combina-
tions of experiences; it is a continuous reconstruction of experience
which is also a "construction of good." To be properly understood,
what he says about growth must be interpreted in terms of what he
says about good in the chapter "The Construction of Good" in
The Quest for Certainty. Its appearing there is no mere coincidence.

SOME GOOD EXPERIENCES

What sorts of experiences does Dewey regard as consummatory
or satis*factory*? He does not give us any fixed list. In fact, he cannot, since he believes that every valuation or judgment about what
is good depends on a prediction that the thing in question *will do*,
and hence may turn out to be false. Besides, what will do for one
person may not do for another. Perhaps no sort of experience can
be said with any confidence to be good for everyone or at all times.
Still, Dewey does believe that there are "certain goods" which "are
likely to be approved upon searching reflection," so that "a *pre-
sumption* exists in their favor."[48] He mentions "art, science, culture,
interchange of knowledge and ideas, etc.," and, no doubt, he would
include freedom, friendship, democratic living, and many other things
among the *et ceteras*. Dewey does not, however, divide goods or values
into spiritual and material ones. For him all actual goods are ideal

or spiritual in the sense of being approvable upon searching reflection, and all sorts of things may turn out to be approvable in this way on one or another occasion.

> There are circumstances under which enjoyment of a value called spiritual because it is associated with religion is mere indulgence. . . . There are occasions when attention to the material environment constitutes the ideal good because that is the act which thoroughgoing inquiry would approve. . . . There is . . . a place and time . . . in which the satisfactions of the normal appetites, usually called physical and sensuous, have an ideal quality. . . . The business of reflection in determining the true good cannot be done once for all, as, for instance, making out a table of values arranged in a hierarchical order of higher and lower.[49]

Against Aristotle, Dewey argues that even "work" may have an ideal intrinsic value, and should be reconstructed so that it has such a value, as far as possible, not assigned to a separate class of human beings.

THE TWO STANDARDS AGAIN

Now we must return to the question we raised earlier about the two standards. Is the education of an individual to promote his growth and welfare or is it to promote the general growth and welfare? Is it to foster in him the dispositions that will give him the best life possible for him, or is it to foster in him the dispositions which will be conducive to the best life of society? To which standard does Dewey finally give priority, the growth and good life of the individual, or the all-around growth and good life of everyone?

There are passages in which Dewey seems to take the side of the former standard, and other passages in which he seems to take the side of the latter. The truth is that, although it is logically possible for the two standards to come into conflict, Dewey seems to hold that they in fact coincide, so that he need not choose between them. That is, he believes, as an empirical hypothesis which will be confirmed by scientific research and the future experience of mankind, that every individual will find his own greatest growth and happiness if he makes himself the kind of a person whose interest "focuses in objects that contribute to the lives of all."

> The final happiness of an individual resides in the supremacy of certain interests in the make-up of character; namely, alert, sincere, enduring interests in the objects in which all can share.[50]

Dewey's belief on this point, which is part of his "common faith," has been attacked by Niebuhr and others as naive and simple-minded in view of the demonic element in man, to which Kant also called attention. It must be admitted that Dewey is not obviously right as against Niebuhr, but it may be added that he has not been proved wrong by empirical evidence (which he takes as alone legitimate), and that Niebuhr himself somewhat similarly believes, as part of *his* religious faith, that the law of love and the requirements of self-realization coincide. We saw earlier that Aristotle, like Dewey, assumes that the good of the individual and that of his society are the same. Even Kant makes a somewhat similar assumption in postulating that there is a God who will see to it that the greatest happiness comes in the long run to the man of good will. In fact, Kant thought that man's natural predispositions are to good, and hence that he is such that he can find his happiness in being moral.

In one interesting passage Dewey says that a kind of *choice* is required if there is to be "an equation between personal and general happiness"—if one chooses to be a self of a certain sort then one's personal happiness and the general welfare will coincide.

> Many an individual solves the problem . . . not by any theoretical demonstration that what gives others happiness will also make him happy, but by a voluntary choice of those objects which do bring good to others. He gets a personal satisfaction or happiness because his desire is fulfilled, but his desire has first been made after a definite pattern. This enjoyment may be shorter in duration and less intense than those which he might have had some other way. But it has one mark which is unique and which for that individual may outweigh everything else. He has achieved a happiness which has *approved* itself to him, and this quality of being an approved happiness may render it invaluable, not to be compared with others. By personal choice among the ends suggested by desires of objects which are in agreement with the needs of social relations, an individual achieves a *kind* of happiness which is harmonious with the happiness of others.[51]

There is here an existentialist suggestion that one chooses his character much like the suggestion we found in Kant, but Dewey does not think of choice as something transcendental or contracausal, as Kant and the existentialists do. Free choice for him, as for Aristotle, is simply intelligent choice, and so can be affected by education. In fact, we may perhaps say that for him one role of education is precisely to bring us to a voluntary choice of those objects that are in agreement with the needs of social relations, and thus into a conformity with both standards at the same time.

CONCLUSION

What, then, is Dewey's answer to the question why education should foster the dispositions described earlier? It is a threefold answer: (1) that the formation of these dispositions is required for the growth of a human being, that is, for the construction of a life of consummatory or truly good experience, (2) that their formation is also conducive to the common good, which is the standard of the moral life, and (3) that their formation will lead an individual to choose to be the kind of a self that finds its good in objects that bring good to others, thus making the happy life and the morally good life one. Of course, these three claims are hypotheses that may turn out to be false, and Dewey does not marshal much direct empirical evidence for them, but they are at least plausible.

I should like to put Dewey's answer in another way by returning to a passage cited early in this chapter. There he says that man is faced with three problems:

(a) that of controlling the occurrence of consummatory experiences,
(b) that of enriching such experiences by clarifying and deepening their content or perceived meaning, and
(c) that of increasing the number of those who enjoy such experiences.

He also says that the method of intelligent empirical inquiry is man's only available and effective instrument for dealing with these problems: it enables one to control the course of his own subsequent experience and to do something to enhance the experiences of others, and, at the same time, it serves to clarify and deepen one's perception of the meaning of one's experiences. The end, if one may use this term, is consummatory experience, the means scientific intelligence. Put in these terms, the task of education is to help solve these three problems, first, by fostering the disposition to construct a good life by controlling the course of one's experience intelligently, the desire to enrich one's experiences by increased knowledge of their connections, and the benevolent concern to help bring consummatory experiences to others; second, by developing the abilities, knowledge, and traits needed to control and enrich one's own experiences and those of others—in short, by promoting the dispositions listed earlier.

It may be worth noting here that each of Dewey's consummatory experiences is a *bonum consummatum* in Kant's sense. For it is not only enjoyed or enjoyable; it is also approvable or morally good. Similarly, the good life as Dewey understands it is not just the happy life as Kant defines it; it is a happy life which can be approved upon an intelligent reflection which considers it in all its bearings. To this extent Dewey's end of education resembles Kant's.

A comparison with Aristotle may also be mentioned. Dewey's "consummatory experiences" are much like the "excellent activities" with which Aristotle identifies happiness. Both are supposed to be actual events, not just dispositions, and both are regarded as intrinsically worthwhile. The difference is that Aristotle believes (a) that happiness, or at least the highest happiness, consists of events of the same kind, viz. acts of contemplation, and (b) that such acts of contemplation are unconditionally good in themselves, apart from their consequences—while Dewey denies both of these propositions. For Dewey, happiness consists of consummatory experiences of various sorts, and no sort of experience is unconditionally good just in itself; a consummatory experience is good in itself and is unconditionally good, but only because it is good in its entire context, good even when considered together with its conditions and consequences. Dewey does not agree that an act of contemplation is necessarily good in its entire context, though he does seem to hold that a kind of contemplation (perception of meaning) is present in every consummatory experience.

One more point must be made here. Dewey's followers often proceed as if the end of education (in America at least) is simply to promote democracy, that is, as if its whole job is to foster democratic dispositions. They suggest that the reason education should foster the dispositions described above is simply because they promote democracy. My point is that, though Dewey gives some countenance to this way of thinking, he would not regard it as the whole story. Why should education promote democracy? Not merely because we happen to have a democratic constitution, but also because we ought to have one, and we ought to have a democratic society because

> democratic social arrangements promote a better quality of human experience, one which is more widely accessible and enjoyed, than do non-democratic and anti-democratic forms of social life.

Thus for Dewey

> the ultimate reason for hospitality to progressive education, because of its reliance upon and use of humane methods and its kinship to democracy, goes back to the fact that discrimination is made between the inherent values of different experiences.[52]

That is, the justification of progressive education does not rest on democracy; rather, the justification of both democracy and education rests on the fact that they are most conducive to growth or goodness of life.

THE METHODS AND PRACTICES OF EDUCATION

THE QUESTION

It is not easy to summarize in a systematic way all of what Dewey has to say in answer to our third question—namely, how educators and teachers are to go about forming the dispositions listed in answer to the first question. He wrote a great deal on this subject; it is really here that most of his criticisms of traditional education and proposals for its reform make their appearance, for, although he gives us a somewhat different list of dispositions from those of the proponents of traditional education and defines the dispositions listed somewhat differently than they do, most of his contrasts between the "old" and the "new" in education have to do with school practices and teaching methods. He joins issue with the proponents of the older education, not only at the level of philosophy, but also at that of practice. Even when he agrees with them about what is to be taught, he disagrees with them about the methods to be used.

Earlier we saw that Dewey sometimes in effect distinguishes three things in talking about education: (1) the dispositions to be formed, (2) the end to which these dispositions are conducive, which he describes both as "release of personal potentialities" and as "a bettered community life," and (3) the "educative processes" by which the dispositions (including beliefs and ideas) are to be formed. Kilpatrick, in a passage quoted in the first chapter, calls these, respectively, the "intermediate aim" of education, the "remoter and inclusive guiding aim," and the "immediate aim." The question is: What are Dewey's views about (3)? What are educators and schools actually to do?

The point is that if A desires to form a certain disposition in B, he must do something to B, he must set some "educative process" in motion. This means, for Dewey and his followers, that A must provide B with the appropriate "experiences" (they often say "life-experiences" but this is hardly necessary, since there are no other kinds of experience). Education, as Dewey once put it, is "of, by, and for experience,"[53] and it is the "by" that concerns us now. Not all experiences are educative, but all education comes about through experience. This is a generalization of Aristotle's remark that a moral excellence is acquired by performing actions of a certain kind. Dispositions are formed only by having experiences of the appropriate kind. Experiences are not magic, but they are all we have to work with.

There is nothing in this that a proponent of the older education need disagree with, for even listening and being told to do something are experiences. Neither need the traditionalist disagree when Dewey insists, as he does, that all experiences involve an interaction between an individual and his environment, and hence are both active and passive. For, if experiences are both, there is no necessary virtue in stressing activity or vice in stressing passivity. The question is: just what sorts of experiences is the educator to provide for the child?

Dewey likes to say here that no education can take place by any direct transfer of an item (idea, belief, attitude, etc.) from teacher to pupil, and that the teacher can educate his pupil only by transforming his environment in some way.

> The educator's part in the enterprise of education is to furnish the environment which stimulates responses and directs the learner's course. In last analysis, *all* that the educator can do is modify stimuli so that response will as surely as is possible result in the formation of desirable intellectual and emotional dispositions.[54]

This tells us that an educator can provide a pupil with experiences only by doing something to his environment, but it does not advance the discussion very much. For a traditional educator is also doing something to a child's environment—even if he is only reciting words. The question remains: Just what environment must an educator furnish in order to provide the sorts of experience that will bring about the formation of the desired intellectual and emotional dispositions?

In dealing with this question Dewey does not say as much about preschool education in the home as Aristotle or Kant do. Though he tends to take the family (which he idealizes) as a model for the school, what he is concerned about is school education. What he says about its practices rightly rests partly on his view of the dispositions to be formed, partly on what he takes to be the conclusions of science about the effects of various practices, and partly on the ethical principles he thinks should be observed by teachers and administrators. On these grounds he both attacks the practices of the old education as he sees them and advocates the practices of a new education as he thinks it should be (which is not what some of his "followers" think it should be).

OBJECTIONS TO TRADITIONAL EDUCATION

In attacking the older education Dewey is not so much criticizing the views of previous philosophers of education, though he does that too, as the methods previously prevailing in the schools and the more or less conscious theory that seemed to go with them. His objections are many and various. (1) The older educational practices fostered, intentionally or not, a number of undesirable intellectual dispositions: supernaturalistic beliefs, authoritarianism, worship of the past, and reliance on intuition, revelation, tradition, etc. They fostered a distrust of or at best only a limited trust in experience and science. (2) They were themselves not based on the findings of scientific research into the psychology of learning, etc. (3) They were also not sufficiently imbued with the spirit of democracy. (4) The older education sought to inculcate fixed conclusions rather than to develop intelligence as a method. It was too wholly concerned to pass on the skills, the bodies of information, and the rules and standards of conduct arrived at in the past, and too little interested in transmitting the disposition to extend and revise them or the abilities needed to do so. (5) It relied too completely, in passing on the former, on drill, lecturing, reading, and telling by the teacher, and on listening, memorizing, and "studying" by the child, and not enough on learning by doing and experience. (6) It mistrusted the natural interests and free activity of the child as an ally, and relied too much on the teacher's authority supplemented by *ad hoc* sanctions and extrinsic motivations of various sorts. (7) In general, it left the child too purely passive and inculcated attitudes "of docility, receptivity, and obedience" (not to mention conformity, which Deweyan education is now also charged with producing). (8) It treated the child's school years too much as a mere means to or preparation for later life either here or hereafter. (9) Yet at the same time it made his school life too different and too separate from the rest of his life. (10) It centered on subject-matter rather than on the child, and organized its subject-matter (divided into several subjects, each calculated to foster certain dispositions) in a "formal" or "logical" way suitable for adults, not in a "psychological" way, which would adapt it to children. (11) In all this it bred a socially undesirable kind of individualism and self-interestedness.

DEWEYAN EDUCATION

In contrast Dewey advocates freedom, scientific intelligence, democracy, looking to the future, learning by doing and experience, making connection with the interests and capacities of the child, continuity with life outside school, cooperative activity, unifying method and subject-matter and adapting both to the child, and making his school experience "worthwhile in its own immediate having" so that his education is "literally and all the time its own reward."[55]

To get a more systematic understanding of Dewey's view of what the practices of the new education should be, we may begin with the following passage. Talking about the problem of method, he says,

> It is no longer a question of how the teacher is to instruct or how the pupil is to study. The problem is to find what conditions must be fulfilled in order that study and learning will naturally and necessarily take place, what conditions must be present so that the pupils will make the responses which cannot help having learning as their consequence. The pupil's mind is no longer to be on study or learning. It is given to doing the things that the situation [which has been instituted] calls for, while learning is the result. The method of the teacher . . . becomes a matter of finding the conditions which call out self-educative activity, or learning, and of cooperating with the activities of the pupils so that they have learning as their consequence.[56]

What, then, are the general conditions under which pupils will "naturally and necessarily" acquire the knowledge and other dispositions Dewey regards as desirable? Dewey holds, of course, that they are not those which he takes to be characteristic of traditional education. Rather, the appropriate conditions are the following:

(a) The pupils must be engaged in activities, occupations, etc.

(b) These activities must involve physical action and be somewhat prolonged.

(c) Each activity must involve a problem to be solved by thinking.

(d) Activity must be carried out in cooperation with other pupils and the teacher.

(e) Activities must be related to the normal interests of the pupils and within their capacities, though challenging them.

(f) The atmosphere in the group must be free and as democratic as possible.

(g) The whole experience of the activity must be "worthwhile in its own immediate having," not just in the sense of being enjoyed, but in the sense of being good, not just good *for* something, but "good for itself." It must, however, also "promote having desirable future experiences," else it is not educative.

Something must now be said about each of these points.

Let us begin with (g). This point connects with what was said earlier about the growth and the end of education. It is really a principle which, according to Dewey, must govern all thinking about school practices. The job of education is to construct good in life of the pupil, or, rather, to aid him in constructing good in his own life. Dewey is particularly concerned to emphasize, however, that, while the school must have an eye to the future, it must also treat the child's present life as an end in itself and not as a means only. He is at least as emphatic on this point as Kant was. One reason for this is that he believes more and better learning will take place if the child finds the experiences involved to be satis*factory*, enjoyable upon reflection on their conditions and consequences, than will take place if he does not enjoy them or if he enjoys them but finds he cannot approve them on reflection. The other reason is a moral one: just as no person's life should be treated as a mere means to another's, so no part of a person's life should be treated as a mere means to or preparation for another part.

The main practical implication of (g) is that attention must be given to the appreciations or intrinsic values in school studies as well as to their utilities. The child's life is

> . . . not an end to which studies and activities are subordinate means; it is the whole of which they are ingredients. . . . every study in one of its aspects ought to have just such ulti-mate [appreciative or intrinsic] significance. It is as true of arithmetic as it is of poetry that in some place and at some time it ought to be a good to be appreciated on its own account—just as an enjoyable experience.

It is also true of science.

> Science . . . may have *any* kind of value, depending upon the situation into which it enters as a means. . . . All we can be sure of educationally is that [it] should be taught so as to be an end in itself in the lives of students—something worth-while on account of its own unique intrinsic contribution to the experience of life. Primarily it must have "appreciation value."

It is true of manual activities and of laboratory exercises, as well as of play. Their educative value

> . . . depends upon the extent in which they aid in bringing about a sensing of the *meaning* of what is going on. In effect,

. . . they are dramatizations. Their utilitarian value in forming habits of skill to be used for tangible results is important,
but not when isolated from the appreciative side.

In general, apparently admitting that some topics must be studied
for some end beyond themselves and certainly holding that all of
them may have values as means, Dewey concludes that

. . . what is desirable is that a topic be presented in such
a way that it either have an immediate value, and require no
justification, or else be perceived to be a means of achieving
something of intrinsic value.

About the latter alternative he writes,

The way to enable a student to apprehend the instrumental
value of [say] arithmetic is not to lecture him on the benefit
it will be to him in some remote and uncertain future, but to
let him discover that success in something he is interested in
doing depends upon ability to use number.[57]

Even so, (g) is not a wholly separate requirement added to
others, for, according to Dewey, an activity which fulfills the other
requirements will normally be found to be good or satisfactory for
itself by those engaged in it.

INTEREST

Point (e) is closely related to (g) and easily confused with it.
The need in educative activity of staying within reach of the child's
capacity, though at the same time developing it, is obvious. More
controversial is the need of education's making a connection with
the child's natural interests. By this Dewey means that the activities
the child is asked to engage in should be such as to enlist his present
interests, not just some hypothetical interests he may come to have
later. Moreover, they must enlist his present interests "naturally,"
that is, without the use of commands or the introduction of sanctions
in the form of extrinsic rewards or punishments. His claim is that
more effective learning takes place under these conditions. There
may not be very much learning sometimes, but it will be more than
will take place if he is bored, hostile, or unmotivated. Besides, even
if some of the desired learning does take place under extrinsic
motivations, these conditions also foster the development of undesirable dispositions—docility, self-interest, fear, mercenary attitude,
indifference, etc.

Dewey does not mean, however, that the child's desires are simply to be indulged, and he warns progressive educators about this in his later writings, though he makes the point already in his early ones. The end is not just pleasure or satisfaction; it is education, growth, the construction of a life found good on reflection.

> . . . the question of education is the question of taking hold of [the child's interests and] activities, of giving them direction.[58]

The child must learn self-control and discipline, but he can and should do so within the framework of interests which he already has or develops as he goes along under guidance. Present interests are the starting point, and though a necessary one, they must be interpreted, guided, and developed into interests in other people and in enduring objects in which all can share.

> Education . . . must begin with a psychological insight into the child's capacities, interests, and habits. It must be controlled at every point by reference to these same considerations. [But] these powers, interests, and habits must be continually interpreted—we must know what they mean. They must be translated into terms of their social equivalents—into terms of what they are capable of in the way of social service.[59]

The teacher's task—and this must determine his classroom methods—is to see to it that day by day the conditions are such that his pupils' *own* interests and activities *move* in the direction of the knowledge and dispositions desired.

ACTIVITY

Mention of activities brings us to points (a) and (b). The child, according to Dewey, is by nature active, and education should proceed by engaging and directing his activities. Now, one might say that a child is being active in a sense even if he is only listening, understanding what is said, memorizing it, etc., whether of his own volition or not, and Dewey sometimes recognizes this, but when Dewey calls for activity he calls for more than this—he calls for bodily movement as well as thought, and he calls for more freedom and decision on the part of the child. He wants *all* education to be active in Kant's sense, not only moral or practical education. Education is to be not only in and by experience, but in and by experience that is fully active. Learning is to be in and by doing. Why? Partly because, as Kant pointed out, we learn best when we are doing something; our motivation is better then, we remember better, and we see better the meaning of what we learn. Partly also because we find our experience more worth having for itself if we are active in this way.

Dewey's emphasis on activity also has a basis in his pragmatism. This pragmatism consists of four doctrines. First, thought, ideas, knowledge, theory, etc., have a practical function, the guidance of *action*. Second, to believe a proposition, *p*, is to be ready to *act* on it in the appropriate circumstances. Third, the meaning of any proposition, what it says (if it says anything), is that if one performs such and such an *action,* one will experience such and such consequences. Fourth, the test of truth of any proposition is to perform such and such an *action* and see if such and such consequences are experienced. From these four doctrines it follows that if one is to learn any proposition or come to know it, first-hand, one must perform a certain *action* and observe its consequences for oneself. Otherwise one has only opinion and second-hand knowledge. If we add the premise that we should try to know everything first-hand (which Dewey sometimes suggests but is too realistic wholly to commit himself to), it follows further that all learning should be by *doing*.

Followed out logically, this conclusion would mean, and seems sometimes to be accepted as meaning, that each generation must rediscover all knowledge from scratch, with at most some advice from the previous generation about how to do it and thus speed up the process, but Dewey does not really accept it in this sense, though first-hand knowledge is his ideal. He points out that children will have to consult teachers and books for information and ideas to be used in solving their problems and advancing their enquiry, thus resting on other people's shoulders. He is not wholly opposed to such "short-circuited" learning. All that he really insists is that such second-hand knowledge must always come in only in the context of a first-hand activity on the children's part, and, of course, that they must learn how to check up on it if necessary.

As examples of activities or occupations for which schools should provide opportunities—but only for purposes of using them educationally—Dewey mentions making a box, cooking an egg, drawing a picture, sewing and weaving, etc. Any sort of activity is suitable for education if it can be used to develop the dispositions desired, and all teaching should consist in initiating and cooperating in such activities in such an order and in such a way as to bring about those dispositions (attitudes, skills, knowledges, etc.). In a way the methods and the subject-matters are dictated by the activities, but in another way the ordering and guiding of the activities are determined by what the teacher's experience and knowledge tell him about methods and by what he knows are the dispositions to be produced.

> How, then, stands the case of Child *vs*. Curriculum [the list of dispositions to be formed]? . . . The case is of Child. It is his present powers which are to assert themselves; his present capacities which are to be exercised; his present attitudes which are to be realized. But save as the teacher knows, knows wisely and thoroughly, the race-experience which is embodied in that thing we call the Curriculum, the teacher knows neither what the present power, capacity, or attitude is, nor yet how it is to be asserted, exercised, and realized.[60]

Of course, the activities, occupations, or projects engaged in should not always be elementary manual ones, even though "it is possible and desirable that the child's introduction into the more formal subjects of the curriculum be through the medium of these activities."[61] The nature of the activities must be varied and they must become more and more adult. The purpose is the fullest possible growth as earlier construed. But throughout

> . . . the true center of correlation on the school subjects is not science, nor literature, nor history, nor geography, but the child's own social activities.[62]

If the pupils are to be active in this way, it does not follow for Dewey that the teacher is to be a passive spectator. It is still primarily the teacher's responsibility to find the conditions that call out self-educative activity, and to cooperate in and guide this activity so that it leads to the formation of the desired dispositions. He must know "wisely and thoroughly" a great deal, not only about psychology, methods, and his pupils, but also about subject-matter ("the race-experience which is embodied in that thing we call the Curriculum"), and he must bring that knowledge to bear.

> . . . the teacher, as the member of the group having the riper and fuller experience and the greater insight into the possibilities of continuous development found in any suggested project, has not only the right but the duty to suggest lines of activity. . . . [63]

It is also his duty

> . . . to select the influences which shall affect the child and to assist him in properly responding to these influences.[64]

Still in relation to points (a) and (b), it is easy to see why Dewey insists that school activities must have "a sufficiently long time-span"; otherwise nothing very educative can come of them— no discipline, no development of mind, no elaboration of subject matter. But why does he hold that school activity must be physical, at least in part? Philosophically his reason is that he regards mind-body dualism as false. More empirically it is that he does not believe there is any purely mental activity; even the mathematician thinking out a new proof is wrinkling his brow, staring into space, reciting sub-vocal words, or making marks on paper. I do not think he means to deny that there are educative activities which are physical only in this rather minimal way (if he did I should think he was wrong). His point seems to be that a much larger amount of overt physical behavior is normally involved in significantly educational activities—much more than was recognized in traditional education. This is the point of his early and now well-worn story about looking for desks and chairs suited to what he regarded as the educational needs of children.

> We had a good deal of difficulty in finding what we needed, and finally one dealer, more intelligent than the rest, made this remark: "I am afraid we have not what you want. You want something at which the children may work; these are all for listening."[65]

Whether Dewey thought that children should always be moving about is another question, which I shall not try to answer. He certainly did admonish the progressivists that "bare doing, no matter how active, is not enough."[66]

THINKING

We have already noticed the central importance in Dewey's philosophy of the habit of reflective thought. The main point to be added here, in connection with (c), is that Dewey believes that the school activities of the pupils must have to do with a problem and center around the thinking needed to solve it. This is the main reason that bare doing is not enough. Speaking in 1910 of the proximate end of education Dewey says,

> . . . the *intellectual* (as distinct from the *moral*) *end of education is entirely and only . . . the formation of careful, alert, and thorough habits of thinking.*[67]

In 1916 he put it even more strongly, as covering moral as well as intellectual education.

. . . all which the school can or need do for pupils, so far as their *minds* are concerned (that is, leaving out certain specialized muscular abilities), is to develop their ability to think. . . . The sole direct path to enduring improvement in the methods of instruction and learning consists in centering upon the conditions which exact, promote, and test thinking. Thinking *is* the method of intelligent learning, of learning that employs and rewards the mind. . . . the important thing to bear in mind is that thinking is method, the method of an intelligent experience in the course which it takes. The essentials of method are therefore identical with the essentials of reflection.[68]

In other words, according to Dewey, the main principle of method in teaching is to center on activities which promote good habits of thinking, that is, all of the dispositions belonging to the habit or method of intelligence as described earlier.

Given Dewey's conception of the origin and pattern of intelligent thought, this means

. . . first, that the pupil have a genuine situation of experience—that there be a continuous activity in which he is interested for its own sake; secondly, that a genuine problem develop within this situation as a stimulus to thought; third, that he possess the information and make the observations needed to deal with it; fourth, that suggested solutions occur to him which he shall be responsible for developing in an orderly way; fifth, that he have opportunity and occasion to test his ideas by application, to make their meaning clear and to discover for himself their validity.[69]

The practices of the school and the methods of the teacher must then be such as to provide these conditions. In addition, the teacher must take "a sympathetic attitude toward the activities of the learner by entering into a common or conjoint experience"—sharing in such a way that he too is a learner and the pupil a teacher, with neither being unduly conscious of either giving or receiving instruction. The rest, Dewey says, lies with the child.

If he cannot devise his own solution (not of course in isolation, but in correspondence with the teacher and other pupils) and find his own way out he will not learn, not even if he can recite some correct answer with one hundred per cent accuracy.[70]

Concerning the provision of the conditions just listed and the activity of the school and teacher, Dewey has a number of points to make, among them the following. (1) The first stage of contact with any new material, whatever the pupil's age, must inevitably be of the trial and error sort. He must do something, and see what happens. This is the way of real life. Hence the entry to any subject in school must be as unscholastic as possible. It must not be rigged by the teacher. (2) The problem must be the pupil's own problem, not a problem set for him as a pupil by the teacher, and it must be as much as possible like a problem of life outside school. (3) Data, information, knowledge of fact are of crucial importance and must be acquired, as we saw earlier, but they should be acquired for use in enquiry in connection with an activity, not just piled up for their own sake or for purposes of reproduction in recitation and examination. This piling up of knowledge, Dewey says, is an obstacle to educative development and swamps thinking. At the same time, he insists that schools must make a great deal of information available to their pupils in books, pictures, talks, etc. Direct observation is the most vivid and vital source of information, but it has limitations. Memory, reading, and "telling" must also be relied on, though not to excess. (4) The teacher must be ready with ideas and suggestions but should avoid supplying ready-made solutions either through lecturing or reading. The child should be required to do "original," but responsible thinking, and experience "the joy of intellectual constructiveness." (5) If the child does not have substantial opportunity to test his ideas by application, his thinking remains truncated, artificial, and isolated from life, and his learning scholastic and incomplete. (6) It follows that schools should be equipped with kitchens, laboratories, shops, museums, and gardens, as well as libraries, and make free use of dramatizations, plays, and games—not so much for training in vocational skills as for complete and responsible training in thinking.

COOPERATION AND DEMOCRACY

We may take points (d) and (f) together: the educative activities are to be free, cooperative, and democratic. Why? Primarily because, as Dewey conceives of it, reflective enquiry itself is a cooperative and democratic activity. It is typified by science, and science is an activity in which no man is an island. The scientist is a member of a community of enquirers, and science is a cumulative enterprise in which many take part. Within it the atmosphere is one of freedom, openmindedness, objectivity, tolerance, intellectual integrity, cooperation, impartiality, and absence of self-concern. Within it, too, there are seniors who teach and juniors who learn as part of a genuinely cooperative activity. Thus it is the very genius of thinking to be cooperative, social, and democratic.

Dewey also believes that man is essentially social. He does not carry this to the point of agreeing with Aristotle that the individual belongs to the state as his arm belongs to his body, but he does hold that apart from society a man would be no man. Man would not even be able to think, since thought depends on language, which is social. He becomes aware of himself only in relation to others. For these and similar reasons, Dewey thinks that our activities are always at least implicitly social and ought to be explicitly so.

Even if he did not hold this, Dewey would still contend that schoolwork should center in activities which are cooperative and democratic; for only then can it foster the dispositions he regards as desirable—respect for others, concern for the common good, being democratic, etc. Here Dewey is adapting in his own way Aristotle's principle that one becomes just by doing just actions. If this principle is correct, as he thinks it is, school life must be so organized as to furnish occasion for and encourage the performance of actions that will bring into being the desirable dispositions. These dispositions cannot be produced by lecturing—the direct method—but only by the indirect method, and this means, Dewey maintains, that the school life must itself be a cooperative and democratic one. The "older" education, even in nominally democratic countries, was in his eyes too individualistic in one sense and too undemocratic in another to foster truly social interests or thoroughly democratic dispositions.

How far are the teacher and the school administrator to go in being cooperative and democratic? There is a real question here for progressive educators. One hears of pupils being permitted, not only to choose their own projects, but also to decide their grades by vote—or even to decide by majority vote the correct answer to a question. Dewey does not give very clear or specific guide lines in these matters. He does criticize teachers who are afraid to even make suggestions. There must be give and take, "the teacher taking but not being afraid also to give."[71] The essential point is that the occasion be taken educational advantage of, and that the desired dispositions grow and take shape through the process of social intelligence; and this is "the teacher's business." He must not abuse his office, but he must be an educator.

Perhaps it will help here if we remember that Dewey's model seems to be the case of a senior scientist engaged with junior ones in a joint enquiry freely carried on. Here there is cooperation, give and take, and an essential equality, but there is also leadership of a significant kind—and no disposition to use majority vote to decide what is good or what is true. Only the results of experiment can decide this, for what is good or true is what checks out as such in experience.

So much for points (a) to (g). The upshot for Dewey is that the school is to be "a form of community life," as real life is, but "simplified" in such a way as to be conducive to the formation of desirable dispositions—which for him are scientific, social, and democratic ones. It must be a center of democratic living and intelligent enquiry in the form of free cooperative activities involving the solving of problems genuinely suited to the child's interests and capacities.

> . . . the entire spirit of the school is renewed. It has a chance to affiliate itself with life, to become the child's habitat, where he learns through directed living; instead of being only a place to learn lessons having an abstract and remote reference to some possible living to be done in the future. It gets a chance to be a miniature community, an embryonic [ideal] society. This is the fundamental fact, and from this arise continuous and orderly sources of instruction. . . . To do this means to make each one of our schools an embryonic community life, active with types of occupations that reflect the life of the larger society, and permeated throughout with the spirit of art, history, and science. When the school introduces and trains each child . . . into membership within such a little community, saturating him with the spirit of service, and providing him with the instruments of effective self-direction, we shall have the deepest and best guarantee of a larger society which is worthy, lovely, and harmonious.[72]

One of Dewey's illustrations may help to show something of what he has in mind, even though it is incomplete because it does not mention how aesthetic or moral values are brought in.[73] In it boys and girls of ages ten to thirteen are engaged in sewing and weaving, not for any narrow or utilitarian purpose, but because

> . . . this work gives the point of departure from which the child can trace and follow the progress of mankind in history, getting an insight also into the materials used and the mechanical principles involved.

In connection with these occupations the children learn (by use of the library, etc.) the history of man's use of cotton, wool, and other textiles. They learn by observation the difference between cotton and wool fibers, and by experience the importance of the invention of the cotton gin. Thus they come to understand why our ancestors wore woolen instead of cotton clothing. They work this out for themselves "with the actual material, aided by questions and suggestions from the teacher." They even go on to reinvent the first frame for carding wool, and to redevise the simplest process for spinning it. They see the need and the effects of various inventions, and "all that goes with the application of science in the use of our present available powers"; and they review the geography and economics of the sources of materials, the centers of manufacture, and the distribution of products. They study the biology, chemistry, and physics involved in the materials or in the machinery of production. Thus, Dewey contends, they get a better historical and scientific grasp of all that is relevant to their activity than they would by other methods of teaching the same subject matter.

> The occupation supplies the child with a genuine motive; it gives him experience at first hand; it brings him into contact with realities. It does all this, but in addition it is liberalized throughout by translation into its historic values and scientific equivalencies. With the growth of the child's mind in power and knowledge it ceases to be a pleasant occupation merely, and becomes more and more a medium [of education].

Add the aesthetic (appreciative) and the moral or social dimensions which Dewey points to elsewhere, and one has a picture of Deweyan education in its ideal form. One also sees why Dewey says that the teaching involved is harder, not easier, than that of the traditional school—and why it requires more knowledge of various subject-matters on the teacher's part rather than less.

COMPARISON

It will be clear from our account so far that Dewey is opposed to the general use in education of discipline in Kant's sense. He also is opposed to what Aristotle and Kant call instruction, except when it takes the form of Socratic discussion or carrying into practice what is learned. Certainly he seeks to eliminate "work" as Kant defines it from school life; he does not wish school life to be all play in Kant's sense, but it must be made enjoyable for its own sake and intrinsically motivated, even though it must not be merely pleasing and may require self-control and effort. It may even be that Dewey is against what Aristotle calls "habituation" or "practice" and

Kant "exercise"; at least insofar as we know how they conceive these, it appears that the child is more passive than Dewey thinks he should be. For Dewey all learning is to be by freely living through activities and situations in which the desired dispositions are "naturally and necessarily" formed, and all discipline, knowledge, and acquisition of skill is to be integral (not just incidental) to such living.

DISCIPLINE, INFORMATION, AND SKILL

Dewey firmly believes that even if the school is thus made "a place in which the child should really live," it can at the same time give him "the necessary discipline, culture and information" more effectively, more usefully, and with a more liberalizing effect than the older kind of school could.[74] He reminds us that interest is not incompatible with effort, as even play shows, and he argues that in group activities of the sort he envisages there will be several important kinds of discipline—there will be discipline in the fact that the child is required to refrain from merely satisfying momentary impulses, in the fact that he learns to consider others, in the fact that he comes to form interests that include both his own future and that of others, in the fact that he must take a responsible part in the development of the activity, in the fact that he must learn to be impartial, objective, and true to the facts of experience, and in the fact that he is required to think carefully over a considerable period of time. In all this the individual child is helped by the fact that the group, though free, exercises a discipline of its own—a point which gives some countenance to the charge that Deweyan education produces conformity but at least does something to free it of the charge of not providing any discipline. To counter the charge of fostering conformity is the fact that among the dispositions being fostered in and presumably by the group is that of careful independent thought or critical intelligence.

How the acquisition of knowledge comes into Deweyan education has already been indicated. As for skills—a variety of them are almost inevitably acquired, Dewey thinks, by any child who participates actively in a variety of activities and occupations, including possibly reading, writing, languages, weaving, carpentry, etc. What is not so clear is the extent to which Dewey thinks there can and should be planning by the school and the teacher to make sure that certain bodies of information and certain skills are acquired during the course of a pupil's activities and occupations. This question is somewhat neglected in his concern to argue that information and skills should be passed on only in the context of such activities, and not separately for their own sakes or for a possible future use, or just to exercise some faculty (as Kant and the traditionalists thought).

It is important to realize that, although Dewey does give science a unique and central place in education, he does not intend that school children should always be dealing with scientific problems in the strict sense of pure or applied science. Their problem may be an artistic one, like drawing or painting, or it may be social. Dewey does think that the general pattern of reflective thinking should always be used, but he seems to allow that the variety of the activities a child is engaged in during his years in school may be considerable—probably he even thinks that it *ought* to be considerable, but this is another aspect of the question of planning on which he is not very explicit. If the various dispositions he regards as desirable are to be fostered it would seem that the variety of activities should be fairly large.

One might agree with all that Dewey has said so far in this account, and still maintain that education has different kinds or parts, as Aristotle and Kant do, and that different sorts of activities are to be used in the formation of different sorts of dispositions. Dewey, however, rejects such a position. His view seems to be that school materials and methods should be so reconstructed that all desirable dispositions are taught all the time. He refuses, as we saw, to separate moral and intellectual dispositions. Believing that the method of scientific thinking includes certain moral traits of character, he concludes that morality can and should be taught even in the teaching of science. As we also saw, he even suggests sometimes that if only we give children the capacity to think, all the other dispositions will in time be added unto them. If this is so, then, in a sense, for Dewey as for Socrates, excellence is one and it is knowledge, and education is a unity. Even if Dewey does not mean to be quite so intellectualistic, he certainly does believe that if children's problem-solving activities are cooperative in a democratic atmosphere, then all of the desired dispositions will or at least can be effectively fostered, regardless of the particular subject matter. In this sense he definitely is in favor of a unified education.

Thus Dewey argues forcefully against assigning specific educational values to different subjects, as is so often done, and for breaking down boundary lines between subjects, at least for pedagogical purposes. He also contends that for pedagogical purposes, subjects like geometry, chemistry, etc., should at least in the elementary years be de-organized; they should be presented to the pupil not in the "logical" form they have for the expert or for the educated adult, but in a more "psychological" form, namely in the form and to the extent called for by the activity the child is engaged in.

What governs method and subject-matter alike, in Dewey's view, is the activity or occupation in progress and the requirement of using it to promote thinking and the other desirable dispositions. "Subject matter" is "identical with all the objects, ideas, and principles which enter as resources or obstacles into the continuous intentional pursuit of a course of action." "Method" is arranging subject-matter so that it is used most effectively in a course of action for the promotion of the desired dispositions. Method and subject-matter are therefore not separable, as is sometimes thought; they are held together in a unity by the developing course of action.[75] What these rather abstract statements mean will be reasonably clear if one looks back at the illustration of learning about textiles cited earlier.

EDUCATION AND VOCATION

Thus, for Dewey, method is one, subject matter is one, at least pedagogically, and method and subject-matter are one. There is a strong tendency in Dewey's philosophizing to break down all dualisms, distinctions, and separations, and, as his critics have often pointed out, the result is not always a gain. However, even if this tendency does have a somewhat blurring effect, perhaps what has been said will at least be clear enough to convey what Dewey means. Another aspect of his conception of the unity of education comes out in his discussion of vocational education. Dewey does not exclude vocations from the educational picture, as Aristotle does. Certainly he has no wish to disparage the doing of the sorts of things involved in occupations, no matter how manual they may be. Still, he does not believe that any part of education should be specifically or primarily vocational as distinct from being intended to foster the general dispositions listed earlier. Such a vocational education would be "an instrument of perpetuating the existing industrial order of society, instead of operating as a means of its transformation." It would, moreover, tend to train people along such definite lines as to make them unadaptable to social change. Dewey also attacks the notion that there should be two kinds of schools and two kinds of education, a "liberal" one for the relatively few, and a "narrow technical" one for the masses, such as Aristotle in effect subscribes to.

> This scheme denotes . . . simply a perpetuation of the older social division, with its counterpart intellectual and moral dualisms. . . . under conditions where it has much less justification for existence.[76]

All education should be of the kind described above—starting from "various forms of occupation typifying social callings" and bringing out their "intellectual and moral content" through the introduction of relevant historical background, scientific knowledge, and economic, civic, and political understanding. Such an education, Dewey is convinced, would be at once liberal and vocationally effective by virtue of the dispositions it would form; it would prepare the young both for work and for the enjoyment of leisure insofar as one can ask the schools to do so.

SOME SUBJECTS

Dewey has, of course a good deal to say about the usual school subjects, but we can give only a few samples.[77] (1) He sometimes speaks rather cavalierly of history, as pragmatists often do.

> The past just as past is no longer our affair. If it were wholly gone and done with, there would be only one reasonable attitude toward it. Let the dead bury their dead.

But, he hastens to add,

> knowledge of the past is the key to understanding the present. . . . The function of historical and geographical subject matter . . . is to enrich and liberate the more direct and personal contacts of life by furnishing their context. their background and outlook. . . . Perhaps the most neglected branch of history in general education is intellectual history.
> (2) The problem of an educational use of science is . . . to create an intelligence pregnant with belief in the possibility of the direction of human affairs by itself. . . . Science represents the fruition of the cognitive factors in experience. . . . The function which science has to perform in the curriculum is that which it has performed for the race: emancipation from local and temporary incidents of experience, and the opening of intellectual vistas unobscured by the accidents of personal habit and predilection.
> (3) Even in our so-called progressive schools, science is usually treated as a side line, an ornamental extra, not as the chief means of developing the right mental attitudes. It is treated generally as one more body of ready-made information to be acquired by traditional methods, or else as an occasional diversion. That it is the method of all effec-

tive mental approach or attack in all subjects has not even gained a foothold. . . . It should be axiomatic that the development of scientific attitudes of thought, observation, and inquiry is the chief business of study and learning.

(4) Greek and Roman art and institutions made such important contributions to our civilization that there should always be the simplest opportunities for making their acquaintance. But to regard them as *par excellence* the humane studies . . . tend[s] to cultivate a narrow snobbery. . . . Knowledge is humanistic in quality not because it is *about* human products in the past, but because of what it *does* in liberating human intelligence and human sympathy. Any subject matter which accomplishes this result is humane, and any subject matter which does not accomplish it is not even educational.

(5) Education has no more serious responsibility than making adequate provision for enjoyment of recreative leisure; not only for the sake of immediate health, but still more if possible for the sake of its lasting effects upon habits of mind. Art is again the answer to this demand.

SUBJECT MATTER ONCE MORE

One more word is needed about subject matter in Dewey's way of thinking. We saw that he is against a logical or formal presentation of subject matter, e.g. biology, for its own sake. The child, he insists (and Kant agrees), is not up to such a presentation, either intellectually or emotionally; subject matter must come to him in the context of his own problems and activities. Dewey does not leave this matter here, and it would be unfair to represent him as if he did—as both his followers and critics sometimes do (and as he himself sometimes does). He always insists that "the organized subject matter of the adult and the specialist" cannot be taken as the starting point in education, as it was in the traditional school; but he sometimes adds that "it represents the goal toward which education should continuously move."

. . . finding the material for learning within experience is only the first step. The next step is the progressive development of what is already experienced into a fuller and richer and also more organized form, a form that gradually approximates that in which subject-matter is presented to the skilled, mature person.[78]

I am not convinced that Dewey's conception of what this entails is entirely satis*factory*. but his point should go far toward answering some of his critics and restraining some of his followers.

In this connection we should remember that Dewey wrote mainly about elementary education, and that we know rather little about his views about education in high school or college. The passage just quoted at least suggests that he might have had a somewhat more traditional conception of education at these levels. Even if he did, however, he certainly thought that teaching at these levels should be more in accord with that just described than it has been, for he complains that colleges and universities constitute a serious obstacle to the new education he is outlining, because, except for some schools of education, they tend to keep to the old ways in the training of parents and teachers.

MORAL EDUCATION

This is not a separate topic in Dewey's discussion. As we saw, he refuses to regard moral dispositions as distinct in kind or in condition from others, and to think of moral knowledge as distinct from non-moral. He constantly contends that moral education does not call for activities of a different kind from the others belonging to the education of the child. Moral education is part and parcel, an aspect or phase, of all educational activity, requires no separate method and involves no separate subject matter. It consists of acquiring (1) the habit and method of reflective intelligence as a basis of belief and action, (2) the empirical knowledge needed for knowing what to do and what not to do, and (3) the dispositions of benevolence, faithfulness, etc. The acquisition of all of these is provided for by the above scheme.

All of this should be clear on the basis of what has been said, but a few other points need attention. (a) Dewey attacks Kant over and over for saying that good will is the sole moral good, arguing that "meaning well" is not enough even for morality; it is the road to hell that is paved with good intentions, as the saying has it, not the one to heaven. Kant would reply, in part at least, that he means by good will not a mere wish but an actual will to do what is right, but it still remains true that he does not stress the need for empirical knowledge in applying the principles of morality as much as he should, though he does mention that a truly good will will try to get the necessary factual information. (b) Dewey also attacks the method of "direct instruction in morals" which is part of Kant's conception of moral education, if not of Aristotle's, specifically mentioning the use of "catechetical instruction, or lessons about morals" on which Kant relied so much (though by no means entirely).

> Lessons 'about morals' signify as matter of course lessons in
> what other people think about virtues and duties . . . direct
> instruction about morals has been effective only in social.
> groups where it was part of the authoritative control of the
> many by the few.[79]

(c) Dewey does not wholly exclude the use of praise and blame,
approval and disapproval, as instruments of moral education, or even
the use of punishment; but he emphasizes that such instruments must
be thoughtfully used in accordance with the standard of reflective
morality—namely the promotion of the common good—and he seems
to think that, in fact, their use, in anything like their familiar forms,
will tend to disappear as morality becomes more reflective and more
humane.

(4) The most interesting point remaining has to do with the
Socratic-Platonic teaching that identifies knowledge and virtue, referred to earlier in this chapter. Dewey mentions that it was attacked
by Aristotle (and he might have added Kant), and proceeds to defend
it.[80] "The issue turns," he says, "upon what is meant by knowledge."
A "second-handed, largely symbolic" knowledge such as comes from
books and lectures "does not guarantee conduct"; but there is also
first-hand knowledge, gained and tested in one's own experience—
and knowledge of this kind does find direct issue in conduct. This
is proved "every time a man sits on a chair rather than on a stove,
carries an umbrella when it rains, consults a doctor when ill. . . ."
Dewey goes on to say,

> There is every reason to suppose that the same sort of knowl-
> edge of good has a like expression [in conduct]. . . . In truth,
> the problem of moral education in the schools is one with
> the problem of securing knowledge—the knowledge connected
> with the system of impulses and habits. For the use to which
> any known fact is put depends on its connections. The knowl-
> edge of dynamite of a safe-cracker may be identical in verbal
> form with that of a chemist; in fact, it is different, for it is
> knit into connection with different aims and habits, and thus
> has a different import.

The last lines remind us of Aristotle's distinction between cleverness and practical wisdom. Dewey's claim is that knowledge gained
first-hand in the morally well-constructed activities of the ideal school
will bear fruit in similar activities outside of school.

> What is learned and employed in an occupation having an
> aim and involving cooperation with others is moral knowledge.

> . . . For it builds up a social interest and confers the intelligence needed to make that interest effective in practice.

Knowledge acquired through a prolonged education of the right kind—previously described—*is* virtue. That is Dewey's hope, as it was Plato's.

In truth—to borrow Dewey's phrase—there is some unclarity in his statement of this point. It is not the knowledge gained in the course of school activities of the sort described which by itself issues in moral conduct; it is the dispositions formed in and through the activities which also bring knowledge that do so. As far as I can see, the safe-cracker and the chemist might actually have the same knowledge of dynamite, both of them having acquired it first-hand in the course of their own active experience. What really makes them different is the fact that the activities through which they acquired it are different and connected with different aims and habits. It certainly is not the fact that the safe-cracker's knowledge is second-hand and largely symbolic while the chemist's is first-hand and experiential. The whole process is what forms the resulting dispositions, not the knowledge as such. That is all Dewey needs to claim. It must be admitted, however, that, because of the difference in the contexts of the two cases, the knowledge of the safe-cracker is almost certain to be different in itself from that of the chemist, that is, the one will almost certainly know some things the other does not. My point is only that this is not why one of them goes to his own office to work and the other to those of other people.

UNIVERSAL PUBLIC EDUCATION

Dewey accepts our American system of free, compulsory, public education so whole-heartedly that he hardly discusses it. The education he is talking about all the time is such public school education. Whether or not he believes there should also be private schools is not very clear. He does believe that education should make for social unity rather than division, and hence refrain from teaching religion in any sense other than that explained earlier—even though it should also promote individual diversity. At any rate, he, unlike Aristotle and Kant, holds that everyone, boys and girls alike, should have the kind of school education described. Should they have the same education, as some of our contemporary Aristotelians are maintaining? We have already seen that Dewey is opposed to a dual system of general and vocational educations. The same general dispositions are to be fostered in and formed by everyone, but this does not mean that all must go through exactly the same activities or subject-matters in the same order. No particular activity or subject-matter, or arrangement of them, is indispensable, according to Dewey. Besides, the interests and capacities of children vary a great deal—Dewey always attacks the notion that human nature is something fixed and the same in all of us—and hence the methods and subject matters used must be considerably diversified. They must be as diversified as they need be to bring about the greatest construction of good in the lives of individuals that can be consistent with their cooperating democratically for the common good. Robert M. Hutchins reasons as follows in a striking passage:

> Education implies teaching. Teaching implies knowledge. Knowledge is truth. The truth is everywhere the same. Hence education should be everywhere the same.[81]

Now, while there is a sense in which Dewey accepts this conclusion, he denies it in the literal sense in which Hutchins understands it. Even so, he could accept the four premises stated by Hutchins, though he might not—for Hutchins needs a fifth premise to reach his conclusion, namely, that we should *all* be taught *all* the same truths *in the same way*. This is what Dewey denies and Hutchins does not show.

It goes without saying that Dewey is an advocate of academic freedom (as Hutchins is) and of democracy in school government. These are necessary conditions, as he sees it, of school activities being such as to develop in the young the dispositions required for intelligent and democratic living.

> He who would put the freedom of [teachers] in bond, especially freedom of inquiry and communication, creates conditions which finally imperil his own freedom and that of his offspring. . . . The ultimate stay and support of [our] liberties are the schools.[82]

It follows among other things, that

> . . . every teacher should have some regular and organic way in which he can, directly or through representatives democratically chosen, participate in the formation of the controlling aims, methods and materials of the school of which he is a part.[83]

For one thing, he will be a more interested and responsible teacher of the desired excellences if he has a share in determining what goes on. We do not know just what Aristotle thought about these matters, if he thought about them at all, but Kant, at least, would have agreed heartily.

CONCLUSION

It will be observed that, for all his emphasis on experience and practicality, Dewey's discussions of school practices are rarely as concrete and specific as those of Aristotle and Kant. He is concerned to paint his new picture of education only in rather general strokes. Perhaps this is due in part to his belief that more specific recommendations must be even more tentative and are better left for the educational scientist and the teacher to work out by experimental enquiry. After all, philosophy for Dewey is only "the theory of education in its most general phases." At the same time, this generality in his strokes remains one of the reasons his foes have interpreted his picture as a vague one or as meaning what he did not intend, and many of his friends sought to finish it in ways which he could not approve and which made him even more anathema to his enemies. It must be added, however, whatever one thinks of his painting as a whole, that his strokes were often so unclearly articulated or so emphatic in tone as to justify or at least excuse both groups of viewers in their responses to it. My own reproduction of it is intended to be as objective as possible, but it is idealized in much the same way in which Dewey thought the school should be a "simplified" version of society. This is an attempt to help spectators in both camps, as well as others who are viewing Dewey's picture for the first time.

•

CHAPTER FIVE

Comparison of the

Philosophies

•

The primary purpose of this book is to give the reader an opportunity to look long and deeply into three rather different historical philosophies of education, and thus to learn, not only about their authors and the history of the philosophy of education, but also how to think philosophically about education at length and in depth. It is more concerned that he come to know *how* to do philosophy of education for himself than it is that he acquire knowledge *that* Kant believed thus and Aristotle so. "In short," to quote from Kant's announcement of his lectures for 1765–66, "he is to learn, not *thoughts*, but *thinking;* he must be *guided,* not *carried,* if he is to be able to *walk* by himself later."[1] As Kant goes on to explain, it is impossible to *learn philosophy* as one learns history or mathematics; one can only *learn to philosophize.* Moreover, the best way to learn this is to do it, as Kant and Dewey agree. To generalize Aristotle, as we become just by doing just acts, so we acquire any disposition by doing the corresponding acts, and we become philosophers by doing philosophical acts. The hope behind this book is that one may become something of a philosopher of education by doing it three times, at least if one has enough of that maturity that both Aristotle and Kant regard as necessary for philosophy.

This being my purpose, I have sought to help the reader by making frequent comparisons between our three authors, but have only occasionally made comments criticizing or defending one or another of them. I shall not now summarize the various comparisons, but do wish to restate some of them and to add a few more.

COMPARISONS ON THREE BASIC QUESTIONS

COMPARISON OF VIEWS ABOUT DISPOSITIONS

(1) Aristotle and Kant both distinguish intellectual and moral excellences, Aristotle exalting the first and Kant the second. Dewey attacks the distinction. (2) They also distinguish theoretical and practical reason, Aristotle giving primacy to the first and Kant to the second. Again, Dewey attacks the distinction. (3) Kant holds that one is morally virtuous if one has good will or acts from a sense of duty, whether what one does is right or not, and Aristotle that one is morally virtuous only if he does what he thinks is right and if what he thinks is right *is* right. On this point Dewey tends to attack Kant and to agree with Aristotle. (4) The three have different criteria of what is right. Kant is a deontologist, and Dewey a teleologist of a utilitarian kind. Aristotle's position is not entirely clear, but he probably is also a teleologist. If so, he is either an ethical egoist or nationalist, not a utilitarian. (5) In his conception of intellectual excellence Aristotle exalts the kind of intuitively and demonstratively certain knowledge of reality which he believes we have in mathematics, physics, and metaphysics. Dewey denies that we can have this kind of certainty or should even seek for it, and instead conceives of intellectual excellence as being best exemplified by the methods and tentative results of experimental science. Kant largely agrees with Dewey, except that he holds that we have some a priori knowledge of the *phenomenal* world and may and must make certain postulates about the *noumenal* world. Dewey, of course, denies this distinction between the two worlds, while Aristotle in a sense accepts and in a sense rejects it. (6) For Kant, practical reason gives us a priori knowledge of the principles and ends of moral action, but for Dewey all such knowledge is also experimental, though he does not clearly show how it can be. Aristotle is ambiguous; he denies that we can attain mathematical-like certainty in ethics and politics, but still seems to think of the basic propositions of his ethics and politics as fixed and final truths (as do his followers).

COMPARISON OF VIEWS ABOUT AIMS

(7) If we use for our comparison Kant's notion of the *supremum bonum* or unconditionally good, then Aristotle says that it is happiness, and, in fact, that it is contemplation, in direct opposition to

Kant, who says that it is good will. Against both, Dewey insists that neither contemplation nor good will is unconditionally good— for him there is no disposition or activity that can be said always to shine by its own light regardless of its setting. He does believe that each consummatory experience is unconditionally good, but only because it represents an enjoyment which approves itself on reflection inspired by good will and guided by empirical knowledge. (8) If we use for comparison Kant's notion of the *summum bonum,* or complete good, then Aristotle's position is less clear; sometimes he seems to identify it with happiness and happiness with contemplation, sometimes with a combination of contemplation and morally excellent activity. Kant identifies it with happiness (which he identifies with satisfaction) combined with "natural perfection" and conditioned by moral virtue or good will, and Dewey in a way agrees, for he identifies happiness and consummatory experience and regards a consummatory experience as a fusion of enjoyment, good will, and knowledge. (9) Kant, however, talks as if the mere possession of certain *dispositions* (i.e. "perfection") is the ultimate end, whereas Aristotle and Dewey insist that the end must be certain kinds of intrinsically desirable *activities* or *experiences.*

COMPARISON OF VIEWS ABOUT METHODS

(10) Aristotle does not write as much about methods of teaching as Kant or Dewey. Intentionally or not, he stresses subject-matter, and this may in itself betoken what is now called a "subject-centered" approach. Certainly his followers tend to take this approach. Kant and Dewey, under the influence of Rousseau, are more "child-centered." (11) Aristotle regards education as taking a relatively long time, and does not put much stress on the child's being free, autonomous, or even happy during that time. Neither does he emphasize the importance of the child's eventually becoming autonomous, though he does seem to have a certain kind of autonomy in mind for adult citizens, at least implicitly, since he assigns them a turn at taking part in the government. Kant thinks of education as taking a relatively short time and as ending in relatively complete freedom and autonomy. He is also more insistent on treating the child as an end while he is in school, on keeping him happy and allowing him an increasing autonomy, though he stresses the necessity for discipline and work too. Dewey conceives of education as always going on, as involving a minimum of discipline and work, and as being always concerned that the agent-patient (child or adult) be active, free, autonomous, and happy. (12) Aristotle correspondingly puts a stress on the need

for a long period of rather rigorously controlled habituation; Kant and Dewey are equally concerned to prevent the formation of bad habits, but Kant is cautious about the formation of any habits whatsoever, and Dewey, who prefers the word "habit" where I use "disposition," is careful to emphasize that our habits must be flexible and intelligent.

SOME GENERAL COMPARISONS

(13) Socrates' hope was that excellence is basically one—a single basic disposition, namely knowledge—and that it can be taught by a single method, his own method of Socratic discussion. Even though there is a sense in which Aristotle agrees that virtue is knowledge, we may think of him as rejecting Socrates' vision. Excellence is many; there are moral excellences and intellectual ones, and there are several of each kind; and they are taught and acquired by two different methods, neither of which is quite Socratic (though there is a kind of Socratic dialectic in Aristotle's own method of composing his lectures). For Kant too excellence is many; even if moral virtue is in a way one (good will), it is also in a way many (honesty, benevolence, etc.), and, in any case, there are also non-moral excellences; and five different methods are required in teaching or achieving them, the Socratic method being only the best form of one of these. He even seems to hold that, though empirically moral virtue is a product of education, virtue is noumenally or transcendentally (i.e. really) not a product of education at all, but of a free choice whose ground is unknowable—if it has a ground. As I intimated earlier, Dewey can be thought of as returning to Socrates' vision, though with a difference. Dewey is more of a pluralist about the good or happiness than Socrates implicitly was; but he is trying to find a single, if complex, disposition that will generate all the others and that is teachable by a single, if complex, method. The disposition is the habit or method of scientific intelligence—this corresponds to Socrates' knowledge but is differently conceived; and the method of teaching it is a kind of expansion of the Socratic method—this too did in a way start from the pupil's eros and enlist his participation in any inquiry carried on by a group—an expansion that makes it suitable to everyone and not only to the elite who followed Socrates. Neither the method used nor the result envisaged is as simple or monolithic as that of Socrates', for the whole conception of a common and fixed human nature implied in the Socratic notion of a single eros in all men with a single definable or intuitable end is given up by Dewey, but the vision is essentially the same.

It may be of interest here to see, in this light, what alternatives are open to one who rejects Dewey's position—though I do not mean this as an argument in favor of Dewey. (a) He may keep the Socratic vision of the disposition to be sought and the Socratic-Platonic conception of the method to be used. (b) He may keep the vision and form some other conception of the disposition or method—and this conception may be either an intellectualistic one as Plato's and Dewey's are, a moralistic one, one which is both anti-intellectualistic and anti-moral, or perhaps a neutral (e.g. an aesthetic) one. (c) He may give up the vision for some form of the line Protagoras is represented as taking in Plato's dialogue: that excellence is many and can be taught, but not by the single method of instruction (including discussion). Then he may follow Aristotle or Kant, or take off on some line of his own. (d) He may give up education, conceived as a planned and purely human enterprise, for all or at least some of the basic excellences, and rest his hopes on divine revelation or infusion, on some existential choice (as Kant may be doing), or on both. Something of this sort is done by many existentialists and theologians.

(14) As the last comparison shows, Dewey is an optimist, believing that *everyone* can be given *his* kind of education with a reasonable chance of success. That is one possible program for us. A second is that of Aristotle—to give a rather different kind of education to a relatively select class (people with the intellect and spirit of the Greeks). He too is an optimist, but on a smaller scale; he hopes that his education will succeed with the few, and that the few are enough to keep the rest of the world at bay, in submission, or in a state of unrebellious content. Kant offers us a third program—an intermediate kind of education for an intermediate-sized group (all male human beings). He is more pessimistic than Dewey and perhaps even Aristotle, for he sees a factor of "radical evil" in man and posits an ultimate and possibly uneducable choice that may go either way. At the same time, he believes that man is predisposed to good, that there is an active God behind nature and history, and that a world republic of perpetual peace is part of the destiny of man on earth. There is a fourth alternative, not represented by our authors, namely, to adopt Kant's position, but give up his belief in a temporal kingdom of God and substitute for it a belief in a non-temporal one. This is what Niebuhr and many others do, but it takes us out of philosophy and into something else.

(15) Aristotle stands resolutely for the view that what we all want in life is to exercise our faculties excellently, that the good, the happy, and the virtuous life is a life of excellent activity, and that this excellent activity consists primarily of rational cognition and secondarily of rational feeling, choice, and conduct. In short, he stands for the life of reason. As Santayana saw it,

> In Aristotle the conception of human nature is perfectly sound; everything ideal has a natural basis and everything natural an ideal development. His ethics . . . [is] therefore entirely final. The Life of Reason finds there its classic explication.[2]

Moreover, Aristotle believes that with luck, practical wisdom, and education, such a life is possible for a sufficient number of men and that the rest may find such fulfillment as they are capable of in doing well the sorts of things (art, crafts, work, etc.) that subserve and maintain the good life for those who can live it (or alternatively in doing well those things which they are capable of doing and which come closest to embodying such a life). All men and all things, for Aristotle, strive to imitate God's life of pure intellectual contemplation, and "irrational man" is neither natural, nor inevitable, nor ideal. His vision may seem to contemporary realists to be utterly romantic, but it is the epitome of classicism.

Kant and Dewey too are on the side of the life of reason, of rational as against irrational man, although they were influenced by Christianity and Rousseau, and although Kant was one of the progenitors of romanticism and Dewey one of its many progeny. In a sense Kant gives us another classical ideal. Like Aristotle he believes that our lives should be governed by reason and distinguishes practical and theoretical reason; unlike Aristotle he gives practical reason primacy over theoretical reason and, like Rousseau, ranks morality above contemplation. But he regards morality still as entirely rational; for him it is rational morality that should be supreme in life, not just as a means, but as an end. Where Aristotle exalts knowing, Kant exalts doing. And Kant, even more than Aristotle, believes in the a priori, non-experimental character of moral insight.

Dewey's picture is modern and unclassical (though not therefore true). He breaks down the distinctions between intellectual and moral excellence and between theoretical and practical reason. He conceives of all reason as practical but thinks of practical reason as empirical, or, rather, as scientifically experimental, rejecting the belief in a priori bases of thought or action; and he asserts that practical reason so conceived—in other words, scientific intelligence—should be taken as a basis for all our knowing, feeling, and action. The good, the happy, and the virtuous life is a life of scientific intelligence and of the consummatory experiences it makes possible. This is Dewey's explication of the life of reason to which education is to minister. Where Aristotle exalts knowing, and Kant doing, Dewey exalts active knowing and knowing action in tandem; but while they neglect making, Dewey advocates a life in which knowing, doing, *and* making, all experimentally based, find an equal place in the generation, enrichment, and control of consummatory experience.

The reader should not be left, however, without any indication of the direction in which I think he should walk by himself when he no longer has a guide. I shall end, therefore, with a personal statement that is not intended to be exhaustive but may be of some use even though it is presented without the argumentation needed to make it properly philosophical.[3]

(1) I do not accept the general philosophical position of any of our three authors. As far as I can see, however, this does not preclude my subscribing, in essentials, to any one of the three philosophies of education presented by them.

(2) When I view the sets of dispositions listed by the three men, I find myself with Kant and Dewey as against Aristotle. Aristotle's moral virtues do not include benevolence and equal respect for all men, as theirs do, and his intellectual excellences do not include anything like the scientific intelligence so important for Dewey and even Kant. Again, Aristotle ranks the intellectual above the moral excellences, as if the first take priority over the second in case of conflict, while Kant and Dewey do not. Moreover, like them, I doubt that we have the kind of intuitively and demonstratively certain knowledge of the world that forms the core of the excellences of theoretical intellect as Aristotle sees them. Also, although Aristotle's excellences may be given a more democratic rendering, it remains that they are conceived by him in aristocratic terms, especially justice and greatnesss of soul. In any case, his criterion of right, wrong, and moral virtue, whether it be egoistic or nationalistic, seems to me quite unacceptable.

On the other hand, I am inclined to join Aristotle and Kant in distinguishing theoretical and practical reason, moral and intellectual excellences, etc., and, in fact, to make all of the distinctions Dewey tries to unmake.

As between Kant and Dewey—well, I remain somewhere between them, especially in moral philosophy. Dewey's moral standard is rather vague but appears to be a utilitarian one, and I do not see that it can account for all legitimate moral claims, especially those of justice; on this point it seems to me that the deontologists are right. But I agree with Dewey that Kant is too drastic in his tendency to disregard the value of consequences for the determination of what is right (I also mistrust Aristotle's deontological suggestion in one passage that some kind of "perception" tells us what is right or wrong). I side with Kant against Aristotle in thinking that one need not do what is actually right in order to be virtuous, but I join Dewey in thinking that mere good intention is not enough either. "The harm that good men do," as Bertrand Russell calls it, must be deplored and somehow prevented, as well as that done by bad men. I very much question, as Kant would, Dewey's apparent belief that a disposition to be benevolent is somehow contained in or generated by the habit or method of scientific intelligence. Like Kant, I am much less sure that virtue is knowledge than Dewey is, in spite of the plausibility of much of what Dewey says. And, finally, I am not persuaded that all intellectual excellences follow the pattern of the experimental sciences. Some philosophers even deny that Dewey understands scientific method correctly, but, whether this is so or not, it does seem to me that mathematics and history cannot be fitted into the same experimental pattern as readily as Dewey thinks they can.

(3) About the ultimate end of education, as I have indicated, Kant seems to me to be wrong in so far as he suggests that the end is simply the possession of good will and/or of other *dispositions*. The ultimate end must be some kind of activity or experience, as Aristotle and Dewey hold (though Dewey does not like the phrase "ultimate end"). I doubt, however, that the end can even be morally good *activity* as such, and nothing else, for it seems to me that morality must involve a concern about something besides itself, namely the happiness or unhappiness of people's lives. Hence Kant seems to me wiser when he says that the end is a combination of good will, happiness, and natural perfection. In any case, I am not convinced by his arguments to show that good will is unconditionally good, any more than Dewey is or Aristotle would be.

Aristotle construes the end as excellent intellectual activity, especially pure contemplation, Dewey as consummatory experiences of all sorts, but all including a contemplative element, namely, a perception of their meaning, and all approvable in the light both of their conditions and their consequences. Aristotle is more monistic here, Dewey more pluralistic. Dewey argues, as Kant does, that contemplation by itself is not unconditionally good; in fact, he goes further and contends that *no* kind of activity or experience is *always* unconditionally good and that *any* kind of activity or experience may *sometimes* be unconditionally good if its being engaged in or enjoyed is compatible with good will and reliable knowledge. In all this Dewey seems to me to be on the whole on the right track, both when he is with Aristotle against Kant and with Kant against Aristotle.

(4) About teaching methods, etc., I cannot but approve the general trend of thought from Aristotle through Kant to Dewey— the increasing recognition of the importance of empirical science as a "subject" in the curriculum and as a basis of belief and action both in education and in other areas, the increasing emphasis on autonomy, freedom, democracy, and on the happiness of children,

and the decreasing role of discipline, pain, punishment, and the like. However, I do somewhat deplore the increasing neglect of the importance of knowing the truth, though I sympathize with Dewey's insistence on the need to develop "intelligence as a method" instead of merely inculcating "fixed conclusions." As a university professor still guilty of the rather traditional methods and notions Deweyans complain of as lingering on in our centers of higher education, I doubt that education can or should dispense with discipline, telling, etc., as completely, or confine itself to what can be learned by first-hand doing as wholly, or disorganize and recombine subject-matters quite so much, as Dewey and his followers appear to think (and I have indicated that Dewey himself does not carry such thinking to the furthest extreme). I doubt too that we have the time or the teaching skill to use his methods without modification. Hence I tend to pull back somewhat in the direction of Kant and Aristotle. At the same time, I find most approvable those items in Aristotle and Kant in which they approach Dewey in one way or another, and have put some stress on these; and I see much justice in the principles underlying Dewey's critique of traditional education, especially the ethical principles. As for his empirical claims, it is hardly in my capacity as a philosopher to pronounce for or against them, for they can and should be challenged, if at all, only on empirical grounds. All in all, I can discern a version of Dewey—more or less like the one given earlier—which strikes me as a statement of what education ought to be like. If it only could be like that! If it—or at least public education—could be like that in its main outlines, if not in detail, and effectively produce the sorts of dispositions Dewey calls for on his positive side (leaving religion to the home, the church, and private schools), what a "bettered community life" we would have.

FOOTNOTES

CHAPTER ONE

1. *The Principles of Psychology* (New York: Henry Holt and Co., 1890), I, p. 127.

2. John Dewey, *Democracy and Education* (New York: The Macmillan Company, 1916), pp. 3f.

3. *Laches, Protagoras, Meno, Enthydemus,* trans. W.R. M. Lamb (New York: G. P. Putnam's Sons, 1924), p. 265.

4. *Mysticism and Logic,* (London: George Allen and Unwin, 1917), p. 37.

5. *Nicomachean Ethics,* Book I, Chapter 9, 1099b; trans. H. Rackham (Cambridge, Mass.: Harvard University Press, 1934), p. 47.

6. *Philosophy of Education,* (New York: The Macmillan Company, 1951), p. 427; cf. p. 301.

CHAPTER TWO

1. Plato, *Laches, Protagoras, Meno, Enthydemus,* trans. W.R. M. Lamb (New York: G. P. Putnam's Sons, 1924), pp. 7f.

2. Aristotle, *Nicomachean Ethics* (hereafter called *Ethics*), Book X, Chapter 9, 1179b.

3. *Ethics,* I, 9, 1099b.

4. *Politics,* Book IV, Chapter 1, 1288b.

5. *Ethics,* I, 3, 1095a; trans. W. D. Ross, (New York: The World's Classics, Oxford University Press, 1954), p. 3.

6. Ernest Barker, *The Politics of Aristotle* (New York: Galaxy Books, Oxford University Press, 1962), p. lii.

7. *Ethics,* I, 3, 1094b; cf. 1098a, 1104a; trans. H. Rackham (Cambridge, Mass.: Harvard University Press, 1934), p. 9.

8. *Ethics,* I, 7, 1098a.

9. *Ethics,* I, 7, 1098a; Rackham, p. 33.

10. *Ethics,* I, 7, 1098a.

11. *Ethics,* I, 13, 1102a.

12. See William K. Frankena, *Ethics* (Englewood Cliffs, N.J.: Prentice-Hall, Inc., 1963), pp. 13–16.

13. *Ethics,* II, 2, 1103b.

14. *Ethics,* II, 6, 1107a.

15. *Ethics,* II, 9, 1109a; cf. II, 6, 1106b; Rackham, p. 111.

16. *Aristotle: The Nicomachean Ethics* (Oxford: Oxford at the Clarendon Press, 1951), pp. 87–88.

17. *Ethics,* II, 9, 1109b; cf. IV, 5, 1126ab; Rackham, p. 113.

18. *Ethics,* VII, 3, 1147a.

19. *Ethics,* VI, 5, 1140ab.

20. *Ethics,* I, 2, 1094b.

21. W. D. Ross, *Aristotle* (Cleveland: Meridian Books, Inc., The World Publishing Company, 1959), pp. 184, 199f., 211, 215, 226f.

22. Joachim, *Aristotle: The Nicomachean Ethics,* pp. 164, 188, 214, 218.

23. *Eudemian Ethics.*

24. *Aristotle* (New York: Oxford Paperbacks, Oxford University Press, 1962), pp. 231-246.

25. *Ethics,* II, 4, 1105a; cf. VI, 12, 1144a.

26. *Ethics,* II, 3, 1104b.

27. Jacques Maritain, *Education at the Crossroads* (New Haven: Yale Paperbounds, Yale University Press, 1960), p. 52.

28. *Ethics,* IV, 3, 1123b-1125a.

29. *Politics,* I, 13, 1260a.

30. *Ethics,* VII, 10, 1152a.

31. *Posterior Analytics,* 100ab; cf. *Metaphysics,* 980–981b; *The Basic Works of Aristotle,* ed. Richard McKeon (New York: Random House, 1941), p. 185.

32. *Ethics,* I, 7, 1098b.

33. See *Ethics,* VII, 3, 1147a; VI, 7, 1141b; VI, 11, 1143b.

34. *Metaphysics,* 981a; McKeon, p. 689

35. *Ethics,* VI, 13, 1144b.

36. *Ethics,* VI, 12, 1144a; Rackham, p. 369.

37. *Ethics,* V, 2, 1130b; Rackham, p. 267.

38. *Politics,* VIII, 1, 1337a; Barker, p. 332.

39. *Metaphysics,* 1047b.

40. *Politics,* VII, 13, 1332b.

41. *Metaphysics,* 1048a; *On the Soul,* 417ab.

42. *Ethics,* II, 1, 1103ab.

43. *Ethics,* X, 9, 1179b; cf. I, 3, 1095a.

44. *Politics,* VIII, 1, 1337a.

45. D. Riesman, *The Lonely Crowd* (New York: Anchor Books, Doubleday & Company, Inc., 1950).

46. Joachim, *Aristotle: The Nicomachean Ethics;* A. E. Taylor, *Aristotle* (New York: Dover Publications, Inc., 1955), Chapter V.

47. *Ethics,* X, 9, 1180a; Ross, p. 272.

48. *Politics,* VIII, 1, 1337a.

49. *Politics,* I, 2, 1252b.

50. *Politics,* VII, 13, 1332a.

51. *Politics,* VIII, 2, 1337ab.

52. *Loc. cit.*

53. *Politics,* VII, 14, 1333a.

54. *Politics,* VIII, 3, 1338b.

55. *Politics,* VIII, 5, 1339a.

56. *Politics,* VIII, 4, 1338b.

57. *Politics,* VII, 16, 1335b.

58. *Poetics,* 1447a-1448a; McKeon, pp. 1457ff.

59. *Poetics,* 1451b; in Greek *historia* includes history, natural history, etc.

60. *Ethics,* VI, 8, 1142a.

61. *A History of Education in Antiquity* (New York: Mentor Books, New American Library of World Literature, Inc., 1964), pp. 193ff.

62. *Politics*, VIII, 3, 1337a.

63. *Politics*, VIII, 6, 1340b.

64. *Politics*, I, 13, 1260b.

65. R. M. Hutchins, *The Higher Learning in America* (New Haven: Yale Paperbounds, Yale University Press, 1962), p. 66.

CHAPTER THREE
1. I. Kant, *Education*, trans. Annette Churton (Ann Arbor: Ann Arbor Paperbacks, University of Michigan Press, 1960), pp. 7–8.

2. There have been two English translations, the one by A. Churton in 1900 and another by E. F. Buchner in 1904. References in this book are to the former in the Ann Arbor Paperback edition, though I have often used my own translation.

3. See *Education*, p. 14.

4. See *Education*, p. 22.

5. *Education*, Churton, pp. 1, 6.

6. See *Education*, pp. 1, 18-20.

7. See *Education*, p. 23.

8. *Education*, Churton, p. 45.

9. See *Education*, p. 26.

10. *Lectures on Ethics* (London: The Century Co., 1930), pp. 138f.

11. See *Education*, p. 19.

12. *Education*, Churton, p. 60.

13. See *Education*, p. 77.

14. Kant lists the faculty of cognition thus in *Education*, p. 78, but this seems a mistake, for he usually lists reason, judgment, and understanding as faculties of cognition.

15. *Critique of Pure Reason*, trans. N. K. Smith (London: Macmillan and Co., 1929), p. 177.

16. *Critique of Judgment*, trans. J, H. Bernard (London: Macmillan and Co., 1892), pp. 189–191, 253.

17. See *Education*, p. 30; Miss Churton mistranslates this to include a reference to vocations.

18. Miss Churton says "discretion" where I say "prudence." For quotations in this discussion see *Education*, pp. 95f., 19.

19. See *Education*, p. 20.

20. See *Education*, p. 30.

21. Part II, A, 3. See also *Education*, pp. 84, 98f.

22. Quoted by E. F. Buchner, *Kant's Educational Theory* (Philadelphia: J. P. Lippincott Co., 1904), p. 227.

23. Quotations in this paragraph are from *The Doctrine of Virtue* (Part II of *The Metaphysics of Morals*), trans. Mary J. Gregor (New York: Harper Torchbooks, Harper & Row, Publishers, 1964), pp. 54, 41f., 65.

24. *Religion Within the Limits of Reason Alone*, trans. T. M. Greene and H. H. Hudson (New York: Harper Torchbooks, Harper & Row, 1960); see pp. 20, 51 here.

25. *Doctrine of Virtue*, Gregor, p. 53.

26. *Education*, Churton, pp. 96f.

27. Quoted by Ernst Cassirer, *Rousseau, Kant, and Goethe* (New York: Harper Torchbooks, Harper & Row, Publishers, 1963), pp. 1f.

28. *Doctrine of Virtue*, Gregor, p. 149.

29. This list is based on *The Doctrine of Virtue*.

30. *Doctrine of Virtue*, Gregor, p. 44.

31. *Doctrine of Virtue*, Gregor, pp. 44f.

32. *Doctrine of Virtue*, Gregor, p. 45.

33. *Doctrine of Virtue*, Gregor, p. 52.

34. *Doctrine of Virtue*, Gregor, pp. 52, 107.

35. *Doctrine of Virtue*, Gregor, p. 47.

36. *Doctrine of Virtue*, Gregor, pp. 53f.; cf. 154.

37. *Education*, Churton, pp. 30, 66.

38. *Education*, Churton, pp. 14, 15; see *Lectures on Ethics*, p. 253.

39. *Education*, Churton, p. 11; see also p. 9.

40. *Foundations of the Metaphysics of Morals*, trans. L. W. Beck (New York: Liberal Arts Press, The Bobbs-Merrill Co., Inc., 1959), p. 9.

41. *Loc. cit.*

42. See *Foundations of the Metaphysics of Morals*, Beck, pp. 18, 42.

43. *Foundations of the Metaphysics of Morals*, p. 19, cf. p. 40.

44. *Foundations of the Metaphysics of Morals*, p. 47.

45. *Doctrine of Virtue*, Gregor, p. 55.

46. *Doctrine of Virtue*, Gregor, pp. 55f.

47. See *Lectures on Ethics*, pp. 247-251.

48. See *Perpetual Peace* and *Idea for a Universal History with Cosmopolitan Intent*.

49. See *Education*, Churton, p. 1.

50. *Education*, Churton, pp. 23f.

51. See *Education*, Churton, p. 77.

52. *Education*, Churton, pp. 39, 64f; cf. *Lectures on Ethics*, p. 248.

53. *Education*, Churton, pp. 26, 85f.

54. *Education*, Churton, p. 88.

55. *Education*, Churton, p. 89.

56. *Education*, Churton, pp. 68, 70.

57. *Education*, Churton, pp. 86f.

58. *Education*, Churton, p. 75; cf. pp. 78f.

59. *Education*, Churton, p. 80.

60. *Education*, Churton, p. 81.

61. *Education,* Churton, p. 99.

62. *Doctrine of Virtue,* Gregor, p. 150; cf. p. 74.

63. *Education,* Churton, pp. 103f.

64. See *Foundations of the Metaphysics of Morals,* Beck, p. 25.

65. *Doctrine of Virtue,* Gregor, p. 159.

66. *Critique of Practical Reason,* trans. L. W. Beck (New York: Liberal Arts Press, The Bobbs-Merrill Co., Inc., 1956), p. 158.

67. *Loc. cit.*

68. *Doctrine of Virtue,* Gregor, p. 152.

69. *Loc. cit.*; cf. *Education,* Churton, pp. 105f.

70. *Critique of Practical Reason,* Beck, pp. 158f.

71. *Education,* Churton, p. 112.

72. *Religion,* Greene and Hudson, p. 3.

73. See *Education,* Churton, pp. 11, 15, 108.

74. Cf. esp. Book I.

75. *Religion,* Greene and Hudson, p. 40.

76. *Education,* Churton, p. 93; cf. pp. 31f.

77. *Education,* Churton, p. 26.

78. *Loc. cit.*

79. Quoted by Buchner, *Kant's Educational Theory,* p. 226.

CHAPTER FOUR
1. *The Problems of Men* (New York: Philosophical Library, Inc., 1946), p. 20.

2. *Democracy and Education* (New York: Macmillan Paperbacks. The Macmillan Company, 1961), pp. 328, 332.

3. John Dewey, *On Experience, Nature, and Freedom,* ed. B. J. Bernstein (New York: Liberal Arts Press, The Bobbs-Merrill Co., Inc., 1960), p. 14.

4. *Democracy and Education,* p. 329.

5. *The Quest for Certainty* (New York: Minton, Balch and Co., 1929), p. 252.

6. *The Philosophy of John Dewey,* ed. P. A. Schilpp (New York: Tudor Publishing Co., 1939), p. 563.

7. *Quest for Certainty,* pp. 107, 256, 284.

8. See *Rationalism in Politics* (London: Methuen and Co., Inc., 1962); the quotations in the text are from pp. 61, 66f.

9. John Dewey, *Theory of the Moral Life* (New York: Holt, Rinehart & Winston, Inc., 1960), p. 12.

10. *Theory of the Moral Life,* p. 36.

11. *How We Think* (Boston: D. C. Heath & Company, 1910), p. 6. Italics removed.

12. For accounts of this pattern, see *How We Think,* chapter VI, and *Democracy and Education,* chapter XI.

13. *Human Nature and Conduct* (New York: Modern Library, Inc., 1922), p. 133.

14. *Human Nature and Conduct*, pp. 295f.

15. *Theory of the Moral Life*, p. 144.

16. *Reconstruction in Philosophy* (New York: Mentor Books, New American Library of World Literature, Inc., 1950), p. 133; *Democracy and Education*, p. 179.

17. *Problems of Men*, p. 91.

18. *Theory of the Moral Life*, p. 147.

19. *Theory of the Moral Life*, pp. 66f.

20. *Human Nature and Conduct*, p. 326.

21. *Theory of the Moral Life*, pp. 69f.

22. *Theory of the Moral Life*, p. 83.

23. *Theory of the Moral Life*, p. 147.

24. *Theory of the Moral Life*, pp. 142f.

25. *Theory of the Moral Life*, p. 168.

26. *Theory of the Moral Life*, p. 163.

27. *Quest for Certainty*, pp. 221f.

28. *Democracy and Education*, p. 238; cf. *Quest for Certainty*, p. 262.

29. See *A Common Faith* (New Haven: Yale University Press, 1934).

30. *Democracy and Education*, p. 238; cf. pp. 79, 99, 322.

31. *Quest for Certainty*, p. 252.

32. *Dewey on Education*, ed. M. S. Dworkin (New York: Bureau of Publications, Teachers' College, Columbia University, 1959), p. 30.

33. *Democracy and Education*, p. 79.

34. *Intelligence in the Modern World*, ed. J. Ratner (New York: Modern Library, Inc., 1939), p. 692.

35. See *Experience and Education* (New York: Macmillan & Co., 1938), pp. 13, 16.

36. *Theory of the Moral Life*, p. 147.

37. *The Public and Its Problems* (New York: Henry Holt & Co., Inc., 1927), pp. 200f.

38. *Reconstruction in Philosophy*, p. 147.

39. *Loc. cit.*

40. Resp., *Democracy and Education*, pp. 76, 239f., 76f.; *Experience and Education*, p. 16.

41. *Theory of the Moral Life*, pp. 45f.

42. *Theory of the Moral Life*, pp. 50f.

43. *Theory of the Moral Life*, pp. 53f.

44. *Quest for Certainty*, pp. 259, 260f., 264, 268, 286; cf. also *Theory of Valuation* (Chicago: University of Chicago Press, 1939).

45. *Quest for Certainty*, p. 267.

46. *Democracy and Education*, pp. 241f.

47. *Theory of the Moral Life*, p. 100.

48. *Theory of the Moral Life*, p. 62.

49. *Theory of the Moral Life,* pp. 61f.

50. *Theory of the Moral Life,* p. 167.

51. *Theory of the Moral Life,* p. 104.

52. *Experience and Education,* pp. 25f.

53. *Experience and Education,* p. 19.

54. *Democracy and Education,* p. 180.

55. *Democracy and Education,* p. 109.

56. *Dewey on Education,* p. 125.

57. For these quotations, see *Democracy and Education,* pp. 240, 237, 242f., 240, resp.

58. *Dewey on Education,* p. 54.

59. *Dewey on Education,* p. 22.

60. *Dewey on Education,* p. 111.

61. *Dewey on Education,* p. 26.

62. *Dewey on Education,* p. 25.

63. *Dewey on Education,* p. 124.

64. *Dewey on Education,* p. 24.

65. *Dewey on Education,* p. 50.

66. *Dewey on Education,* p. 122.

67. *How We Think,* pp. 57f.

68. *Democracy and Education,* pp. 152f., 163.

69. *Democracy and Education,* p. 163.

70. *Democracy and Education,* p. 160.

71. *Experience and Education,* p. 85.

72. *Dewey on Education,* pp. 41, 49.

73. *Dewey on Education,* pp. 43ff.

74. *Dewey on Education,* pp. 54, 68.

75. *Democracy and Education,* p. 138; cf. chapters XIII and XIV.

76. For quotations, see *Democracy and Education,* pp. 316, 319.

77. For quotations, see *Democracy and Education,* pp. 214, 211, 216, 225, 230; *Philosophy and Civilization,* p. 326; *Democracy and Education,* 205.

78. For these passages, see *Experience and Education,* pp. 103, 87.

79. *Democracy and Education,* p. 354.

80. See *Democracy and Education,* pp. 354–356.

81. *The Higher Learning in America* (New Haven: Yale Paperbounds, Yale University Press, 1962), p. 66.

82. *Intelligence in the Modern World,* Ratner, pp. 725, 723.

83. *Intelligence in the Modern World,* Ratner, p. 717.

CHAPTER FIVE

1. Quoted by Buchner, *Kant's Educational Theory,* p. 264.

2. George Santayana, *Reason in Common Sense* (New York: Charles Scribner and Sons, 1905), p. 21.

3. Throughout, for my ethics and theory of value, see Frankena, *Ethics* (Englewood Cliffs, N.J.: Prentice-Hall, Inc., 1963)

BIBLIOGRAPHICAL ESSAY

In the text I approached the educational philosophies of our authors mainly by way of their ethical and political theories, because I believe that one's answers to the three questions of a normative philosophy of education are or should be determined primarily by his ethical and political views. I shall accordingly make ethical and political works central in this bibliographical note, along with educational ones. Where possible I shall list the works cited in readily available editions.

There are, of course, many books and essays on the philosophy of education that might be mentioned in connection with Chapter I, besides those referred to in the footnotes. Among them, three of the most helpful are D. J. O'Connor, *An Introduction to the Philosophy of Education* (London: Routledge & Kegan Paul, 1957), especially chapters 1 and 5; John Lenz, *Philosophy of Education* (Englewood Cliffs, N.J.: Prentice-Hall Inc., 1964); and the introduction to the book by Kingsley Price listed below. I make another, closely similar statement in the introduction to my book, *Philosophy of Education* (New York: The Macmillan Company, 1965). The reader may also consult the works by Israel Scheffler and R. S. Peters in the Scott, Foresman Keystones of Education series.

Of Aristotle's works the central ones are the *Nicomachean Ethics* and the *Politics,* which are available in a number of paperback editions, e.g. the Penguin Classics series. E. F. Barker's *The Politics of Aristotle* (New York: Galaxy Book Oxford University Press, 1962) is useful because of its introduction and notes. I have made my references to Aristotle's works in such a way that any edition of them can be used, and have followed no single translation, frequently preferring my own. Aristotle's psychology and epistemology are to be found especially in *De Anima* (*On the Soul*) and *Posterior Analytics,* both available in *Introduction to Aristotle,* edited by Richard McKeon (New York: The Modern Library, 1947). Practically all of Aristotle's relevant works are included in McKeon's *The Basic Works of Aristotle* (New York: Random House, 1941).

Good general introductions to Aristotle's philosophy are W. D. Ross, *Aristotle* (Cleveland: Meridian Books, Inc., The World Publishing Company, 1959); A. E. Taylor, *Aristotle,* (New York: Dover Publications, Inc., 1955); and D. J. Allen, *The Philosophy of Aristotle* (London: Oxford University Press, 1952). *Aristotle: The Nicomachean Ethics,* by H. H. Joachim (Oxford: Oxford at the Clarendon Press, 1951) is an excellent commentary and contains much material bearing on Aristotle's philosophy of education. There are very few useful and available accounts of his philosophy of education as such, besides those given in such general histories as are listed below, but I may mention in this connection E. F. Barker's account in *Political Thought of Plato and Aristotle* (New York: Dover Publications, Inc., 1959), Chapter X. Some important references to Aristotle may be found in H. I. Marrou, *A History of Education in Antiquity* (New York: Mentor Books, New American Library of

World Literature, Inc., 1964); and W. Jaeger, *Paideia*, Volumes I–III (New York: Oxford University Press, 1939–1945).

On Kant's book on education, see footnote 2, Chapter 3 of the present text. All of Kant's works contain passages on education and materials bearing on his philosophy of education. For the most part these are indicated above in the text and footnotes. Many of the passages are quoted by E. F. Buchner, in *Kant's Educational Theory* (Philadelphia: J. B. Lippincott Co., 1904), pp. 225–292. Kant's ethical theory is contained in the following works, all available in popular editions: *Foundations of the Metaphysics of Morals*, translated with an introduction by L. W. Beck (New York: The Liberal Arts Press, The Bobbs-Merrill Co., Inc., 1959); *Critique of Practical Reason*, translated with an introduction by L. W. Beck (New York: Liberal Arts Press, The Bobbs-Merrill Co., Inc., 1956); Part II of *The Metaphysics of Morals*, on which I have relied a great deal, translated by J. Ellington (New York: Liberal Arts Press, The Bobbs-Merrill Co., Inc. 1964) and, under the title *The Doctrine of Virtue*, by Mary J. Gregor (New York: Harper Torchbooks, Harper & Row, Publishers, 1964); and *Lectures on Ethics*, translated by L. Infeld (New York: Harper Torchbooks, Harper & Row, Publishers, 1963). Pages 242–253 of *Lectures on Ethics* are especially important for Kant's views on education. Kant's political philosophy is contained mainly in *Perpetual Peace*, edited by A. R. Caponigri (New York: Liberal Arts Press, The Bobbs-Merrill Co., Inc., 1948); and *Idea for a Universal History with Cosmopolitan Intent*, edited and translated

by W. Hastie (Edinburgh: T. and T. Clark, 1891). Selections from these works and others as well are provided by C. J. Friedrich, *The Philosophy of Kant* (New York: Modern Library, Random House, 1949). Kant's *Religion Within the Limits of Reason Alone* (New York: Harper Torchbooks, Harper & Row, Publishers, 1960) is also important for his views on education.

S. Körner gives a handy introduction to Kant's philosophy in *Kant* (London: Pelican Books, Penguin Books Ltd., 1955). Good studies of Kant's ethics are H. J. Paton, *The Categorical Imperative* (Chicago: University of Chicago Press, 1948); W. D. Ross, *Kant's Ethical Theory* (Oxford: Oxford at the Clarendon Press, 1954); and L. W. Beck, *A Commentary on Kant's Critique of Practical Reason* (Chicago: University of Chicago Press, 1960).

A complete bibliography of works by Dewey on education and by others on his philosophy of education would be endless. A useful small volume of the former is M. S. Dworkin's *Dewey on Education* (New York: Bureau of Publications, Teachers College, Columbia University, 1959). It contains "My Pedagogic Creed" (1897), *The School and Society* (1899), *The Child and the Curriculum* (1902), and two later essays. Dewey's chief work on education is *Democracy and Education* (1916), now in paperback (New York: Macmillan Company, 1963). His *Experience and Education* (1938) was his last full presentation of his views, and is somewhat critical of more extreme forms of progressive education. It is also in paperback (Collier Books, P. F. Collier, Inc., 1963). Dewey's psychology is presented in *Human Nature and Conduct* (New York: Modern Library, Random House, 1922). For his ethics see especially *Theory of the Moral Life* (New York: Holt, Rhinehart and Winston, 1960), and Chapter X of *The Quest for Certainty* (New York: Capricorn Books, G. P. Putnam's Sons, 1960); for his political theory *The Public and its Problems* (New York: Henry Holt and Co., 1927) and *Liberalism and Social Action* (New York: Capricorn Books, G. P. Putnam's Sons, 1962). A good account of Dewey's thought in general is given by Sidney Hook in *John Dewey, an Intellectual Portrait* (New York: John Day Company, Inc., 1939).

The places of our authors in the history of educational thought may be seen by reading such books as: E. B. Castle, *Ancient Education and Today* (Baltimore, Md.: Pelican Books, Penguin Books, Inc., 1961);

E. B. Castle, *Educating the Good Man* (New York: Collier Books, P. F. Collier, Inc., 1962); S. J. Curtis and M. E. A. Boultwood, *A Short History of Educational Ideas* (London: University Tutorial Press Ltd., Third Edition, 1961); E. P. Cubberley, *The History of Education* (New York: Houghton Mifflin & Co., 1920); J. S. Brubacher, *A History of the Problems of Education* (New York: McGraw-Hill Book Co., Inc., 1947). K. Price's *Education and Philosophical Thought* (Boston: Allyn and Bacon, Inc., 1962) has selections from Kant and Dewey with good introductions; and *Philosophers on Education* by R. S. Brumbaugh and N. M. Lawrence (Boston: Houghton Mifflin Company, 1963) has penetrating essays, rather different in approach from mine, on all three of our authors.

INDEX

A

Abilities: as dispositions, 2. *See also* Skills.
Academic freedom, 190
"Active intellect," 38
Active learning: Aristotle on, 55, 57; Dewey on, 173-176; Kant on, 114, 173-174
Activities: Aristotle on "excellent," 22-28; "consummatory experiences" compared with "excellent," 166; worthwhile, 2-4. *See also* Excellences.
Actualization, 23-25. *See also* Growth.
Adler, M.J., 13, 140
Administration: Aristotle on, 60-61; Dewey on, 179, 190
Adult education, 133
Aesthetic culture: Aristotle on, 69-70; Dewey on, 152; Kant on, 89-90
Aims of education: 7-8; Aristotle on, 20-40; comparison of views on, 193-194; Dewey on, 154-167; Frankena on, 199; Kant on, 104-112
Akrasia, 44
Amusement: Aristotle on, 66. *See also* Pleasure.
Analytical philosophy: defined, 8. *See also* Philosophy of education.
Anthropology, 93, 104
Appetitive soul, 23, 26, 27-28
Aquinas, 90
Arete, 15
Argument: as method of education, 113, 121
Aristocracy: excellence in an, 53-54
Aristotle: on aims of education, 7, 20-40; on curriculum, 69-75; Dewey compared with, 136, 137, 139, 140, 141, 142-143, 144, 147, 148, 150, 152-153, 154, 155, 156, 158, 159, 163, 164, 166, 167, 168, 179, 181, 183, 184, 187, 188, 189, 190, 191; on dispositions, 1, 2, 3, 5, 40-54; Greek philosophy and, 15-17; influence as philosopher, 13-14; Kant compared with, 79, 81, 83, 86, 87, 90, 93, 94, 96, 100, 103, 105-106, 112, 113, 115, 116, 119-120, 131-132, 133, 134; on methods of education, 54-69, 75-78; other views compared with, 193-200; on philosophy of education, 8, 9, 10, 12, 17-20, 192; writings on education, 17

Arithmetic: Aristotle on, 70-71
Arts: Aristotle's methods for education in, 57-58; Aristotle's productive excellence as, 48-49, 51. *See also* Aesthetic culture, Fine arts.
Asceticism: Dewey on, 160; Kant on, 125-127
Ascholia, 66
Autonomy: Aristotle on, 59-60, 93; comparison of views on 92-93, 194; Frankena on, 199-200; Kant on, 92-93. *See also* Freedom.

B

Barker, Ernest, 20
Basedow, J.B., 79, 80
Bodily skills: Kant on, 86-87. *See also* Physical education.
Body: Aristotle on soul and, 22
Bonum consummatum: "consummatory experiences" compared with, 165; as Kant's highest good, 111. *See also* Summum bonum.
Broudy, H.S., 13
Bürgerliche Gesellschaft, 103

C

Campbell, C.A., 131
Capacities: of the soul, 22-23
Catechism: in Kant's method of education, 113, 119, 120, 123-124
Categorical imperative, 82, 107-108
Certainty (in educational philosophy): Aristotle on, 20; comparison of views on, 193; Dewey on, 138-140; Kant on, 82
Character: as aim of education, 2, 7; Dewey on, 144; Kant on, 93. *See also* Excellences.
The Child and the Curriculum, 136
Children: Aristotle on education of, 59, 67-68; Kant on discipline of, 117-118; Kant on education of, 109-110, 132-133; Kant on nurture of, 84
Christianity, 5-6, 12, 135, 139, 197
Citizens: Aristotle on education of, 63-66, 75; Aristotle on the good man and, 52-54; in Aristotle's ideal state, 62-63; comparison of views on good man and, 102-103; Dewey on good man and, 152-153; Kant on good man and, 102-104
Classicism, 197
Common good: Dewey on growth and, 163-164; as Dewey's moral standard, 150-151, 156
Conscientiousness: Dewey on, 148

"Consummatory experiences": as *bonum consummatum*, 165; comparison of views on, 194; Dewey on, 138, 161-163, 165; as "excellent activities," 166
Contemplation: Aristotle on, 29, 34-36; comparison of views on, 194, 197, 199; Dewey on, 166; Kant on, 106
"Contra-causal freedom," 131, 132
Cooperation: in educative activities, 178-179
Counsel of prudence, 82
Courage: Dewey on, 148
Critique of Judgement, 80, 81, 88, 89
Critique of Pure Reason, 80, 81, 88, 90
Culture: Kant on, 86, 118-121
Curriculum: Aristotle on, 69-74; Dewey on, 174-175. *See also* Dispositions, Subject-matter.

D

Demands: in human relationships, 149
Democracy: Dewey on, 151-152; education and, 136, 166-167; in school activities, 178-179, 190
Democracy and Education, 136
Deontologist: Aristotle as, 30, 33, 35; defined, 30; Dewey as, 149; Kant as, 106-107
Descartes, 79
Dessau Institute, 80, 83, 104
Dewey, John: on aims of education, 7, 154-167; Aristotle compared with, 26, 28, 30, 37, 38, 39, 55, 59, 60, 65, 66, 68, 70, 71, 74, 77; on dispositions, 2, 4, 5, 140-153; influence as philosopher, 13-14; Kant compared with, 80, 83, 85, 87, 92, 93, 114, 115, 116, 119, 120, 121, 122, 132; on methods of education, 167-191; modern developments and, 135-136; other views compared with, 193-200; on philosophy of education, 8, 10, 12, 136-140, 192; on subject-matter, 185-187; writings on education, 136
Dialogue: in Kant's method of education, 123-124, 126
Didactic: Kant's method for teaching, 123-125
Dignity of humanity: Kant on, 95-96
Discipline: Dewey on, 146, 160, 182; Frankena on, 200; Kant on, 85-86, 113, 117-118
Discussion: in Kant's method of education, 113, 119, 121, 124
Dispositions: Aristotle on, 40-54; comparison of views on, 193; cultivation

of, 3-4; Dewey on, 140-153; Frankena on, 198-199; Kant on, 83-104; in normative philosophy, 8-12
Distribution of education: Aristotle on, 77-78; Dewey on, 189-190; Kant on, 134
"Doctrinal" method, 123
Doing: Aristotle on, 26-27, 28, 58; comparison of views on, 55, 197; Dewey on, 174
Drama: in Aristotle's curriculum, 70
Duty: Kant on, 96-97, 108-110
Dynamis, 22

E

Education: defined, 6-7
Egoist: defined, 30; Aristotle as, 30, 34, 37
Emile, 96
Empiricism: in Dewey's philosophy, 138-149. *See also* Experimentalism.
Energeiai, 3, 22
Enjoyments. *See* "Consummatory experiences."
Enlightenment, 79
Environment: Dewey on, 168
Equipment: for schools, 176, 178
"Erotematic" method, 123
Ethics. See Nicomachean Ethics.
Ethics (Dewey), 142
Eudaimonia, 20-21. *See also* Happiness.
Eudemian Ethics, 35
Eupraxis, 27
Evil: Kant on, 129-130
Evolution: theory of, 135, 136, 137
Examples: in Kant's method of education, 113, 119, 124-125, 126
Excellences: acquisition of, 5-6; Aristotle on activities as, 27-28; as Aristotle's actualization, 23-25; defined, 1-3; in Greek philosophy, 15; need for, 3-4; in normative philosophy, 8-12. *See also* Intellectual excellence, Moral excellence.
Exercise: Dewey on, 182; in Kant's method of education, 113, 118-120, 123. *See also* Habituation.
Existentialists, 92, 131, 164, 196
Expectations: in human relationships, 149
Experience and Education, 136
Experimental schools, 80, 82-83
Experimentalism: comparison of views on, 193; Dewey on, 138-140; Frankena on, 199

F

Faithfulness: Dewey on, 148-149
Fine arts: Aristotle on, 49; Dewey on, 152, 186. *See also* Aesthetic culture.
Form: soul as, 22-23
Formalist. *See* Deontologist.
Fortune: Aristotle on, 24-25
Frederick William II, 103, 104
Freedom: Kant on moral excellence and, 92-93; Kant on the noumenal self's, 130-132. *See also* Autonomy.
Friendship: Aristotle on, 52
Froebel, 80

G

Games: as method of education, 67, 119
General welfare. *See* Common good.
Geschicklichkeit, 86
God: Aristotle on, 24, 36, 43. *See also* Religion.
Golden Mean. *See* Mean.
Golden Rule: Dewey on, 148
Good: Aristotle on, 20-21, 34-35; comparison of views on, 105, 193-194; Dewey on, 158-162; Kant on, 105-106, 111
Good man: Aristotle on citizen and, 52-54; Dewey on citizen and, 152-153; Kant on citizen and, 102-104
Good will: comparison of views on, 193, 194; Frankena on, 199; Kant on, 94-95, 106, 111
Grammata, 69-70
Greek philosophy, 15-16
Greene, T.M., 80
Growth: Dewey on, 156-158, 162, 163-164
Guidance: in Kant's method of education, 113
Gymnastics: in Aristotle's curriculum, 69. *See also* Physical education.

H

Habit: defined, 2; of intelligence, 144, 147-148. *See also* Dispositions, Excellences.
Habituation: in Aristotle's method of education, 54-60; comparison of views on, 195; Dewey on, 181-182. *See also* Exercise.
Happiness: Aristotle on, 21-25, 29, 34-35; comparison of views on, 193-194; Dewey on, 150, 158-159; Kant on, 97-98, 99-100, 105-106, 109, 110
Hardie, C.D., 8
Harris, W.T., 80

Herbart, J.P., 80
Herodotus, 70
Hexis, 2, 3. *See also* Dispositions.
History: in Aristotle's curriculum, 70; in Dewey's curriculum, 185; in Kant's curriculum, 120
Home: education in the, 60, 133, 168. *See also* Private education.
Homer, 70
Humanity: as Kant's aim for education, 105, 111-112, 129
Hume, 90
Humility: Kant on, 95
Hutchins, Robert M., 13, 77, 139, 140, 190
Hypothetical imperative, 82

I

Imperatives: in Kant's philosophy of education, 81-82
Incontinence: Aristotle on, 44
Industrial revolution, 135, 136
Infancy: Aristotle on education in, 67; Kant on education in, 84, 117. *See also* Children.
Instruction: in Aristotle's method of education, 54-60; in Kant's method of education, 113, 114, 119-127
Intellectual activity: vs. moral activity, 28-29. *See also* Activities.
Intellectual excellence: Aristotle on, 37-39, 44-49, 55, 56-57, 58; comparison of views on, 193; Dewey on, 141, 146, 147; Frankena on, 198. *See also* Mental skills.
Intelligence: *See* Reflective intelligence.
Intelligent soul. *See* Rational soul.
Interest: Dewey on, activities related to pupils', 172-173
Intuition: Aristotle on, 46

J

Jaeger, Werner, 36
James, William, 3, 13
Joachim, H.H., 29, 30, 32, 34, 35, 54
Judgement: Kant on, 87, 88-89, 120

K

Kalos, 27
Kant, Immanuel: on aims of education, 7, 104-112; Aristotle compared with, 30, 37, 39, 45, 53, 54, 66, 71, 77, 78; Dewey compared with, 135, 136, 137, 139, 140, 141, 142, 143, 144, 147, 148, 149, 151, 152, 153, 155, 156, 158, 159, 160, 164, 165, 168, 171, 173, 181,

183, 186, 187, 188, 189, 191; on dispositions, 1, 5, 83-104; eighteenth century and, 79-80; influence as a philosopher, 13-14, 80; on methods of education, 112-134; other views compared with, 193-200; on philosophy of education, 8, 9, 10, 12, 81-83, 192; writings on education, 81
Kilpatrick, W.H., 7, 167
Knowing: Aristotle on actualization as, 38-39; comparison of views on, 197; Kant on, 87-88. *See also* Intellectual excellence.
Knowledge: Aristotle on virtue as, 56, 58; comparison of views on virtue as, 195, 199; Dewey on virtue as, 188-189; Kant on historical and rational, 88

L

Laches, 16
Law of morality, 82
Learning: Kant on, 88
Lectures on Ethics, 85, 110, 111
Leibniz, 79
Leisure: Aristotle on education for, 64
Lenin, 155
Literature: in Aristotle's curriculum, 70
Locke, 79, 115

M

Maintenance. *See* Nurture.
Making: Aristotle on, 26-28, 49; comparison of views on, 197
Maritain, Jacques, 13, 139, 140
Markham, Edwin, 78
Marrou, H.I., 71
Marx, 139
Mathematics: Aristotle on, 46, 70-71; Kant on, 88, 120
Matter: body as, 22
Maxims: Kant on morality and, 107, 122-123
Mean: Aristotle's doctrine of, 31-34; Kant's criticism of, 94
Memory: Kant on, 87, 88, 120
Meno, 5, 16, 17, 58, 132
Mental skills: Kant on, 87-89, 93
Metaphysics, 57
Metaphysics: Aristotle on, 46; comparison of views on, 12; Dewey on, 142; Kant on, 90
Methods for education: Aristotle on, 54-69; comparison of views on, 194-195; Dewey on, 167-182; Frankena on, 199-200; Kant on, 112-134

Mill, John Stuart, 7, 9, 10, 11, 12, 30, 106
Montaigne, 80
Moral activity: vs. intellectual activity, 28-29. *See also* Activities.
Moral education. *See* Practical education.
Moral excellence: Aristotle on, 30-37, 41-44, 50-51, 55-56, 58-60, 72-73; comparison of views on, 193, 194; Dewey on, 141, 143-147, 150-151, 187-189; Frankena on, 198; Kant on, 92-100, 107, 122-127
Moral imperative, 82
Music: in Aristotle's curriculum, 69, 71-74
Mussolini, 155
"My Pedagogic Creed," 136, 153

N

Nationalist: Aristotle as, 30, 34, 37; defined, 30
Nature: Kant on, 116, 129-130
Newton, 79
Nicomachean Ethics, 17, 19, 21, 28, 29, 30, 33, 36, 47, 52, 53, 54, 63, 64, 65, 69, 71, 81, 93
Niebuhr, 139, 164, 196
Non-citizens: education of, 63, 75-77
Normative philosophy, 8-12
Noumenon: comparison of views on, 193; Kant on, 90, 101, 129-130, 130-131
Nurture: Kant on, 84-85, 113, 117
Nutritive soul, 23, 26, 27

O

Oakeshott, Michael, 143
O'Connor, D.J., 8
Odes, 16
On the Parts of Animals, 65
Opportunity for education. *See* Distribution of education.

P

Paideia, 15
Painting: in Aristotle's curriculum, 69-70
"Passive intellect," 38
Passive learning. *See* Active learning.
Pauson, 73
Perfection: comparison of views on, 194; Kant on, 98-99, 109-110
Pestalozzi, J.H., 79, 80
Peters, R.S., 13
Phenomenon: comparison of views on, 193; Kant on, 90, 101, 129-130
Philanthropinists, 79
Philosophy of education: analytical and

normative, 8-12; Aristotle on, 17-20; comparison of views on, 8, 9, 10, 12; Dewey on, 136-140; Kant on, 81-82; for the student, 12-13, 192-193

Phronesis, 46

Physical education: Aristotle on, ·67-69; Kant on, 84-85, 100-102, 113-114

Pindar, 16

Plato, 5, 13, 16, 17, 20, 40, 58, 59, 70, 74, 77, 78, 132, 188, 196

Pleasure: happiness vs., 22, 158-159

Poetics, 57, 69, 70

Poetry: in Aristotle's curriculum, 70

Poiesis, 26

Politics, 17, 19, 21, 28, 29, 40, 42, 43, 53, 54, 57, 81, 93

Politike, 17-20

Polygnotus, 73

Practical action, 26-27. *See also* Doing.

Practical education: Kant on, 100-102, 114

Practical reason: Aristotle on, 26, 28, 37-38, 46-48, 50-51; comparison of views on, 193, 197; Dewey on, 146; Kant on, 81. *See also* Prudence.

Practical science: Aristotle on, 18

Practice. *See* Habituation.

Pragmatic imperative, 82

Pragmatism, 137, 174

Praxis, 26

Predispositions: Kant on, 129-130

Private education: Aristotle on, 60-61; Dewey on, 189; Kant on, 122, 133-134

Productive action, 26-27. *See also* Making.

Productive science: Aristotle on, 18

Productive thinking: Aristotle on, 38, 48-49, 57-58. *See also* Making.

Professionalism: Aristotle on, 65-66, 74

Protagoras, 16, 196

Prudence: Dewey on, 144, 160; Kant on, 91-92, 121-122. *See also* Practical reason.

Public education: Aristotle on, 60-61; Dewey on, 142, 189-190; Kant on, 133-134

Punishment: Dewey on, 150, 188; Kant on, 113, 118

Q

The Quest for Certainty, 162

Questioning: in Kant's method of education, 123-124, 126

R

Rational soul, 23, 26, 28

Reading: in Aristotle's curriculum, 69-70

Reason: comparison of views on, 196-197; Kant on, 87, 90, 121. *See also* Practical reason, Theoretical reason.

Reflective intelligence: comparison of views on, 195-196, 197; Dewey on, 142-143, 145-146, 176-178

Religion: Dewey on, 142, 152; Kant on, 127-129

Religion within the Limits of Reason Alone, 129

Republic, 5, 59, 77

Responsibility: Dewey on, 144

Rewards: Dewey on, 150; Kant on, 118

Riesman, David, 59

Right principle: Aristotle on, 32-37

Rights: in human relationships, 149

Rink, Theodor, 81

Romanticism, 135, 197

Ross, W.D., 29, 30, 34, 35

Rousseau, Jean-Jacques, 5, 6, 13, 14, 79, 80, 96, 115, 116, 129, 130, 133, 134, 194, 197

Rule of skill, 82

Ruskin, 7

Russell, Bertrand, 6, 159, 198

Ryle, Gilbert, 87, 88

S

Santayana, 196-197

Schole, 64

School: Dewey on, 180-181

The School and Society, 136

Science: Aristotle on, 46; in Dewey's curriculum, 171, 185-186; and Deweyan education, 136, 145

Scientific intelligence. *See* Reflective intelligence.

Self-mastery: Dewey on, 148; Kant on, 85, 95

Self-realization. *See* Actualization, Growth.

Senses: Aristotle on education of, 45; Kant on education of, 86, 87

Sensitive soul: 23, 26, 27-28

Skills: Dewey on, 146, 182-183; as dispositions, 2; Kant on, 86-89, 118-121. *See also* Dispositions.

Slaves: Aristotle on education of, 42-43, 62-63, 76, 77-78

Social relationships: Dewey on, 148-149; dispositions and, 4; Kant on, 122

Socrates, 5, 13, 16, 17, 51, 54, 55, 56, 58, 96, 132, 188

Socratic method, 121, 123-124, 195-196

Sophia, 46

Sophocles, 76

Soul: as form, 22-23
Sparta, 64, 68
Speculative thought: Kant on, 90. *See also* Reason.
Stages of education: Aristotle on, 67-69; Kant on, 132-133
Standard of morality: Dewey on, 150-156
State: Aristotle on education and, 60-61; Aristotle's ideal, 61-63; Kant on education and, 103-104, 133. *See also* Citizens, Public education.
Subject-matter: comparison of views on, 194; Dewey on, 183-187. *See also* Curriculum.
Success: Dewey on, 159
Summum bonum: comparison of views on, 194; Kant on, 111, 112, 128
Supremum bonum: comparison of views on, 193-194; Kant on, 111
System of Logic, 9

T

Taylor, A.E., 60
Teacher: Dewey on freedom of, 190; Dewey on tasks of, 173, 175, 177, 178, 179
Techne, 46
Technical imperative, 82
Teleologist: Aristotle as, 30, 33-37; defined, 30; Dewey as, 149, 150; Kant's criticism of, 106-107
Theoretical reason: Aristotle on, 26, 28, 37-38, 46; comparison of views on, 193, 197; Dewey on, 146; Kant on, 81, 90
Theoretical science: Aristotle on, 18
Theoretikon, 69
Theory of the Moral Life, 142
Thoughtfulness: Dewey on, 150
Traditional education: Dewey on, 168-169; Frankena on, 200
Tragedy: Aristotle on, 18
Training. *See* Discipline.
Traits of mind: Dewey on, 147

Transcendentalism: Kant's, 80
Truth: Aristotle on, 37-39; Frankena on, 200

U

Über Pädagogik, 81
Understanding: Kant on, 87, 88
Unified education: Dewey on, 183-184
Uniformity of education: Aristotle on, 77; comparison of views on, 77; Dewey on, 189-190; Kant on, 134
Universalist. *See* Utilitarian.
Utilitarian: defined, 30; Dewey as, 30, 149, 150; Mill as, 30

V

Values: defined, 3; Dewey on, 160-161
Vice: Aristotle on, 43-44
Virtue (as knowledge): Aristotle on, 56, 58; comparison of views on, 195, 199; Dewey on, 188-189. *See also* Good will, Moral excellence.
Visual arts: Aristotle on, 73
Vocational education: Aristotle on, 28; Dewey on, 184-185; Kant on, 90-91

W

Watching: in Aristotle's method of education, 67-68
Wild, J.D., 13
Wisdom. *See* Practical reason, Prudence.
Wittgenstein, 73, 76
Women: Aristotle on education of, 42-43, 76, 78; Kant on education of, 134
Work: Aristotle on, 28; Aristotle on education as, 66; Dewey on education as, 163; Kant on education as, 119-120
Workers: Aristotle on education of, 42-43, 62-63, 76-78
World government: Kant on, 111-112
Worthwhileness: Dewey on, 170-172
Writing: Aristotle on, 69-70
Writings on education: Aristotle's, 17; Dewey's, 136; Kant's, 81

2 3 4 5 6 7 8 9 10 11 12 13 14 15 16 17 18 19 20 21 22 23 24 25 SH 74 73 72 71 70 69 68 67 66